UNDERSTANDING GLOCAL CONTEXTS IN EDUCATION

WHAT EVERY NOVICE TEACHER NEEDS TO KNOW

DAVID SCHWARZER
JAIME GRINBERG

Kendall Hunt
publishing company

Cover design created by Noa Sela.

Kendall Hunt
publishing company

www.kendallhunt.com
Send all inquiries to:
4050 Westmark Drive
Dubuque, IA 52004–1840

Copyright © 2018 by Kendall Hunt Publishing Company

ISBN: 978-1-5249-9018-3

Published in the United States of America

TABLE OF CONTENTS

LIST OF AUTHORS AND AFFILIATIONS

Daniel K. Abuabasa a student enrolled in the Mathematics Education doctoral program at Montclair State University, who is also very interested in Special Education. His research interests include culture and mathematics education, mathematics appreciation, and disability studies. His current projects focus on culture and its impact on mathematics education.

Yelena Adelman has a BA in Economics from the University of Michigan and an MA in Alternative Education from the University of Haifa. For the last 10 years, she has been working in informal education and in the last 2 years has worked as a teacher in an alternative high school called Man, Nature and Society, in Karmiel, Israel. The school is based on a dialogical pedagogy with an emphasis on creating social change by empowering students to be partners in their education and in shaping a more equal society. Yelena is currently studying toward a teaching degree through a unique track, Beit Hamidrash at Beit Berl College. This track is co-built by professors and students and has a high emphasis on dialogue and community-based learning.

Hanan A. Atiyat is a program assistant in the Student Success Center at Montclair State University. She is currently working toward completing her MA in Educational Leadership with a concentration in higher education. For seven years, Hanan taught English Language and Literature abroad at an International Baccalaureate Organization. She is interested in international education and humanitarian relief efforts, as she volunteered with the International Rescue Committee (IRC) in the Middle Eastern and North African region to respond to a humanitarian crisis by helping Syrian refugees rebuild their lives.

Nicole Auffant is a PhD candidate in Global Urban Studies with a concentration on Women's and Gender Studies at Rutgers University-Newark. She holds a BA in Sociology and Women's and Gender Studies from Rutgers University. Her research interests include the intersections of policy, gender, race, culture, and well-being. Her dissertation explores the relationship between school policies and female students' bodies.

Susan Baglieri is an associate professor in the Department of Secondary and Special Education at Montclair State University. Her research interests include disability studies, inclusive education, and teacher education. She is coauthor of *Disability Studies and the Inclusive Classroom* (Routledge, 2017, with Arthur Shapiro). Her current projects focus on universal design in education, inclusive postsecondary education, and democratic free schools.

Clarissa Barrios, BA, is a certified second-grade teacher working in a Northern New Jersey inner city for 11 years. She has taught both general and inclusion classrooms. She hosts parent workshops on involvement in mathematics and navigation of standardized testing. Her work ethic and educator success have afforded her the opportunity to mentor novice educators in her district.

Veronica R. Barrios, PhD, is an Assistant Professor in the department of Family Science and Social Work at Miami University. Her research involves working with Latinx college students in understanding their Latinx identity through a college curriculum. She is also interested in the culture of nondisclosure of sexual abuse, applications of intersectionality theory, and using intersectionality as a methodology.

Ellen Cahill is a teacher in an inclusion kindergarten class and a doctoral student in the Teacher Education & Teacher Development program at Montclair State University. Her research interests include culturally relevant teaching and social justice in education. Her current project is a participatory action research project that studies social inequity at her school and its impact on teacher practice.

Debra H. Cho is a biology and environmental science teacher at KIPP: Newark Collegiate Academy in Newark, NJ. She graduated from The College of New Jersey with a degree in Women in Gender Studies. While pursuing a masters in biology, she discovered a way to combine her passion for social justice and fascination with science in secondary education. Ms. Cho joined Teach for America and found her niche serving in the vibrant city of Newark. Outside of school, Ms.Cho is serving the United States as a Company Commander in the New Jersey National Guard. Currently, she is pursuing a masters in biology pedagogy at Montclair State University. She is an activist for education equity, women's rights, and lifelong academic success.

Charity Dacey is the Director of Teacher Education Admissions and Retention in the Center of Pedagogy at Montclair State University and an adjunct faculty member of the Educational Foundations department. She is a PhD student in the Teacher Education Teacher Development program in the same institution. She is an expert in assessment and its implications to classroom practices.

Heather Frank is an early elementary classroom teacher with over 14 years of teaching experience in New Jersey public schools. She has served on various school and district committees and in leadership roles during her tenure. She holds a BA from Gettysburg College and an MAT from Montclair State University. Currently, she is a doctoral student in the Teacher Education and Teacher Development program at Montclair State University. Her research interests include teacher leadership, professional learning, and literacy.

Dr. Carolina E. Gonzalez is a higher education professional with over 10 years of experience in both academic and student affairs serving students, particularly those from diverse racial and ethnic backgrounds. As a scholar-practitioner, she advocates and actively challenges assumptions about the experiences of minoritized students and calls for practitioners to shift away from a deficit-based paradigm when working with underrepresented populations. Her academic work and research interests include intersectionality of identities; experiences of immigrant children; parental involvement; and access, equity, and the academic success of underrepresented students in higher education. She currently serves as the Director of the Teacher Education Advocacy Center in the Center of Pedagogy at Montclair State University.

Jaime Grinberg, PhD, is Department Chair and Professor of Educational Foundations at Montclair State University. His research covers progressivism; teacher preparation; critical studies; leadership; history of education; and cultural studies. He published *Teaching like that: The beginnings of teacher education at Bank Street* (Peter Lang Pub. 2005), as well as edited five anthologies (Kendall Hunt Publishing Co.), in which he authored many chapters. He co-edited with D. Schwarzer *Successful Teaching, What Every Novice Teacher Needs to Know*, published in 2017 by Rowman & Littlefield. He also published numerous research articles in academic journals such as Teachers College Record, Review of Educational Research, Theory Into Practice, and Educational Administration Quarterly among others. Also, he has written research review chapters in academic handbooks, numerous book chapters, and has written journal articles and book chapters in Spanish for Latin-American publications.

LaChan V. Hannon is a doctoral candidate in Teacher Education and Teacher Development at Montclair State University. Her research interests include culturally responsive school practices, parent engagement, and teacher education. She is the founder of Greater Expectations Teaching and Advocacy Center.

Dr. Rafael Inoa is a Kean University Lecturer with a PhD in Educational Research and Program Evaluation. He has an extensive background in research both as an instructor and analyst. He has taught directed research to various cohorts of teaching professionals and has been both lead researcher and assistant to senior researchers at various schools districts across New Jersey and New York. His experience extends to both quantitative and qualitative research methods, with a strong background in qualitative research and analysis.

Maria Sara Kopczynski is a MAT student in the Department of Secondary and Special Education in the College of Education and Human Services at Montclair State University.

Dr. Maya Levanon has a MA in philosophy, with specialization in ethics from the Hebrew University in Jerusalem; EdD in Philosophy for Children from Montclair State University. She served as an assistant professor in National Louis University, interdisciplinary graduate program. She now serves as a lecturer and a pedagogical instructor at Beit Berl college elementary program. She also works extensively with the Martin Buber School for Informal Educational Leadership. She now again lives in Israel.

Tanya Maloney, EdD, is an Assistant Professor in the Department of Secondary and Special Education at Montclair State University in Montclair, New Jersey. She began her career in education as a high school mathematics teacher in Chicago, IL. Her diverse experiences teaching mathematics as well as preparing and developing teachers in various contexts, inform her research interests in teacher education and mathematics education. Her scholarship to date has examined how teacher preparation programs support and inhibit positive racial identity development among teacher candidates.

Justin Matyas is a current graduate student at Montclair State University pursuing his Master's Degree in Social Studies Education and a Certification in Special Education, which he expects to have completed by January 2018. He previously worked as a Graduate Assistant under Dr. Susan Baglieri and has always had a passion for inclusive education research as he has an older brother who is on the Autism spectrum. Upon graduation, Justin hopes to teach in a Middle or High School setting as a Social Studies educator.

Dr. Tammy Mills is an Assistant Professor of Curriculum, Assessment, and Instruction at the University of Maine. She teaches undergraduate and graduate courses that address assessment literacy, effective instructional strategies, aspects of planning, and schooling in multicultural contexts. She serves on the Penobscot River Educational Partnership and works with practicing teachers and principals to develop expertise in classroom-based assessment for instructional decision making.

Dr. Evan Mooney is an adjunct faculty member of the Educational Foundations department at Montclair State University. His research focuses on social studies teacher education, citizenship and social justice education, and the intersections of science and social studies education.

Caroline Murray has over 25 years of experience in education in the public, private, and nonprofit sectors. She holds a BA from Boston College and an MA from Teachers College Columbia University. For the past 13 years she has served as the Assistant Director of the Center of Pedagogy at Montclair State University. The Center of Pedagogy is the hub of teacher education and is a frequent focus of study by education researchers in the United States and around the world. Currently she is a doctoral student in the Teacher Education and Teacher Development program at Montclair State University.

Erika Oliveros is a Senior Lecturer at Fairleigh Dickinson University. She also directs the English as a Second Language (ESL) efforts for the HACER and Puerta al Futuro Programs. She is currently a doctoral student in the Teacher Education and Teacher Development Department at Montclair State University. Her areas of interest include professional development and teachers working with English Language Learners (ELL) in multicultural classrooms of the 21st century.

Tina Powell, EdD, is the Director of Mathematics and Science for Orange Public Schools in Orange, New Jersey. Prior to her role in Orange, she served as the Director of Mathematics for Newark Public Schools. She earned her PhD from Teacher College, Columbia University.

Dr. Jennifer J. Robinson is a faculty member and Executive Director of Montclair State University's Center of Pedagogy, which coordinates initial teacher preparation and the simultaneous renewal of teacher education and partner schools. She also established a center at Montclair State to increase the recruitment and retention of students from minority groups into teaching. She has written and presented extensively about minority teacher recruitment and retention, urban education, and sustaining school–university partnerships.

Dr.Alison Price-Rom is an adjunct faculty in the Departments of Secondary and Special Education and Educational Foundations at Montclair State University. She is also an international education consultant and previously managed State Department-funded international exchange programs for students, teachers, and scholars in the Washington DC area. She is interested in teacher education abroad, and has worked on USAID and Asian Development projects in Central Asia and Eastern Europe.

Dr. Elizabeth Iris Rivera Rodas is an Assistant Professor of Quantitative Research Methods in the Department of Educational Foundations at Montclair State University's College of Education and Human Services. She holds a joint PhD in Urban Systems with a concentration in urban educational policy and in management with a concentration in economics from Rutgers University–Newark, a MS in Social Research from Hunter College, CUNY, and a BA in economics from Barnard College, Columbia University. As an economist of education, Dr. Rivera Rodas' scholarly interests involve the economics of urban education, residential and school segregation, and teacher quality.

Dr. David Schwarzer is a professor in the Department of Secondary and Special Education in the College of Education and Human Services at Montclair State University.

Laurie Summer is a school-based speech language pathologist in New Jersey. She is a doctoral student with the Teacher Education and Teacher Development PhD program at Montclair State University. Her research interests include narrative inquiry, relational beliefs and practices within education, disability studies, and inclusive education.

Dr. Pablo P.L. Tinio is Associate Professor at the Department of Educational Foundations, Montclair State University. He holds a Doctorate from the University of Vienna, Department of Psychology, an MA in Educational Psychology: Learning, Cognition, and Development from Rutgers University, and an MA in Behavioral Science from Kean University. His research is focused on the psychology of aesthetics, creativity, and the arts; arts and aesthetics in education; and learning and engagement in cultural institutions. Dr. Tinio is Editor of the APA journal, Psychology of Aesthetics, Creativity, and the Arts. He is also co-editor of the Cambridge Handbook of the Psychology of Aesthetics and the Arts. Dr. Tinio has been awarded the 2011 Frank X. Barron Award; the 2014 Daniel E. Berlyne Award for Outstanding Early Career Achievement in Psychology of Aesthetics, Creativity, and the Arts by the American Psychological Association; and the 2016 Alexander Gottlieb Baumgarten Award for Outstanding Contributions to the Field by an Early Career Scientist from the International Association of Empirical Aesthetics.

Sofia A. Tinio works at the Teaching Performance Center at the College of Education, Kean University. She holds a Master of Public Administration degree and a Bachelor of Arts degree in English from Kean University.

Jaclyn Weisz is currently a MAT student in the Department of Secondary and Special Education in the College of Education and Human Services at Montclair State University. She is pursuing her Master's Degree in Biological Sciences Education and a Certification in Special Education. While at MSU, she worked as a Graduate Assistant under Dr. Jaime Grinberg. Upon graduation, Jaclyn hopes to teach in a high school setting as a Biology educator and extend her love and passion for science to her students.

Jacqueline Wells is currently a MAT student in the Department of Secondary and Special Education in the College of Education and Human Services at Montclair State University. She is pursuing her Master's Degree in Socials Studies Education along with a Certification in Special Education. She currently works as a Graduate Assistant under Dr. Jaime Grinberg. After achieving her Master's Degree, Jacqueline aspires to teach Social Studies in a high school setting, hoping to pass along her knowledge and love for Social Studies.

INTRODUCTION

DAVID SCHWARZER AND
JAIME GRINBERG

The book you are about to read *Understanding Glocal Contexts: What Every Novice Teacher Needs to Know* is an edited volume that is a part of a book series mostly designed to help undergraduate students like you to determine if joining the teaching profession is for them. This book focuses on the historical and sociocultural foundations of education and its importance for novice teachers. It also provides the global and local (glocal) foundations for understanding the current context of public education, utilizing historical, sociological, cultural, and economic and political sciences contexts and perspectives.

This book is also constructed as a scaffolding tool for you on your quest to understanding the foundational historical and sociocultural underpinnings of the teaching profession during the last fifty years. Reading and reflecting on the following chapters helps you connect the conceptual themes of each chapter to the global, national, current policies, and current understandings of the phenomenon at hand. For example, when we talk about family involvement, we present information about how families were understood fifty years ago, and how this understanding has changed both in the United States and in the world. Moreover, we present pertinent policies that were created to help families to be more engaged in their children's lives in schools and classrooms. Finally, this book aims to illustrate the ways in which educational foundations impacted in the past and are still impacting the teaching profession in the 21st century. Each chapter ventures into a description of the authors' takes on future trends on each one of the issues to help navigate novice teachers' academic journey. As experienced teacher educators, we have found over the years that students entering the profession have difficulty understanding education as a transdisciplinary phenomenon. Therefore, this book is designed to facilitate the beginning teacher's decision-making process. Preparing conscientious teachers that are aware of the global forces, national forces, policies, and understanding the phenomena at hand are crucial for different societies, schools, and communities (the three sections of our book—Society, School and Community are central to the conceptualization of this volume and will be explained in the next section). This understanding is of particular importance given the current pressures of teacher education programs to implement standardized testing as part of their curriculum, alongside the implementation of common core standards, PARCC testing, teacher evaluations, and other new initiatives.

Several different audiences are guiding our writing. As stated before, the primary target audience of this project are students who are thinking about entering the teaching profession. A potential secondary audience might be teacher educators interested in better understanding the complexity of the sociohistorical foundations of current educational practices. The last potential audience would be individuals who are seeking an alternative career in education. In all cases, some of the features used in the book could become an indispensable tool for all audiences interested in reflection and deeper understanding of a current educational trend in its glocal historical context. Moreover, its design as a dialogical transdisciplinary analysis of primary documents is a noteworthy feature. In this dialogue, an experienced theoretician/researcher engages in a dialogue with a practitioner about their different understandings and/or questions related to the primary sources or texts that were chosen to discuss the issues at hand. Furthermore, the writing style of the book is reader friendly with minimum "jargon" as well as the inclusion of definition of terms at the end of each chapter suitable for newcomers to the educational profession. Finally, each chapter includes practical applications, questions, and/or activities for teachers to use as another tool to further self-reflection and/or group discussions to help the reader make a more informed decision about their professional journey into the teaching profession in the 21st century.

BOOK SECTIONS

This book has three sections: Society, Schools, and Teachers. As you can see, the sections are designed as a funnel—from the more general concept (society), to the more specific one (teachers), moving through a more intermediate concept (schools). This approach is called deductive—from the general to the specific. A deductive approach for an historical book makes sense since it implies that general understandings of education have a clear impact on the particular examples or new policies being created and enforced in schools and finally adopted by teachers in their daily practices.

Each of these sections contains more specific chapters that are devoted to a particular concept such as language, culture, family, and funding (among others). Although each one of these topics were assigned to one particular section of the book, it is important to state that all the phenomena discussed in each one of the chapters are connected to the three sections discussed (society, school and teachers). Placing them in ONE particular section of the book, does not imply that can ONLY be there. It only makes the interconnected nature of the topics center in ONE major aspect of its conceptualization to make the overall content of the book accessible to a broader audience. An interesting activity for a class/group/individual reflection could be to try and see how would YOU place the different topics of the book in your own sections and why.

Following is a list of the features that are anchoring all the chapters of the volume. Therefore, the structure is predictable and yet, each chapter crafted their unique interpretations and flow that suited the authors' personal academic voices. The features are:

1. The definition of the central topic of the chapter that must encompass foundational views including citations from the last 100 years.

2. The relevance of the topic for novice teachers in the 21ˢᵗ century. This section answers the question "Why does the topic matter now?" "Why was the topic relevant in the past?"

3. The definition of conceptual information in as clear as possible language—trying to avoid education "jargon." Moreover, a graphic organizer (a table), in which authors discuss the global forces, national forces, educational policies and practices, and the understanding of the phenomenon at hand on the topic in various time periods are introduced and discussed. The following basic chart is the one used in every chapter to identify and summarize key information for the text analysis.

4. The inclusion of a dialogical text analysis between a theoretician/researcher and a practitioner is included. Authors engage in a dialogic discussion about the topic using primary documents as the framework for their argument in each chapter.

5. Practical implications for teachers: The authors answer the questions: "What are the present implications for teachers regarding the topic presented in the chapter?"

	Global	National (USA)	Policies	Understanding of the Phenomenon
Text 1 (50+ years ago)				
Text 2 (Current)				

6. Extension questions: Authors develop three to five round-table discussion questions and/or self-reflection questions to be used when the readers are reflecting or critically discussing the central topic of each chapter.

7. Glossary of terms: Authors provide definitions of terms they deem relevant and important.

SECTION I: SOCIETY

This section of the book focuses on glocal societal forces that are impacting the historical and sociocultural understanding of each issue described in this section. Moreover, understanding how schools and teaching are heavily impacted by certain movements in the perception of these issues is crucial. For example, the understanding of bilingualism as a right during the 1960s was displaced by an organized effort to promote English-only policies in the 1990s that ended up with a new appreciation for multilingualism in the 21ˢᵗ century. This societal change impacted heavily schools and teachers' practices in the United States and in the world.

SECTION II: SCHOOLS

This section centers in schools as the main context for implementing educational practices and policies. Schools are heavily impacted by societal forces but they also impact the way that teachers practice their crafts by creating mandated curriculum or expectations that might be different from school district to school district and sometimes from school to school in the same school district. For example, the discussion about school funding and its different understanding in the middle of the 19th century and the 21st century are examples how schools can impact the way in which education is perceived and enacted.

SECTION III: TEACHERS

This section centers on the crucial and central role of the teacher in the development of curriculum, activities, lesson plans, and assessments (among other) to enact the understandings and conceptualizations represented in all the other sections of this book. The role of the teacher and teaching as a political practice are central to this section. Decisions taken by the teacher such as the development of curriculum for all students that include students with disabilities in the mainstream classroom are one clear example of the power of teaching and the teacher in translating theoretical and sometimes policy ideas into daily practices for students in their classrooms.

Finally, we also have a postscript, which is a conversation with an experienced expert about education and contexts particularly relevant to novice teachers.

SUMMARY

The book content is designed to draw readers' attention about how the current realities of the educational arena in the United States (that sometimes look puzzling or "strange") are a result of complex glocal sociohistorical processes. It also is based on the understanding that distinct areas of inquiry (history, sociology, politics, philosophy, etc.) are interconnected and better understood through a transdisciplinary approach. Finally, the idea that general ideas and understandings at the society level are impacting schools and therefore they finally change teachers' practice is important to be noted.

The book's structure is designed as a tool to facilitate self-reflection and group/classroom discussion and interactions. Moreover, it can be used as a model when designing curricula since it is organized in a predictable way as well as using graphic organizers to support a variety of learning styles. Finally, the commitment to make this book readable and as "jargon" free as possible and providing different scaffold to facilitate academic language development, makes it more accessible to a variety a students at different levels of academic language proficiency.

Each journey starts with a very important first step—thank you for choosing this book to be one of YOUR first steps in your academic journey!

SECTION I SOCIETY

UNITED WE STAND: UNDERSTANDING THE CONTEXT OF IMMIGRATION IN EDUCATION

CAROLINA GONZALEZ
RAFAEL INOA

Today's schools in the United States have undergone a transformation marked by policy changes, civil rights movements, and an influx of immigrant students. Though not perfect, such transitions have forced our nation to evolve toward a pedagogical culture of inclusion. This chapter will provide an overview of the change in immigration over a period of fifty years and will use two relevant primary resources that showcase the impact of immigration in the United States. The two resources presented in this chapter are contrasting illustrations of how the topic of immigration has evolved in the United States, yet they are not the only viewpoints that supporters and critics may have as it relates to this important matter. The first text we will use in our discussion is the Immigration Act of 1965, which aimed to loosen the restrictive immigration quotas previously implemented in the United States. The second is a report by the Federation for American Immigration Reform (FAIR), which outlines their recommendations for the 45th President of the United States on restricting immigration. The following sections provide a brief overview of both documents along with a contextualization of their relationship to education and schooling in the United States.

IMMIGRATION ACT OF 1965

Sponsored by representatives in the House and Senate, the Hart-Celler Immigration Act of 1965 was designed to end decades of discriminatory immigration restrictions in the United States. Former laws from the 1920s instituted a quota system for some countries and barred immigrants from western and southern parts of Europe. With the new Immigration Act of 1965, restrictions for immigrating to the United States were eased for some non-White groups and those who had relatives in the United States, and they were able to reunite. The Act also provided opportunities for those who had expertise, from which the United States could benefit. The first wave of immigrants came from Korea, China, and Taiwan followed by families from Latin America (Faltis, 2007). With this new repeal of quotas, and subsequent revisions to the Immigration Act, the number of immigrants in the United States increased exponentially. By 1985, immigrants and refugees represented 1 in 12 of U.S. residents; by 2005, this representation had increased to 1 in 9. The children of these immigrant families represented 1 in 4 of all school-aged children (Faltis, 2007).

FEDERATION FOR AMERICAN IMMIGRATION REFORM (FAIR)

The Federation for American Immigration Reform (FAIR) is a nonprofit organization promoting a sharp reduction in the number of people immigrating to the United States from approximately 1 million immigrants to 300,000 immigrants per year. As part of their stated mission, FAIR wants "to educate and increase public awareness of immigration issues, present solutions, hold our leaders accountable for answers, and ensure the public's voice is heard" (FAIR, n.d.). However, FAIR faces much opposition as detailed in a May 2017 article published in *The Washington Post*. This article explains that organizations like the Southern Poverty Law Center (SPLC) have labeled FAIR a "hate group," which is one term, among many, that FAIR sourced as "derogatory name-calling" (Sacchetti, 2017). Regardless of personal views, it is important to take into account the policies that FAIR has chosen to support and their influence in our political system, as well as the reasons behind their support. Not only are these policies and those of the current White House virtually one and the same, but they have also appointed top government officials who have been regarded as allies of FAIR and their views. Such appointments include former FAIR director, who is now ombudsman for U.S. Citizenship and Immigration Services (Sacchetti, 2017). A recent report published by FAIR (i.e., O'Brien, Spencer, Law, & Rehberg, 2016) may help explain the motivations behind the new immigration policies of the current president, as well as the motivations of those 50 private foundations and over 1.3 million FAIR members and supporters.

CONTEXTUALIZING DOCUMENTS' RELATIONSHIP TO EDUCATION

Both documents are important in the context of public schooling for reasons that are both different and similar. The approved federal acts of the mid- and late-1960s are a reminder of how policies from one special interest sector (immigration) can impact policies in another sector (education). For example, consider the Immigration Act of 1965 and its impact on the Elementary and Secondary Education Act (ESEA) of 1965, both respectively signed into law by President Lyndon B. Johnson of that year. The Immigration Act welcomed different segments of immigrants to the United States. As a result, the number of immigrants quadrupled from 9.6 million in 1970 to 43.3 million in 2015; and by that same year, the share of foreign languages spoken at homes grew to 14% from the year 1980 (Zong & Betalova, 2017). The Title III of the ESEA—Language Instruction for English Language Learners—advocated for the rights of those very same immigrants. Title III of this Act affirmed the need for students of immigrant families to achieve at "high levels" and called for schools to institute policies and practices promoting the instruction necessary to meet the needs of English Language Learners.

The policies outlined in the cited FAIR report to the 45th President of the United States, now President Donald J. Trump, do not speak in length about education as they do about immigration reform. However, in separate articles (Farris & Raley, 2016), FAIR discusses their position on education very clearly and explains how educating immigrant youth is crumbling the financial infrastructure of public education. More specifically, FAIR posits that a surge of "Unaccompanied Alien Minors, family units entering the country illegally, people overstaying their visas, higher than average birthrates among families with an illegal head of household, and legal immigrants granted permanent resident status" (Farris & Raley, 2016) cause resources to be "redirected away from American citizens to support programs like . . . English as a Second Language" (Farris & Raley, 2016). Additionally, they convey how despite all of the money spent, the progress of Limited English Proficiency (LEP) students is bleak in all subject areas and drag the achievement rates of all non-LEP students down, due to LEP students' performance on national standardized tests. FAIR's report directly links to educational outcomes as it not only threatens the stability of immigrant families in the country, but it also advocates for the removal of funding designed to educate immigrant youth. Placing reforms that call for deportation, an end to family reunification, and a cut in funding of services will not only impact communities, but also students, educational policy, classroom instruction, and district-level fiscal support for immigrant students.

By studying the relationship between immigration and education policy of 50 years ago, we can get a better picture of how proposed immigration policies of today may impact or align with future policies in education. We must be ready to face such changes if and when they occur, and as educators, we must be ready to take a professional stand as it relates to the children whom we are tasked with serving. Our first step should be educating ourselves on the matter.

WHY SHOULD EDUCATORS CONCERN THEMSELVES WITH IMMIGRATION?

Immigration policy and reform and its impact on the U.S. education system was just as relevant over 50 years ago as it is today. This statement holds true regardless of differences in the popular political and public opinions that moments in U.S. history are defined by. For instance, the Immigration Act of 1965 took a very inclusive stance on immigration and on educating the children of immigrants. Today, new presidential policies and policies proposed by organizations like the Federation of American Immigration Reform (FAIR) are much less inclusive, viewing immigration and the education of immigrant children as a burden on a system with pressures of reform. In both instances, policies and sentiments toward immigrants changed, and educators tasked with the welfare and education of all children were caught in crossfire.

The topic of immigration and its impact on K-12 education will remain of high importance for a multitude of reasons. National and global forces (such as employment and educational opportunities in the United States, protection from political persecution, large immigrant communities and policies protecting human and civil rights) have led to steady immigration to the United States, with situational spikes in migration often bringing this topic to the media forefront. There is also the known impact that education can have on building a safe and prosperous society. Amidst a population that is ever growing in terms of size and diversity, the U.S. educational system becomes one of the primary tools that can be used to effectuate positive and everlasting change. Educators have and will continue to play a major role in helping develop our future citizens and in continuously shaping American society. As such, all within the field of education, but especially teachers who work directly with students on a daily basis, must remain aware of those issues that impact the U.S. populous, and how their roles as educators may be impacted during times of reform.

CONCEPTUAL UNDERSTANDING OF IMMIGRATION

GLOBAL AND LOCAL IMMIGRATION PATTERNS

One way to better understand immigration from a global context is to consider data from the Organization for Economic Cooperation and Development (OECD), of which the United States is a member. Specifically, the OECD (2017) has released its *International Migration Outlook 2017*, which discusses the most pressing issues and recent developments related to international migration policies across its 35 member nations. According to its report, permanent migration to OECD nations has increased for three consecutive years, with approximately 5 million people having migrated to these nations in 2016 alone. While humanitarian and temporary migration have been strong drivers of this increase, it is family migration—in the form of family formation, accompanying family, family reunification, and international adoption—that has played the largest role in driving up international migration numbers.

This is in large part due to what the OECD terms "an expansion of rights" spanning across numerous decades, which has led to more and more family migrants becoming eligible for legal residence in their host nations.

Those considered family migrants vary depending on the policies of the host country. OECD explains that the notion of a family migrant can extend well beyond the nuclear family, which is generally comprised of a spouse or partner and minor children. Sweden and the United States are the most generous in including approximately 12 types of relationships eligible for family reunification. In 2015, the United States accepted more than 700,000 family migrants when compared to Sweden. In fact, the most common destination country for family migrants was the United States with 754,000 family migrants entering in 2015, followed at great distance by Canada who welcomed 159,000 and Australia who welcomed 129,000. Both Canada and Australia may also be considered less welcoming that the United States considering that in Canada fiancés and adult or married children were ineligible for family reunification, while in Australia adult or married children were also ineligible.

As this data shows, the United States has continued to be an immigrant friendly nation when compared to many of its counterparts around the world. In addition to the international commitments toward family unification under the Universal Declaration of Human Rights (1948) and the United Nations Convention on the Rights of the Child (1989), the United States has enacted its own policies in 1924, 1952, and most recently in 1965, which have opened the doors for immigrants to cross its borders and to remain in the country as permanent residents and citizens. While other nations have certainly had their own sets of policies welcoming immigrants across their borders, none have seemingly gone as far or have had the same impact as the United States.

In our more recent times and under a new presidential administration, however, the current goal seems to be to scale back such policies to levels similar or below that of other nations. Whether such policy changes will in fact be realized and whether these changes will in fact realize their intended purpose remains to be seen. However, one thing is for certain: policy reform that attempts to drastically scale back immigration into the United States or that attempts to remove current residents, whether documented or undocumented, will be no easy task for an administration. This is in large part because the United States has welcomed immigrants for very long and those who have immigrated to the United States have helped define this nation's identity and impacted its economy. If their presence in the United States is threatened, it will have detrimental socioeconomic, cultural, and educational implications to the nation.

OUTLINING THE CONTEXT FOR IMMIGRATION AND ITS FORCES

Table 1.1 below provides an illustration of the aforementioned primary resource texts and how their contents relate to (1) global forces, including political persecution, poverty and crime, and public education; (2) national forces, such as job opportunities, large immigrant

Table 1.1 Contextual outline of primary sources

Primary Source Texts	Global Forces	National Forces	Education Policies	Understanding of Phenomenon
Year: 1965 Immigration Act of 1965	Developing countries' desire to reach American dream	"End" of immigration quota systems; Civil Rights Act	Demographic of schools shift; children have different (linguistic) needs, shift in market demands; question of do public schools really teach *all* children?	Shifting pedagogical practices to meet the needs of immigrant children in schools
Year: 2017 Immigration Priorities for 2017 Presidential Transition Report (FAIR Report)	Political persecution, poverty/crime overseas, inferior levels of public education	Job opportunities for immigrant communities, opportunity in American economy	Public school for all, better level of education, ESL, and bilingual education available, DREAM Act/DACA	Threat to: culturally responsive pedagogy, public education (education for all), welcoming and integration of immigrant communities

communities, and social welfare incentives; and (3) educational policies, which include free public education under Plyler v. Doe, bilingual programs, and the Deferred Action for Childhood Arrivals (DACA). The goal of the table below is to provide a contextual outline of the primary resources addressed in this chapter as it relates to phenomenon of immigration in education.

DIALOGUE ANALYSIS OF PRIMARY RESOURCES 1960s VS. 2017

In this section, the authors will engage in a dialogic discussion about immigration using the two primary resource texts and the contextual outline (Table 1.1) as a framework. The authors illustrate their discussion in two different fonts (italic and plain) to represent the differing points of view and use a third font (bold) to represent their agreement about the topic, if there is any. The italic font represents the views aligned with the first primary resource document (Immigration Act of 1965) and the plain font aligns with the discussion of the second primary resource document (FAIR Report).

GLOBAL FORCES

CG: *Immigration in the United States has been in existence since its inception, and it was at the end of the nineteenth century that the country began restricting populations of newcomers based on specific criteria centered on national origin, skill, and profession. But after World War I and the country's fascination with Americanization as a strategy to hold nationalist values intact, immigration legislation in the 1920s became stricter. Teachers used strategies in the classroom to teach immigrant students American values and begin the process of assimilation of these immigrant youths. Assimilation required that students acquired the social, cultural, political, and linguistic characteristics and principles of the United States and its American citizens. Essentially, the school's role was to ensure that immigrant students were prepared to participate and contribute to American society; their needs were subsidiary to that of the greater society. But as the growing needs of immigrants began to conflict with this ideology, the sentiment of assimilation began to change just as the passing of the Immigration Act of 1965 began to change the identity of the United States.*

RI: It's interesting that you would identify this piece of legislation as one of the most impactful on immigration. Organizations such as the Federation for American Immigration Reform (FAIR) identify events such as the Mariel boatlift (a mass emigration from Cuba due to political and economic conflict), along with global pressures of some populations like political persecution and other injustices as key milestones responsible for the increase of immigration. Would you agree that such global forces had a stronger impact?

CG: *The views of a report such as the one you cited is a great example of the controversy related to immigration. The United States has been an aspirational destination for many in foreign countries for its symbolic representation of opportunity and freedom. It became even more desired after political turmoil such as wars, discrimination, economic instability, and request for refugee status emerged in other countries. While the Mariel boatlift increased the population of the United States considerably in 1980, the influx of immigrants began in the late 1960s after the Immigration Act of 1965 was passed. Many nationalists advocated for restrictions on immigration with the goal to restrict and give preference to only those whose national origin stemmed from northern Europe; were highly skilled professionals; or were agricultural workers. In other words, the United States strategically designed its immigration policies to allow people in to the country who either benefitted the U.S. economy or were white.*

RI: It seems like the critics on immigration are not arguing that the immigration system should be eliminated, rather it should be limited and have specific restrictions that help the country succeed. They call for a reduction of immigrants, as this will help the country recuperate from the strain in the healthcare, economic, and education system. Wouldn't this benefit students and families? It seems like a logical argument.

CG: *Oftentimes, positions against immigration stem from nationalism and fear. Immigration critics believed that newcomers would "pollute the nation's bloodstream" (Higham, 1999) and would not assimilate to American life, one of the pedagogical principles in instruction up to the 1960s.*

Many criminalize immigration and frame it as the reason for poverty and crime, when in fact it has benefited our country for centuries. We must be careful when identifying the true intentions of organizations that charge immigrants with the cause for "environmental degradation, displacement of low-skilled American workers, threatening cultural bonds holding Americans together," such as FAIR does in their reporting. It seems like they are more interested in exclusion rather than inclusion. The anti-immigrant narrative is oftentimes extremist and misrepresents the positive impact that immigrants have on the country.

NATIONAL FORCES

CG: *The 1960s was an era of shifting values for the United States with the monumental passing of the Civil Rights Act of 1960. It was a defining moment for the country, as it began shaping the narrative for inclusion, equity, and equality in America, and attempting to end discrimination on the grounds of race, color, religion, sex, and national origin. This era of self-examination for the United States was also marked by the passing of the Voting Rights Act (1965). Civil rights advocates highlighted the hypocrisy in the United States' immigration policies, which discriminated against those seeking to come to the land of opportunity, while having in existence laws that banned differential treatment for diverse people. As America's fundamental values were being redefined, the consequences from the Immigration Act yielded an increase in immigration, providing the opportunity for family reunification, as many were able to sponsor their next of kin to join them in the United States.*

RI: The FAIR report (2016) tries to make a case that because most of the immigrants arriving to the United States are unskilled and rely on social services, that 50 percent are more likely to use welfare. To exemplify this position, a highlighted quote on the report reads, "America is still working to meet the challenges of assisting our own poor and disadvantaged; mass immigration compounds the problem and impedes efforts to raise the standards of living for all" (p. 19).

CG: *Yes, it is true that as a result of "opening the borders" to immigration, the social composition of communities and schools (teachers and children) began to shift. This also made way for the inequitable and incongruent learning experiences of this new wave of students across the country. The FAIR Report's agenda claims to be concerned with "raising the standard of living for all," but with their exclusionary agenda at the forefront, one must question for whom are they really advocating.*

EDUCATIONAL POLICIES

CG: *Historical outcomes have informed us that not providing support for our immigrant youth leads to low achievement and high rates of school dropouts. This is in part, the reason that federal legislation for the rights of those marginalized students were created. The Elementary and Secondary Education Act of 1965 played a significant role in expanding the focus of equal access to education and required high standards and accountability from public schools while providing funding. Its funding formula was linked to academic achievement and its overarching goal was to provide accessible, fair and equitable educational opportunities to children and their families, especially those from low-income households. This influential law aligned with the shifting focus of education in the United States. It helped propel the education of English Language Learners and address the growing need of linguistically responsive instruction with the passing of the Bilingual and Education Act of 1967. This legislation specifically acknowledged the importance of specialized instruction for those non-English speaking students. This, however, did not come without any controversy and has been plagued with inadequate implementation across the country. There are many cited examples of districts placing underprepared teachers in classrooms with English Language Learners or inadequately providing students with the level of instruction necessary for students to transition out of English as a Second Language classrooms.*

RI: The intent of laws such as this one is what FAIR argues to be negatively impacting our education system. They would rather advocate that the specialized services for Limited English Proficient (LEP) students be reallocated to serve the general student population, without providing specialized assistance to LEP students. They, in essence, advocate for the slow disintegration of services for immigrant youth who are in the United States. They also advocate for the elimination of the Deferred Action for Childhood Arrivals (DACA) and the elimination of dual language and English as a Second Language programs in public schools.

CG: *It's important to note that policy changes and passing of legislation did not change the experience for immigrant children overnight. Schools were slow to adjust their practices toward inclusive environments. For example, San Francisco (one of the most linguistically diverse cities) was at the helm of controversy in the 1970s for not providing adequate instruction to English Language Learners. Students were placed in either special education classes, were held back continuously for years, or were sent to other schools designated for truants. Injustices such as this one reached the courts (Lau v. Nichols, 1974) and made a positive indelible impact on the rights of English Language Learners. Other court cases addressed civil rights concerns such as equal rights for Latino students (Keyes v. Denver School District No. 1, 1973) and rights of undocumented children to attend public schools (Plyler v. Doe, 1982).*

Eliminating these services will not serve our country positively. Although many argue that the services to educate immigrant children should be reallocated to better serve those from U.S.-born parents, we cannot forget that immigrant children are the largest segment of school-aged youth. Eliminating such programs will be large detriment to not only those students and families, but for the country as well.

UNDERSTANDING THE PHENOMENON

CG: *Placing the concept of immigration and its impact in schools within the context of the immigrant experience may provide educators with a better understanding of the importance of this* *phenomenon. Leaving one's country and relocating to a new setting is not an easy decision for many. But with its symbolic promise for opportunity and freedom, immigrating to the United States is often filled with hopes. Expectedly, families are met with the challenge of not only learning a new culture, but a new language. Their children also navigate multiple realities, as they receive mixed messages about their identities. On one hand, at home they are speaking their native language, following their customs and paying homage to their heritage; on the other hand, in schools and communities they are receiving messages about delegitimizing their language and hyphenating their ethnic identity (for example, someone who is Chinese becomes Chinese-American). The quest to fit in and transition into the citizenry of the country while maintaining their individualities while having a lack of resources in schools to meet their needs is marginalizing. Schools, in large part, play an essential role in the transition for children. In fact, the schooling that children receive also benefits their immigrant family members, as students bring what they learn in school to the home, especially the English language.*

RI: Many of the policies promoted by FAIR are based on the fear that American resources are limited, and that our societal system overall cannot effectively handle current and future population numbers. Whether that fear is valid or not, the duties of educators remain the same. Teachers are responsible for providing an appropriate education for all children within the least restrictive environment possible. It is also required that this education be fair and equitable regardless of a student's race, ethnicity, religion, gender, sexual orientation, or who their parents are. Many may not be able to control the global and national forces that lead special interest groups and legislative bodies to build their own conclusions and enact new policies among the populous. However, educators can impact their classrooms, schools, and districts in positive ways when they take knowledge from the outside world and use it to advance those they are sworn to educate.

Scholars often cite examples of how history repeats itself. This statement holds true when analyzing the ebb and flow of attention and policies on immigration. The 1960s brought an era of relaxed immigration policies after a bout of decades limiting populations from some parts of the world. In present time, the current administration has employed restrictive measures scaling back the temporary protections and entrance of immigrants into the United States. In part, these measures have been met with appeals, court proceedings, and protests from political organizations and the public, which have slowed down the reform agenda of the current administration promulgated by FAIR's report outlining recommendations of immigration priorities for the 45th President of the United States. This fluctuation in tightening and loosening immigration policies will continue for decades to come, and it is certain that it will not be met without a challenge. Regardless of the patterns of immigration, we must address the current needs of our immigrant population in our schools. Resources such as culturally and linguistically-responsive instruction and diverse and culturally competent educators are not "accommodations," such as FAIR refers to them, but a right of those immigrants to whom we have welcomed and made a commitment.

MEETING THE NEEDS OF IMMIGRANT STUDENT POPULATION: 1960s VS. 2017

THE EDUCATIONAL LANDSCAPE IN THE 1960s

Prior to the 1960s, the dominating narrative in American society and schools stemmed from a desire to Americanize immigrants by implementing strategies for assimilation. But as the vigorous efforts toward equal educational opportunities gradually evolved and the proportion of school children from immigrant families increased, the case for bilingual education and programs for students who spoke a foreign language emerged. This was evidenced by the Elementary and Secondary Education Act (1965), Bilingual Education Act (1968), and Equal Education Opportunity Act (1974). While there was a progressive call to improve the education of the immigrant student population, the implementation of these practices was not evident in many of the classrooms during the late 1960s. Despite the federal government financial incentives, many schools were either unprepared or unwilling to meet the needs of these young newcomers. This was especially evident in the offering of bilingual education in schools.

Bilingual education was at the forefront of criticism during the 1960s, thus impacting pedagogical practices in the classroom. For example, critics argued that instruction in schools should be in English and that learning in two languages would confuse students' sense of being; therefore, English instruction, they argued, could prevent the "inward maladjustment" of students (Duignan, 1998). Some others believed that a student's native language played a temporary role and the English language should eventually be the primary (and only) language in a child's academic life. To complicate matters, there were also issues of segregation of immigrant youth despite the passing of legislation outlawing discrimination. It is no surprise that the instructional practices mirrored antiquated principles that resulted in the marginalization of students. To conceptualize how these practices impacted students, Table 1.2 outlines the detrimental outcomes on these pedagogical practices in the 1960s.

While the examples in Table 1.2 highlight subtractive approaches to students' needs, these began to take a different form as court cases cited schools' inadequacy in mitigating the deficiency in supports and offerings for immigrant youth.

EDUCATIONAL LANDSCAPE IN 2017

The educational trajectory of immigrant students is much different today than in the 1960s, though challenges and injustices still exist. In the current day, educators can find policy briefs, publications, district-wide practices, shared knowledge, and websites that share resources and effective practices in the instruction for English learners that have evolved since those in the 1960s, as described in Table 1.2. Access to all of these resources

Table 1.2 Instructional, pedagogical practices, and outcomes of the 1960s

Instructional and Pedagogical Practices	Impact on Students, Learning, or Outcomes
In the absence of bilingual instruction, students were placed in English-only classes	High drop-out rates; low academic achievement; high rate of absenteeism
Limited English Proficiency students erroneously diagnosed as having a disability	Students were disproportionately and incorrectly placed in special education classrooms
Students speaking a foreign language in schools was regarded as a *problem* that needed to be *resolved*	Bilingual programs were established with a remedial and deficit-based framework, instead of an academic enrichment and strength-based lens
Schools disregarded courses completed in the student's native country	Students were placed in lower level classes; students developed a feeling of inferiority; students were delayed in completing school

signals acknowledgment of the importance of meeting the diverse needs of immigrant student populations. A key point in understanding adequate pedagogical practices is that their experiences are varied; hence, it is important that we not implement the same strategy for all classrooms of immigrant children. For example, the experiences and learning process for students who arrive to the United States around early childhood and elementary school grades (first-generation immigrant) is different from those who arrive around middle and high school grades (generation 1.5). There are also immigrant school children that have interrupted formal education, who due to their refugee status or other obstruction in their continuous formal education, have not attended school consecutively.

Like other immigrant children, those with interrupted formal education can be supported by providing them with the following pedagogical practices: supportive environments with trained staff and educators; newcomer programs to ease student transitions; collaboration models across the school building to strengthen multidisciplinary linguistic and academic development; intentional flexible scheduling; teaching of strategies that they can use in the future; building of the native language's content and literacy instruction in order to later build on English concepts; allowing students to work in cooperative groups; and providing a print-rich environment (Robertson & Lafond, n.d.).

Additionally, there are some curricular and intentional decisions that teachers can make to better impact the learning experience of these students. Table 1.3 below breaks down some practices that can further inform and support the instruction and learning outcomes of immigrant students.

Table 1.3 Current instructional and pedagogical practices and their outcomes on student learning

Instructional Practices	Impact on Students, Learning, and Outcomes
Educators show respect for the student's primary language and home culture	Build confidence and abilities as it relates to academic concepts and settings
Teachers encourage the student to use their native language with others during targeted activities; students are then encouraged to build comprehension by using new English words	Build context familiarity and comprehension in student's native language and allow them to make tangible connections to the English language
Instead of intelligence testing (as it was previously done), schools perform literacy assessments to assign appropriate interventions to students and monitor progress	Accurately address students' needs in academic progress and develop additional enrichment interventions, as needed
For students with interrupted schooling, provide them with extended days, additional task time, weekend academies, and summer school enrichment sessions	Individualized instruction for students; provide them with opportunities to get the most out of instruction; build confidence

BEYOND INSTRUCTIONAL PRACTICES: EDUCATORS AS AGENTS OF CHANGE

With immigration policies becoming as relevant today as they were 50 years ago, it is of vital importance to think about how these policies impact our immigrant students and their families beyond instructional practices in the classroom. The current driving narrative surrounding immigrant families includes imminent threats such as discrimination, ostracism, and deportation—all of which impact the well-being, performance, and success of students. Thus, school officials and teachers must understand and recognize the challenges and fears that immigrant students and families face locally and nationally. This acknowledgment goes beyond implementing culturally responsive instruction in the classroom and involves teachers learning about the students in their classrooms from a sociocultural, sociopolitical, and socioeconomic standpoint. It further requires taking an active role in designing a better context for students and families within and outside of the confines of school by becoming agents of change in the community they serve.

Change can be accomplished by first recognizing that schools are a source of stability and safety to students and their families. Cultivating an environment where students' voices and experiences are heard and validated is important in the process of making a space safe and a haven for those who inhabit it for the majority of the day. Additionally, schools can be agents of change by partnering and collaborating with community organizations that can serve as resources for teachers by providing trainings and workshops that will help educate them on community matters as it relates to the immigrant population. The participation of community organizations in schools can also send the message to immigrant families that the school building is a safe place where they can connect with resources that may be of some help to them. Additionally, teachers and school officials may also benefit from seeking collaboration from local institutions of higher education with scholars and practitioners that are versed in the work that it takes to support students and families in the community. Providing a safe space will also cultivate an environment where immigrant families feel comfortable to engage as parents and have their voices heard as it relates to the schooling of their children.

CONCLUSION

Educators are tasked with serving all youth regardless of personal, social, and political views. These youth are greatly composed of immigrant children and U.S.-born children of immigrant parents, a trend that has not shown signs of slowing. Thus, as educators treat all with equity and perform their jobs with exceptional passion, states and districts have a duty to develop policies and practices, which allow for the servicing all children who walk through school doors. Such constitutes a humanistic approach to education. With this end, the current chapter sought to help future and current educators better understand their roles in the midst of both longstanding and sporadic immigration policy and reform in the United States. We cannot be sure of what the future holds with regards to immigration policy and immigrants in America. However, if the past is any indication of things to come, then we must be prepared to help current and future youth from immigrating families become a longstanding and productive tradition to our nation of immigrants. We must ask ourselves, will we help them reach their destined future, or will we stand aside as their educational process is complicated by political views and fear? Additional questions such as this one are found at the conclusion of this chapter promoting further discussion, multi-pronged perspectives, and critical thinking on the matter. While the answer to these questions may be obvious to many of us, the action that we decide to take may not be the easiest one, though it may be the most fulfilling.

GLOSSARY OF TERMS

Bilingual education—instruction in two languages and their use as mediums of instruction for any part, or all, of the school curriculum (Andersson, Boyer, & Southwest Educational Development Laboratory, 1970).

Bilingual student—someone who has developed proficiency in the English language while having proficiency in their language as well.

Culturally and linguistically responsive—pedagogical practices that focus on students' cultural background, experiences, language, and frames of reference to inform classroom instruction.

Deferred Action for Childhood Arrivals (DACA)—an administrative relief from deportation with the purpose to protect eligible immigrant youth who came to the United States when they were children. Benefits from DACA include giving immigrant youth protection from deportation and a work permit.

English Language Learners (ELL)—learners who are beginning to learn English as a new language or have already gained some proficiency in English.

English as a Second Language (ESL)—an educational program where students are immersed in English as both language of instruction and curriculum content.

Immigrants—persons with no U.S. citizenship at birth. This population includes naturalized citizens, lawful permanent residents, refugees and asylees, persons on temporary visas, and those who are undocumented.

Limited English Proficiency (LEP)—someone who is not proficient speaking, reading, understanding, or writing in English, often because it is not their native language.

EXTENSION QUESTIONS

1. Has legislation for linguistically diverse students had its intended impacts in today's schools? What are examples of its effectiveness or lack of impact?

2. How can teachers learn about their students' environment and background to help better develop culturally relevant instruction?

3. What improvements, if any, could immigrant students benefit from in their educational experience in the United States?

4. What factors can empower educators to provide a safe haven for immigrant students within the confines of school?

REFERENCES

Andersson, T., Boyer, M., & Southwest Educational Development Laboratory. (1970). *Bilingual schooling in the United States*. Austin, Texas: Southwest Educational Development Laboratory.

Duignan, P. (1998). *Bilingual education: A critique* (No. 22). Hoover Institution Press.

Faltis, C. (2007). Immigrant students in US schools: Building a pro-immigrant, English plus education counterscript. *Journal of Global Initiatives: Policy, Pedagogy, Perspective, 2*(1), 2.

Federation for American Immigration Reform. (n.d.). Who we are. Retrieved from http://www.fairus.org.

Ferris, M. & Raley, S. (2016). *The Elephant in the Classroom: Mass Immigration's Impact on Public Education*. Retrieved from https://fairus.org/sites/default/files/2017-08/FAIR-Education-Report-2016.pdf.

Higham, J. (1999). Cultural responses to immigration. *Diversity and Its Discontents: Cultural Conflict and Common Ground in Contemporary American Society*, 39–61.

Massey, D. (1995). The new immigration and ethnicity in the United States. *Population and Development Review, 21*(3), 631–652.

O'Brien, M., Spencer, R., Law, R., & Rehberg, S. (2016). *Immigration priorities for the 2017 presidential transition*. Washington, DC: FAIR Horizons Press.

OECD. (2017). *International Migration Outlook 2017*. Organization for Economic Cooperation and Development.

Robertson, K. & Lafond, S. (2008). How to support ELL students with interrupted formal education (SIFEs). Retrieved from http://www.colorincolorado.org/article/27483.

Sacchetti, M. (2017, May 8). Newly released letter shows growing battle between groups in immigration debate. *The Washington Post*. Retrieved from https://www.washingtonpost.com.

Zong, J. & Betalova, J. (2017). Frequently requested statistics on immigrants and immigration in the United States. Migration Information Source. *Retrieved from* http://www.migrationpolicy.org/article/frequently-requested-statistics-immigrants-and-immigration-united-states.

2

BEYOND CLASS: EXPLORING THE INTERSECTION OF SOCIAL CLASS, CAPITAL, AND STUDENT ACHIEVEMENT

ELIZABETH I. RIVERA RODAS
NICOLE AUFFANT

INTRODUCTION

The educational **achievement gap** separating economically disadvantaged and ethnic minority students from their peers has been the focus of research and school reform for several decades. The gap between African American and White students narrowed considerably through the late 1980s but since then, progress has slowed and reversed. African American and Latino students are much more likely than White students to have lower academic achievement rates and are much less likely to graduate from high school, obtain a college degree, or obtain a middle-class job (National Center for Education Statistics, 2009; National Center for Education Statistics, 2011).

There are a disproportionate number of failing schools, across all grade levels, comprised predominantly of poor, racial, and ethnic minority students. These schools tend to have fewer resources—financial, material, and human—than schools in more affluent areas. Students who attend these segregated schools receive a substandard education, which contributes to the achievement gap.

Differences in student achievement have also been linked to parental expectations, networks between families, school academic climate, and cultural values. Resources within social institutions and relationships are known as **social capital**, which exist in the forms of parental expectations, obligations, and social networks within families, schools, and communities.

The concept of social capital is important when trying to understand differences in learning outcomes among students from different backgrounds. Schools with high levels of social capital are more likely to produce students with better academic performance than those with lower levels.

The fact that lower performing schools have a lack of social capital in comparison to top performing schools has undermined the effectiveness of some of the policies and programs that intended to close the achievement gap in school systems across the country. Low levels of social capital can undercut the effectiveness of many types of school reforms. Policies like increasing teacher quality, improving school leadership and decreasing class sizes are not always successful in closing the achievement gap because of the social dimensions that these policies overlook when they are implemented. The reforms have limited ability to close the achievement gap because they do not take social capital discrepancies into account. However, there is now a movement toward addressing socioeconomic segregation in schools, which would address the social capital gap and therefore, the achievement gap. As you read this chapter, consider the relationship between social capital and educational achievement, as well as the possible role of socioeconomic integration in closing the achievement gap.

CONTEXTUAL INFORMATION

Fifty years ago, the "Equality of Educational Opportunity" report (1966), also known as the Coleman Report, linked low student achievement of racial/ethnic minority students to poverty and parents' education. The table below shows that the Coleman Report was written during a highly charged political climate following the 1954 U.S. Supreme Court decision in *Brown v. Board of Education*. That decision held that state laws establishing separate public schools for Black and White students, segregation, are unconstitutional and it ordered school desegregation. In addition, during the Cold War, the United States wanted to present itself as a society of greater racial harmony. However, there was little change in U.S. race relations by the time the Civil Rights Act of 1964 was passed ten years later.

The Coleman Report was commissioned by Congress in the Civil Rights Act of 1964 as part of the struggle to desegregate public schools in the United States and to prove that segregation by race was continuing in schools across the country. The United States Commissioner of Education was ordered to "conduct a survey and make a report to the President and the Congress, within two years of the enactment, concerning the lack of availability of equal educational opportunity for individuals by reason of race, religion, or national origin in public institutions at all levels in the United States" (Civil Rights Act of 1964, Pub. L. No. 88–352, 78 Stat. 241, 1964).

Prior to the release of the Coleman Report, it was widely believed that increased school funding, which provided schools with better facilities and higher qualified teachers, was the root cause of the achievement gap. However, the Coleman Report found that the differences across schools in average achievement levels were not as profound as those within schools and that the achievement gap was not directly related to differences in school resources. Instead, the Coleman Report stated that "most important variable—in or out of school—in a child's performance remains his family's education background" (Coleman, 1966). In turn, this social capital factor can greatly influence a school's student body performance.

> [I]f a white pupil from a home that is strongly and effectively supportive of education is put in a school where most pupils do not come from such homes, his achievement will be little different than if he were in a school composed of others like himself. But if a minority pupil from a home without much educational strength is put with schoolmates with strong educational backgrounds, his achievement is likely to increase. (Coleman, 1966)

These findings were groundbreaking and focused attention on the social context of children's academic development because the Coleman Report showed that social capital was just as important as school resources.

As racial/ethnic minorities become a larger proportion of the student population, school leaders and teachers must understand how race, ethnicity, and social class impact students' educational experiences and school achievement. As seen in the table below, there has been an increase in the proportion of immigrant students and English language learners across the country. This, coupled with the reversal of mandated desegregation and the end of busing in some of the most historically segregated districts in the country, creates a need for educational reforms to not be completely school focused. The findings from the Coleman Report on the role of social capital are still relevant today and still need to be considered when attempting to close the achievement gap.

School integration based solely on race has been ruled unconstitutional by the Supreme Court's *Parents Involved in Community Schools v. Seattle School District No. 1* (2007). However, several school districts across the country are formally pursuing **socioeconomic integration** as a means to close racial achievement gaps (The Century Foundation, 2016). Most African American and Latino students attend high-poverty public schools in the United States and therefore, socioeconomic integration in schools may equal racial integration.

Revisiting the Coleman Report findings may provide an explanation for the seemingly backward movement and possible solutions that should be included in education policy. The Century Foundation (TCF), a nonpartisan research institute, is interested in economic and socioeconomic school integration. TCF has researched socioeconomic school integration programs for twenty years and has found that low-income students in mixed-income schools perform better than their peers in high-poverty schools (Kahlenberg & Potter, 2012). TCF's *Stories of School Integration* (2016) is a collection of reports on nine school districts across the United States using socioeconomic measures to integrate schools. The report makes clear that diverse cities and school districts do not guarantee diversity within schools. New York City and Chicago are some of the most racially and economically diverse cities in the country, yet most of their schools have an overwhelming poor and minority student body. Segregated neighborhoods within cities, along with the option of private and charter schools, are some explanations for the persistence of segregated schools in diverse districts.

In 2007, TCF released a report that profiled 12 districts implementing socioeconomic integration programs. Currently, there are over one hundred school districts and charter schools serving over 4 million students in 32 states across the country with formal socioeconomic integration plans. As a follow-up to the 2007 report, TCF's *Stories of School Integration* (2016) investigates the effectiveness of socioeconomic integration policies that have been in place for some time. The profiled districts include Cambridge, MA, Hartford, CT, Stamford, CT, New York City, Champaign, IL, Chicago, IL, Eden Prairie, MN, Jefferson County (Louisville), KY, and Dallas, TX. Overall, the report found that well-implemented, socioeconomic diversity policies produced strong academic outcomes for students and that socioeconomic diversity policies lead to racial diversity. In addition, the most successful districts ensured that socioeconomic integration occurred at both the school and classroom level.

The profiled districts implemented socioeconomic integration in various ways. Some districts, such as Jefferson County, consolidated urban and nearby suburban districts, while others, most notably Chicago, instituted socioeconomic policies for particular schools rather than the entire district. Based on the varying results from these districts, *Stories of School Integration* suggests several lessons from socioeconomically integrated schools. The most considerable takeaway is that students performed better, and schools achieved greater racial diversity when they had well-implemented socioeconomic diversity policies. An important point made by the report is that socioeconomic diversity must go beyond family income. Factors such as parental education, non-English speaking households, and single-family households must be considered. Furthermore, reaction to mandated desegregation in the decades following Brown shows the need for community buy-in with educational policies. The report concludes that choice or incentive programs are more likely to result in community support than mandated policies. Socioeconomic integration policy may be key in closing the achievement gap.

Text	Global Forces	National Forces	Education Policies	Understanding of Phenomenon
Text 1 *Equality of Educational Opportunity (Coleman, 1966)*	Cold War; Communists critical of the U.S. when so many U.S. citizens were subjected to racial discrimination	Civil Rights Act of 1964; a decade after *Brown v. Board of Education*, segregation was still the norm; civil rights movement	Changed the way education was studied and evaluated; first to document achievement gap	Family background and the social and economic composition of the student body (social capital) are the most important factors in student achievement
Text 2 *Stories of School Integration (The Century Foundation, 2016)*	Globalization—increase in immigrant students, increase in ELL students	Reversal of mandated desegregation; end of busing	Socioeconomic integration	Coleman's findings are still important when talking about class and social mobility—"The American Dream"

DIALOGICAL TEXT ANALYSIS

In this section, we discuss the Coleman Report and the TCF report, two studies dealing with socioeconomic integration and the achievement gap. We note that even though the studies are over half a century apart, teachers and schools face similar issues. We also explore possible solutions to reducing the achievement gap.

INSUFFICIENT FUNDING

N.A: Lack of funding is often considered a major contributing factor to negative student and school performance. Many districts rely on local property taxes to account for the majority of school funding. Therefore, wealthier districts have more funding than poorer districts. These poorer funded schools tend to serve a majority of students of color, leaving them with fewer resources than students in wealthier districts, who are more often white. States such as New Jersey attempted to address these gaps in funding by rethinking funding formulas. The New Jersey Supreme Court in its landmark ruling in *Abbott v. Burke*, held that money from wealthier districts be rerouted to assist some of the poorest districts in the state.

It is important to note that the Coleman Report does not state that schools' resources are not important to students' achievement. The effects that unequal school resources have on the achievement gap continue to be studied and many policies are enacted to ameliorate these effects. Policies likely focus on unequal resources because it seems to be easier to control. Many state and federal programs allocate extra funding to schools and districts that lack a wealth of resources in an attempt to close racial and economic achievement gaps. However, many of these districts are so overwhelmed by high concentrations of student poverty that the districts are unable to provide the necessary resources students and their families require despite extra funding.

E.R.R: *This is very true. One of the most overlooked findings from the Coleman Report is that it does, in fact, point out that the disparities in financial resources across schools impact student achievement. The Coleman Report stated that the average Black 12th grader in the rural South had a similar achievement level as a White 7th grader in the urban Northeast. Similar performance gaps were never given the attention that they deserved. These gaps were attributed to inequities in school finance and the social capital of families in these areas. In most cases, state and federal funding is supposed to supplant funding for low-income schools in comparison to other schools within the state. Therefore, if a state has low funding overall then federal and state funding will not help low-income schools as much as it would in states with higher educational funding. In addition, financial resources for low-income schools are sometimes stretched thin over several programs that are intended to meet the needs of low-income families.*

N.A: It is clear that insufficient funding plays a role in student achievement, but it is not the only factor and it may not be the most influential factor when it comes to student outcomes. Furthermore, policies that do address insufficient funding are unable to ameliorate the effects of already low funding.

CLASS, CAPITAL, AND STUDENT ACHIEVEMENT

N.A: More than sixty years after *Brown v. Board of Education*, school districts are increasingly segregated by race and socioeconomic status, with suburban schools outperforming urban schools. Schools in urban districts are predominantly Black and Latino, working-class and poor students, while suburban schools have higher concentrations of White, middle-class students. These homogenized districts reduce student exposure to different levels of social capital. If, as the Coleman Report found, students perform better when higher levels of social capital are found within schools, homogenized schools will never close the achievement gap.

Coleman's study found that larger achievement gaps occur within schools than between, suggesting that lack of school resources are not a sufficient predictor of student outcomes. Instead, students' family and socioeconomic background play a larger role in student achievement. Furthermore, students attending schools with children from more varied backgrounds perform better than students attending schools where children come from similar backgrounds. This means that middle-class, working-class, and poor students all perform better academically when they attend socioeconomically integrated schools compared to attending socioeconomically segregated schools. It is worth emphasizing that it is not just poor and working-class students who perform better in socioeconomically integrated schools, it is students from all socioeconomic and class backgrounds. The Century Foundation report supports this finding stating that in Hartford, "Black/White and Hispanic/White achievement gaps in reading were about half as large as the comparable statewide gaps," noting that "achievement differences are smaller not because white students do worse, but because all subgroups of students perform better" (The Century Foundation, 2016). It should follow, then, that any plan to close educational achievement gaps should include fostering socioeconomically diverse schools.

E.R.R: *All students benefit from the social capital that middle-class families bring to schools. Parents from middle-class families will advocate more for their children by demanding smaller class sizes, more rigorous curricula, and higher quality teachers. These improvements not only benefit the middle-class students, but also the rest of the student body in these schools. The positive benefits of being in socioeconomically diverse classrooms have been shown to improve the educational achievement of middle-class students as well, but the percentage of low-income students has been a source of debate.*

Not only that but as students from private school opt back into public schools, overall achievement rates in public school should increase because students from non-socioeconomically integrated public schools outperform students in public schools. In fact, a NAEP study (Braun, Jenkins, & Grigg, 2006) shows that students in private schools achieved at higher levels than students in public schools in grade 8 reading scores when controlling for student characteristics. However, the NAEP study found no differences in grade 4 reading and grade 8 mathematics and students from public schools achieved at higher levels than students from private schools in grade 4 reading when controlling for student characteristics. This would imply that when student characteristics such as socioeconomic status are removed from the equation, students would perform similarly in both private and public schools.

Although the Cambridge case study in the TCF report shows that more middle-class and white people began to enroll their children in the public school districts as its schools became more socioeconomically integrated, in some cases, more affluent parents will opt to send their children to private schools instead of investing in low-income public schools. Adjusting the comparisons for student characteristics resulted in reductions in all four average differences of approximately 11 to 14 points. Based on adjusted school means, the average for public schools was significantly higher than the average for private schools for grade 4 mathematics, while the average for private schools was significantly higher than the average for public schools for grade 8 reading. The average differences in adjusted school means for both grade 4 reading and grade 8 mathematics were not significantly different from zero.

OPTING OUT

N.A: Opting out refers to families choosing not to send their child to their district public school. Instead, families may send their child to private school, charter school, or may even choose to homeschool. However, to achieve the benefits from socioeconomically integrated schools, districts need more families, particularly middle-class families, to opt-in. In this section, we discuss who is opting out, what they are opting for, why they are opting out, and consequences of opting out. Considering these questions may help keep students with high levels of social capital in public schools.

Wealthy families have long turned to private schools for their children's education. Some policy makers and politicians have supported the charter school movement because it provides an alternative option to failing traditional public schools, without the financial commitment that private school demands. Charter schools require families to apply to schools as early as a year in advance of a child's expected enrollment. Depending on the number of applicants, families may be placed in a lottery to decide who gains entry. This lengthy process can be more rigorous than traditional public-school enrollment and requires families to be aware of application deadlines and procedures. Families with high levels of social capital are at an advantage when it comes to navigating charter school enrollment. This is because those with larger social networks are more likely to learn about charter school enrollment periods and have easier access to assistance with navigating the process. Therefore, charter schools may further socioeconomically segregate struggling schools by removing students who come from families with more social capital. It is imperative, then, that policy makers consider the best ways to push back against deepening school segregation.

E.R.R: *As neighborhood public schools become low achieving, many affluent and middle-class parents opt out of traditional public schools. As these parents leave the public schools, it not only lowers the overall enrollment in neighborhood public schools and increases racial and economic segregation in schools, it removes the social capital that middle-class and affluent families have from these schools. In many cases, low-income public schools are left with parents who do not know how to advocate for themselves and their children or do not know what to advocate for because of their lack of social capital. Increased socioeconomic segregation within schools deepens the social capital divide and achievement gap. Adopting socioeconomic integration policies may prevent school districts from experiencing such a social capital drain. For example, since focusing on socioeconomic integration, Cambridge Public Schools is experiencing an increase in student enrollment whereas most other districts are losing their student population to competition with charter and private schools (The Century Foundation, 2016).*

N.A: All families want the best for their children. In seeking the best, families with higher levels of social capital will choose to send their children to schools where they believe their children will perform best. Navigating school options requires a high degree of social capital, therefore, families that opt-out of district schools are often those that would bring higher levels of social capital to public schools. To reap the benefits of socioeconomic integration, school districts must come up with ways to prevent families from opting out. One recommendation is to provide families with choice and incentives. For example, Hartford, Cambridge, and Dallas Public Schools use high-achieving magnet schools to attract middle-class suburban families (The Century Foundation, 2016). The TCF report suggests that policies empowering families to choose schools have better results than policies that mandate socioeconomic integration.

SOCIOECONOMIC INTEGRATION

N.A: In many school districts, pursuing socioeconomic integration means that districts must move beyond the neighborhood school model, and in some cases partner with surrounding districts. Even in racially/ethnically diverse cities such as Chicago, New York, and Dallas, schools are heavily segregated. For example, although Chicago is 32% White, White students account for only 10% of the public-school population (The Century Foundation, 2016).

E.R.R: *New York City is the largest public-school system in the United States and one of the most segregated. Many Black and Latino students in New York City attend public schools with few or no White students, which also translates into socioeconomic segregation. This trend has occurred because of how highly segregated many large cities are and since you attend a public school where you live, public schools look similar to those segregated neighborhoods. This is why many educational policies have not been able to close the achievement gap. Many of the issues that educational programs address do not address the underlying issues of residential segregation that have led to a lack of social capital in these neighborhoods and schools.*

N.A: Socioeconomic integration is not the same as economic integration. Economic integration would entail the use of family income or class status as a factor in enrollment. Instead, families' socioeconomic status is considered. This is not about integrating wealthy and poor students. Socioeconomic status includes social and cultural capital. The districts profiled use different tactics to measure SES, but some of the more common factors include adult educational attainment, home-ownership, single-parent households, English proficiency, and family income (The Century Foundation, 2016). Rather than looking at individual applicants, most of the districts use census data to estimate applicants' SES based on their home address. While families across SES backgrounds may value education, those with higher SES are more likely to emphasize the importance of education. Therefore, as the Coleman Report suggests, integrating families from different SES backgrounds can have a positive effect on all students' education outcomes since all students perform better when high-achieving students are in the classroom.

E.R.R: *It is also important to look at the ways in which many districts are achieving socioeconomic integration. In some cases, school districts are implementing school choice models, which allow families to select into better schools when their neighborhood school is failing. There are also some school districts that are redistricting in order to ensure that schools will be serving students from different neighborhoods. As mentioned earlier, since students attend schools in their neighborhood, it makes sense that the racial and economic segregation found within cities is reflected in the neighborhood public schools. However, redistricting allows for school districts to address the lack of social capital from one neighborhood to the next by shifting the demographics within schools.*

N.A: School busing programs from the 1960s and 1970s teach us that family buy-in is necessary for any school integration plan. The districts profiled use various tactics to gain family complicity. A popular way is to frame schools as selected enrollment or specialized magnet schools. Such schools offer families alternative options to failing schools without families leaving the district. These schools are open to students across the district rather than being bound to neighborhoods. This makes it easier to integrate schools in diverse cities that have segregated neighborhoods, such as Chicago and New York City. Schools in less diverse districts consolidate with nearby towns or the county to achieve integration. For many of these districts, there are only a few of these choice schools, so not all interested students can attend. In Chicago's selective enrollment schools, 30% of students are accepted based on their academic record and test scores while the other 70% of enrollment is based on a formula that uses the census track information discussed above, to rank the applicants' neighborhoods (The Century Foundation, 2016). As these schools perform well, demand for student entry may grow, which in other districts has led to parents challenging acceptance formulas (National Center for Education Statistics, 2011). On the other hand, greater demand may lead to the expansion of socioeconomically integrated schools.

E.R.R: *As formal socioeconomic integration continues to grow across the country in various forms in traditional public schools and charter schools, it will be interesting to see which mechanism* *for achieving socioeconomic integration is the most successful at closing the achievement gap. It will also be interesting to observe how school districts maintain socioeconomic integration as demographics continue to shift.*

N.A: While socioeconomically integrated schools can reduce achievement gaps, they also threaten the existence of neighborhood schools. As some of the profiled districts show, even diverse communities can have segregated schools. Schools bring families together. Students and parents form friendships with other students and their families, and these friendships often continue outside of the school day. In neighborhood schools, parents and children come into contact with the same families both in school and around the neighborhood, strengthening ties to the community and building social capital. If children are not attending their neighborhood schools, however, they have less opportunity of meeting children in their neighborhood. Scheduling playdates and/or enrichment activities with families who do not live close by can be difficult for some families, particularly single-parent, working class, and poor families. This also reduces the chances of building social capital for those families who need it most.

PRACTICAL IMPLICATIONS FOR TEACHERS

As the student population across the United States is becoming more diverse, addressing the achievement gap is becoming even more important. Coleman was the first to point out the glaring differences in educational performance between races and socioeconomic groups. Through his work, he also discovered that the differences between races and socioeconomic groups were not just due to school funding issues, but also due to issues of social capital.

Research has proven that the achievement gap decreases in well-integrated schools because White and middle-class parents bring resources and social capital to schools by advocating for smaller class sizes and more rigorous curricula that would improve conditions for all children. As educational policies shift to address social capital through socioeconomic integration plans, school districts across the country are becoming more racially and economically diverse. Teachers will need to learn how to identify inequalities in their own classrooms, and reconstruct classroom culture to make sure that it is inclusive of all children.

CONCLUSION

Socioeconomic differences between African American and Latino students continue to exist. Persistent patterns of housing segregation coupled with the increasing economic division in many areas has resulted in more residents living in either poor or affluent neighborhoods and fewer in middle-class neighborhoods. There is a strong link between housing policy, economy, and racial segregation. School poverty is a good proxy for the quality of a school because these schools are in less affluent neighborhoods with fewer resources. In addition, these schools have less social capital because the students come from families where fewer parents have college degrees and have the time to volunteer in school. Schools serving the poorest children have fewer resources, both economic and social capital resources.

The economic segregation of low-income students is difficult for schools to overcome when trying to close the achievement gap. Low-income schools have persisted and increased recently, even in neighborhoods experiencing economic growth. The economic isolation in schools creates a barrier to closing the achievement gap because of the lack of social capital in high-poverty schools. However, since economic segregation within schools is so closely tied to housing issues that have created segregated communities, it is difficult to close the achievement gap.

With the reversal of federal mandated segregation and busing laws across the country, it is unrealistic to expect that education policies will be able to close the achievement gap caused by economic segregation and a lack of social capital in low-income schools. Policy makers and educators must develop new strategies aimed at decreasing economic segregation across school districts. Socioeconomic integration is one such promising strategy. Socioeconomic integration, which has proven to be an effective way to increase the social capital within schools, is one such promising strategy.

The number of public school districts that have formally adopted socioeconomic integration in the past twenty years has increased to over one hundred public and charter schools across the country. These school districts consider the socioeconomic status of students when assigning them to schools and attempt to balance it throughout the districts' enrollment. In some cases, school boundaries have been redrawn to create a better balance in socioeconomic status across schools within districts. By changing the make-up of the student population, issues of low social capital are no longer overwhelming low-income schools because of the introduction of middle-class students who bring higher levels of social capital. Overall, socioeconomic integration has helped to close the achievement gap by circumventing the issues that have plagued low-income public schools across the country.

EXTENSION QUESTIONS

1. How does social capital impact educational achievement?
2. Could socioeconomic integration close the achievement gap?
3. How does socioeconomic integration address the lack of social capital in low-income schools?
4. What are some ways that you could grow social capital within your classrooms?
5. What are ways to address demographic shifts within your classroom?
6. How can you help to close the achievement gap in schools and/or classrooms that are low-income?
7. Because of demographic shifts, rich societies will have to learn how to integrate the children of low-income immigrants. In order to achieve socioeconomic integration in

Belgium, educational desegregation is at the heart of educational policy. Considering that racial desegregation is not legal in the United States, what sort of international policies could the United States implement to help close the achievement gap through socioeconomic integration?

GLOSSARY OF TERMS

Achievement gap—differences in measures of educational performance (such as test scores) among subgroups (e.g., socioeconomic status, race/ethnicity, and gender) of students in the United States.

Social capital—resources within social institutions and relationships; exists in the forms of parental expectations, obligations, and social networks within families, schools, and communities.

Socioeconomic integration—educational policy programs that formally ensure that the demographics of schools are diverse; prevents school districts from having schools that are low-income versus affluent, which also addresses racial segregation within districts.

REFERENCES

Braun, H., Jenkins, F., and Grigg, W. (2006). *Comparing Private Schools and Public Schools Using Hierarchical Linear Modeling* (NCES 2006–461). U.S. Department of Education, National Center for Education Statistics, Institute of Education Sciences. Washington, DC: U.S. Government Printing Office.

Brown v. Board of Education of Topeka, 347 U.S. 483 (1954).

Brown v. Board of Education of Topeka, 349 U.S. 294 (1955).

Civil Rights Act of 1964, Pub. L. No. 88–352, 78 Stat. 241 (1964).

Coleman, J. (1966). *Equality of Educational Opportunity*. Washington, D.C.: National Center for Educational Statistics.

Kahlenberg, R. D. & Potter, H. (2012). *Diverse Charter Schools: Can Racial and Socioeconomic Integration Promote Better Outcomes for Students?* The Century Foundation and Poverty & Race Research Action Council.

National Center for Education Statistics. (2009). *NAEP 2009 High School Transcript Study*.

National Center for Education Statistics. (2011). *Condition of Education 2011*.

Parents Involved in Community Schools v. Seattle School District No. 1, 551 U.S. 701 (2007).

The Century Foundation. (2016). *Stories of School Integration*. New York, NY: The Century Foundation.

The Century Foundation (2017). *Do Private School Vouchers Pose a Threat to Integration?* New York, NY: The Century Foundation.

3

FROM BILINGUAL TO ENGLISH ONLY TO MULTILINGUAL? MAKING A CASE FOR A LANGUAGE POLICY TOWARD TRANSLINGUALISM

DAVID SCHWARZER
MARIA-SARA KOPCZYNSKI

INTRODUCTION[1]

The purpose of this chapter is to discuss the national perception of bilingual education and how it has evolved based on the cultural and political climate of the last 50 years. In order to accomplish this task, we have decided to present three texts related to the area of bilingual and multilingual education in the United States (instead of two as it is in most of the other chapters in this edited volume). The importance of discussing language policies in the United States during the last fifty years is important to novice teachers for two reasons:

1. The student body composing of public schools have changed dramatically during the last fifty years (from mostly monolingual to mostly bilingual/multilingual), while the composition of the teacher body has remained the same (mostly White, middle class and monolingual).

2. The perceived pendulum between English-only and bilingual/multilingual education may be better understood as two competing ideas about what is the linguistic nature of the American Dream—monolingual English speakers or bilingual/multilingual citizens.

---

[1] We would like to thank Diana Cedeño and Kasun Gajasinghe M. Liyanage for their comments on earlier drafts.

In this chapter, we will make a case for presenting these two competing ideologies as ever present in the political and educational arenas in the United States. More like a tension between two ideologies that have been accompanying reflective and social justice–oriented teachers since the creation of public schools in this country. We believe that this tension will remain in place for the foreseeable future. Therefore, it is YOUR job as a novice teacher, to reflect on your own ideology or philosophy regarding the linguistic context of schools in your own practice. We will end the chapter by proposing a new term—**translingualism** that might be useful for novice teachers in the 21st century.

The first text used for the purposes of this discussion is the mandate that established bilingual education programs in the United States; the second document is a proposition adopted in California AGAINST bilingual education programs and for English-only proposals; and the third text is a proposition—adopted in California a few years ago—moves away from English-only proposals and furthers the discussion into multilingualism in the United States. We believe that the analysis and discussion between a theoretician (David Schwarzer) and a novice practitioner (Maria-Sara Kopczynski) on the development of bilingual/multilingual policies in the United States will help better understand the historical glocal context of language development and its importance to schooling in the United States.

CONTEXTUAL INFORMATION

The following section provides contextual information surrounding the historical and cultural events, which motivated the propositions behind these legislations (see Table 1 for a summary of this section). This section will be divided into three subsections—the historical and political contexts in which each one of the documents was drafted and adopted—the 1960s; the 1990s and the 2010s.

HISTORICAL AND POLITICAL CONTEXT OF THE 1960S

During the time when the *Bilingual Education Act of 1968* was written, antiracist movements were growing globally due to the national pride that emerged from the liberation struggles of imperialized colonies. Among these changes were movements against linguistic imperialism like in North Africa, where the language spoken in these countries transferred from the colonial language to Arabic. Similarly, the United States was undergoing its own civil rights movement. President Lyndon B. Johnson initiated the Great Society, which was a set of domestic programs set on removing poverty and racial injustice. This program and its ideals significantly impacted discussions regarding race, ethnicity, and gender equality in the country. Among the legislations that sought to eliminate discrimination, the *Immigration and Naturalization Act of 1965* reformed U.S. immigration policy by removing their national-origin quota system and eliminating the policy's preference for northern and western Europeans. Consequentially, this significantly changed later demographics in the United States.

Perhaps the most important education policy that emerged from the Great Society was the *Elementary and Secondary Education Act of 1965*, which was the first comprehensive federal funding program for public schools, allowing schools to start special education programs, especially for low-income youth. Among other education-related initiatives, the *Bilingual Education Act of 1968* was the first federal law to offer funding for school districts launching bilingual education programs. Bilingual education was viewed as the best means for educating nonnative speakers, and immigrant students' bilingualism was considered a right that needed to be protected.

The civil rights movement and the *Bilingual Education Act of 1968* left a significant impact not only in equitable education policies established during this time, but also in proceeding cases regarding fair, quality education for all students. In 1974, the landmark Supreme Court decision of *Lau v. Nichols* (1974) relied on the assertion that providing insufficient language instruction for non-English-speaking students violated the *Civil Rights Act of 1964*. This case consequentially required federally funded school districts in San Francisco to establish multilingual programs to accommodate **English Language Learners** (ELLs) with equal learning opportunities. Likewise, the *Education for all Handicapped Children Act of 1975* (EHA) was enacted to ensure equal education opportunities for students with physical and mental disabilities. The law included provisions such as having students with disabilities in a least-restrictive environment, which maximized the opportunities they had to learn in a mainstream classroom while having the accommodations they needed. Through these legislations schools were increasingly required to provide for the needs of their diverse student population.

HISTORICAL AND POLITICAL CONTEXT OF THE 1990S

However, there was a rightward shift in the United States during the 1990s, which was a reaction against the civil rights and Great Society laws (Affirmative Action, Welfare, etc.). For example, California opposed affirmative action initiatives in their *Proposition 209* (1997) and ruled that government agencies and institutions could not give preferential treatment to individuals because of their race or gender. Other states proposed similar legislations until 2003 where *Grutter v. Bollinger* federally mandated limits on affirmative action. In 1994, after the North American Free Trade Agreement (NAFTA), there was a significant increase of Latino immigration to the United States. Since 1965 there was a rapid rise in foreign-born population from 4.7% to 11% by 2000. This movement lead to xenophobia and a reaction against immigration. Additionally, legislations such as the *Personal Responsibility and Work Opportunity Reconciliation Act of 1996*, which completely reformed the welfare system by including immigrant families in Temporary Assistance for Needy Families (TANF) and Medicaid, further built up resentment toward immigrants.

This political rightward shift toward conservatism in the United States spoke to the international shift of the political center toward the right because of the worldwide rise of neoliberal policies, especially after the collapse of the U.S.S.R. While Russian was the de facto language of officialdom in the U.S.S.R, the republics it birthed reverted to their pre-union languages, with Russian as a significant minority language (in Romania, Ukraine, Poland, etc.), or co-official language (in Belarus, Kazakhstan, and Kyrgyzstan). Thus, there was mass celebration and pride for these countries to use their native language as their official language, promoting a deeper sense of nationalism.

Likewise, in the United States, anxieties surrounding the increasing population of immigrants and preserving a unified cultural identity stimulated the **English-only movement**, which generated a trend of legislations against bilingual education programs. *Proposition 227* (1998) is the first of several state laws legislated in California to implement "English-only" education to counter-act the effects of the *Bilingual Education Act of 1968* at the state level. While not dismantling bilingual education programs in the state entirely, the law made it significantly more difficult for ELLs to receive additional language instruction in their schooling, as the parents of the students would have to go through a process to specifically request these services. Similar propositions were passed in Arizona, Utah, and Massachusetts. Defenders for this movement perceived bilingualism as an impediment for immigrant students from fully assimilating into American culture and English language acquisition. Immigrants' native language was perceived as holding students back academically and hindering their transition into the dominant culture socially. Thus, these legislations promoted the idea that immigrant students would benefit best from full English emersion.

In addition to rethinking the effectiveness of bilingual education programs, the American education system was significantly reformed through the implementation of *No Child Left Behind Act of 2001* (NCLB), from the Bush Administration, which required states to develop their individual academic standards and assessments in basic skills, which would be administered to all students in order to receive federal funding. Additionally, the *Individuals with Disabilities Education Act of 2004* (IDEA), required states to develop guidelines of the accommodations allowed for state assessments as well as alternative assessments for students who were incapable of accessing grade-level curriculum.

THE POLITICAL AND HISTORICAL CONTEXT OF THE 2010S

Within the last few decades we have seen significant remodeling of the education system in the United States. Among these education reforms are the *Every Student Succeeds Act of 2015* (ESSA), which is a reauthorization of the *Elementary and Secondary Education Act* (1965). Following the No Child Left Behind (2001) policy, ESSA maintains some features of NCLB such as standardized testing, but it gives states and school districts more control over determining the standards students are expected to meet.

Additionally, within the education field there has been significant remodeling of teaching practice regarding what it should entail and what should be incorporated into the curriculum, in order to prepare students to function in the 21st century. One of the aspects of education that is being revisited is how to foster **multilingualism** in the American classroom. In recent history, increased globalization leads to a more connected world that requires multilingual individuals for international diplomacy and workforce. Thus, multilingualism has become a desired trait or asset in the modern workforce. While countries around the world have adapted to this multilingual trend, the United States has not been able to keep up with this shift. For the United States' interests, the war on terror has led to an increased need for specialized linguistic skills that are lacking due to past language policies. Immigration has consistently remained high (now 13.5% of the country is foreign-born) and different ideological movements have at times embraced or sought to discourage this trend. Nevertheless, within the education field there is a greater appreciation for multilingualism as a valuable asset and a useful resource for students. This **language ideology** holds multilingualism as an economic, cultural, and social resource that benefits industry, the military, and society as a whole. In an attempt to repurpose multilingualism into the classroom context, a new proposition was passed that promoted multilingualism in California and revoked an earlier proposition that promoted English-only policies. Other states that had previously enacted bans on bilingual education programs, such as Massachusetts, are currently working to overturn these laws as well.

CONTEXTUALIZATION OF THE TEXTS

Following is a table that summarizes the historical and political contexts in which the different policies/texts were created as well as an understanding of how the global forces, the national forces in the United States, the educational policies adopted, and the overall understanding of bilingualism and multilingualism by the academic community influenced its conceptualization.

Table 3.1   Describes the central historical and cultural points that defined and impacted the evolution and perception of bilingual education

Text	Global Forces	National Forces	Education Policies and Laws	Understanding of Phenomena
Text 1 *Bilingual Education Act of 1968*	Growing ant-racist movement and national pride following liberation struggles of colonies Movements against linguistic imperialism	Civil rights movement President Johnson's Great Society	Immigration and Naturalization Act passed in 1965 Elementary and Secondary Education Act (1965) Education for all Handicapped Children Act (1975) *Lau v. Nichols* (1974)	Bilingualism is perceived as two distinct and separate languages in one person's head Bilingual education is viewed as the best means of educating nonnative speakers Bilingualism is right to be protected

(Continued)

Table 3.1 (*Continued*)

Text	Global Forces	National Forces	Education Policies and Laws	Understanding of Phenomena
Text 2 *Proposition 227 (1998)*	NAFTA and globalization lead to increasing Latino immigration to the United States Collapse of the U.S.S.R. The former republics of the U.S.S.R reverted to their pre-union languages, with Russian as a significant minority language	Rapid rise in foreign-born population in the United States Political rightward shift in reaction against Civil Rights and the Great Society Laws (Affirmative Action, Welfare, etc.) Personal responsibility and Work Opportunity Reconciliation Act	Proposition 209 (1997) banned affirmative action in California *Grutter v. Bollinger* (2003) federally mandated limits to affirmative action No Child Left Behind (2001) IDEA (2004) English-only propositions pass in Arizona, Utah, and Massachusetts	Bilingualism is an impediment to socialization and assimilation Bilingual education is perceived as holding students back academically and hindering their assimilation into American culture
Text 3 *Proposition 58 (2016)*	Globalization leads to a more connected world that requires multilingual individuals for communication Economic downturn and increased automation puts pressure on workers and businesses to obtain multilingual skills	The war on terror leads to increased need for specialized linguistic skills Immigration remains high (13.5% of the country is foreign-born)	Every Student Succeeds Act (2015) replaces No Child Left Behind	Bilingualism is understood as two languages interacting with each other within the same individual Multilingualism is a valuable resource that benefits industry, the military, and society as a whole

SUMMARY OF TEXTS

In this chapter, we have decided to present three texts (instead of two as in most other chapters). The first act established the first federally funded public bilingual education programs in the country; the proposition adopted in California to control bilingual education programs and promote English-only public-funded schools is the second text; and the third proposition—also voted into law in California a few years ago—promoted multilingualism in public education.

TEXT 1: *BILINGUAL EDUCATION ACT OF 1968*

Motivated by the civil rights movement, the *Bilingual Education Act of 1968* was an amendment to the *Elementary and Secondary Education Act*, which federally recognized the need for and value of bilingual education programs in the United States. The legislation allocated federal funding to school districts to create innovative education programs for students with limited English-speaking ability. This policy was significant because it reflected a different and more sympathetic cultural outlook toward immigrants, eliminating foreign stigma and accepting these people as American citizens whom the government is also responsible for. For the first time, it established a bilingual education program defined and financially sustained by the Federal Government in the United States.

TEXT 2: *PROPOSITION 227 (1998)*

In 1998, California adopted *Proposition 227*, which limited bilingual education availability to ELLs. While not dismantling bilingual education programs entirely, parents now had to specifically request for their students to be taught bilingually. Thus, general education programs were taught in English exclusively. This proposition likely spoke to the backlash response to the rise of immigration in the United States. This response was motivated by the anxiety that the perceived American linguistic and cultural unity would be lost because of the promotion of a bilingual/multilingual and multicultural approach in public schools. The proposition was essentially the outgrowth to the English-only movement, which asserted that the best way to assimilate immigrants into American culture was by teaching in English only in schools.

TEXT 3: *PROPOSITION 58 (2016)*

In 2016, *Proposition 58* revoked *Proposition 227*, allowing bilingual and multilingual education programs in California. In contrast to the arguments promoted by the English-only movement, this policy assured that bilingual and multilingual education programs were the most effective ways to assimilate new immigrant students into the country, allowing them to learn English while remaining fluent in their native language. This proposition endorsed multilingual curriculums where both ELLs and English native speakers would be exposed to multiple languages in order to attain an awareness and proficiency in recognizing different languages (alphabet characters, syntactic characteristics, etc.).

In summary, the three texts presented in this chapter can be perceived as a pendulum between two different extreme positions on language policy—bilingual/multilingual and English only. As we move into our dialogue about the different texts, we would like to offer a third possible approach to this issue—those two competing ideas (between English-only as a unifier of the American society and bilingual/multilingual approaches as a national resource that should be enhanced and fostered have been present in the public school arena since its inception). The tension between these two competing views comes to light sharply every now and then depending on the political/historical context of the day. We would like to urge novice teachers to start crafting YOUR own philosophical stance on the linguistic nature of schooling.

DIALOGICAL TEXTUAL ANALYSIS

In this section, the authors will engage in a discussion about the critical policies that not only impacted bilingual education in the United States but also spoke to the cultural receptions and attitudes toward multilingualism of the time. Our dialogue will be framed by using Ruiz's (1984) framework of perceiving language as a right, as a problem, and as a resource, which identifies three basic dispositions evolved toward language education. It is quite interesting that a piece published thirty years ago is still so relevant to today's discourse. The seminal work of Ruiz frames language as a right—something that should be provided in school as a human right but only because of the fear of legal actions against school district or as a "requirement" for a socially just linguistic school experience; language as a problem—something challenging that teachers and administrators need to "fix" as part of the schooling experience; and language as a resource—something that is an opportunity that teachers should foster in order to better the bilingual/multilingual lives of their students as well as the future well-being of our society.

LANGUAGE AS A RIGHT

Language-as-a-right model views bilingual and multilingual education as a basic human right. This attitude was motivated by the civil rights movement, which advocated for citizens to be allowed to use their native language in societal contexts. Likewise, in the field of education the policy sought to open access to adequate education to disadvantaged and poor students. However, while this sounded progressive and inclusive, the language-as-a-right model was framed in a way that all students should have quality access to education, despite the "unfortunate" circumstance of their bilingualism, implying that their bilingualism was a deficit or impediment.

MSK: *Upon my first impression of reading the* Bilingual Education Act of 1968 *there is a strong sense of promoting inclusivity, which speaks toward the political climate of the civil rights movement, advocating for humanitarian rights for all citizens. When calling the local, state, and federal levels of the government to collaborate in resolving the struggle for children of immigrants, it is clear that the legislators are taking a national responsibility for immigrant students, and by doing so asserting their American citizenship.*

DS: It is funny that after so many years of this law being written, the section about inclusivity still reads like a current document—today I believe the trend is to include in this discussion not only emergent bilinguals but also students with disabilities.

MSK: *I also thought it was interesting that the federal grants not only went to school districts which catered to bilingual programs, but funding could also go to other educational resources and programs in museums, libraries, etc. which promoted similar causes. I thought this feature was significant because it made bilingual education and information accessible to all immigrants, including those who were not students. This further suggests that the national perception of immigrants was not only that they deserved rights as citizens but that they also should be encouraged to celebrate their own culture and learn in their native language.*

DS: Absolutely! Again, it is impressive to see in how many ways that document still resonates with us fifty years later—the idea that the education of Emergent Bilingual does not ONLY happen in school settings but in large community settings is CRUCIAL: community centers, museums, town libraries, etc. are very important to develop a fully bilingual citizen—not just an English speaker over the shortest period of time. I am wondering if you are seeing some language that we use today in describing our population (emergent bilinguals or English language learners) that the document is using . . .

MSK: *Well that is the thing, while the legislation was written with good intentions, the language that it uses is very different from how we would refer to English language learners. In fact, it would be perceived as being very problematic today. The document consistently refers to immigrant children as having "limited English-speaking ability." It is clear from the language used in this legislation it was motivated by sympathy and understanding toward the struggle ESL students endure when coming to school, and how they were disadvantaged from learning due to the language barrier. However, this derogatory language suggests that these children are "lacking" as if lacking English proficiency equates a lack of intelligence even though they are proficient in another language entirely.*

This idea of lacking is further ameliorated by the fact that these bilingual programs are "designed to meet these special educational needs," (p. 816). Dubbing bilingual programs as resolving special education needs associates having a language barrier with having a language disability, which further amplifies a sense that students who are not proficient in English as a first language as less capable than their English-speaking peers. In this case, bilingual students who come into the school system are perceived as being disadvantaged or having an unfortunate circumstance, because of their bilingualism.

DS: It is very interesting to read any historical document in which the main idea of the text is still current after 100 years and YET some of its language denounces the underlying deficit views that were prevalent while those laws and mandates were created. **Limited English Proficient**, Feeble Minded, and Deaf and Damn are just some examples of how good intentions can be translated into important and ground-breaking laws and mandates and YET still give a sense of the underlying understanding of the phenomenon as something that needs to be "cured." I am always wondering about which one of the aspects of our current legislation that WE believe it to be so cutting edge, will be judged harshly 50 years from today when a new generation of scholars see the hidden agendas that we are probably not acknowledging at the present time . . .

MSK: *Yes, it is an interesting phenomenon to notice how the language we use and its connotations can be modified so drastically over time. Obviously, legislators of the time would not have seen these terms as being problematic or offensive. Given that these were some of the first terms associated to people learning English or people with disabilities, generating these terms alone indicates a sense of progress for the period as it indicates a recognition that certain individuals need additional support.*

I agree with you that not only the Bilingual Education Act, but also throughout all the leg-islations we are covering in this chapter, there is a resounding theme that something needs to be "cured." Even Proposition 58, *which is what we would consider to be a modern and inclusive piece, refers to English language learners as "English learners," and this suggests that the goal of Bilingual Education programs is still primarily to teach English instead of fostering multilingualism as the proposition suggests. With new terms generating like* **"emergent bilingual"** *as a substitute for English language learner or "English learner," in order to eliminate the preference for English, the terms we use today to refer to English language learners may become just as problematic later on.*

LANGUAGE AS A PROBLEM

Language-as-a-problem model sees bilingualism and multilingualism as a deficit or an impediment from learning particularly in English language acquisition. Thus, people who were bilingual or multilingual were perceived as having a deficiency or intellectual limita-tion that needed to be overcome (Ruiz, 1984, p. 20). This ideology motivated policies that sought to *fix* the language problem, by emphasizing the need to learn English. Native lan-guages were something that people needed to be free from, which obscured the debates surrounding the effectiveness of bilingual education programs.

MSK: *When reading* Proposition 227, *I was shocked that the language regarding bilingual educa-tion was completely the opposite from what was written for the* Bilingual Education Act. *While the* Bilingual Education Act *emphasized that all immigrants are American citizens by default, this proposal imposes that there is an "American ideal" to be met, to qualify as a U.S. citizen. It asserts that if immigrant parents want their children to participate in the American Dream and be successful, they need to abandon their own native language in favor of learning only English in school. This sentiment further asserts that without having English proficiency, one cannot fully be a productive member of American society.*

DS: Yes . . . The English-only proposition was voted and accepted as a state law in California—another surprising fact since in the United States we perceive California as a "progressive" and a "safe haven" for immigrants. However, during this par-ticular time, and because of an intense political campaign lead by Unz (the person proposing this state law), the law was passed. This law dramatically changed the amount and quality of bilingual programs in California (one of the biggest and most linguistically and culturally diverse states in the United States). Moreover, it served as a catalyst for several laws to be legislated in other states around the country. Even at international arenas, educators, researchers, and politicians took similar views and tried to implement them into their local contexts. Having a typical American citizen that speaks English only is a very important aspect of this proposal. I think that it was very appealing at the time since there was a sense that there were too many immigrants coming to the country and NOT becoming part of the mainstream American society. Do you think that sentiment has changed in today's schools/ society?

MSK: *I agree with you that the rise in immigration during this period stimulated an anxiety which seemed to drive the English-only movement, where supporters claimed to defend American culture and unity by demanding English be the only official language used in the United States. When evaluating Unz's (1997) argument you can observe a sense of elitism for English when he says, "Fluency in Spanish may provide a significant advantage, but lack of literacy in English represents a crippling, almost fatal disadvantage in our global economy." This prioritization for English then presents bilingualism as an impediment or obstacle, which is detrimental not only for America but for the rest of the world. Thus, within this vein of the argument English is perceived as an advantageous language to have. Proposition 227 frames its stance that the government has a "moral obligation and a constitutional duty to provide for all California's children, regardless of their ethnicity or national origins, with the skills necessary to become productive members of our society," (Unz, 1997) with the English language being one of the most paramount keys to success. The proposition actually takes a similar stance as the Bilingual Education Act, where it emphasizes the government's responsibility to provide for the needs of its citizens. Although we would find the language Unz uses regarding bilingualism to be problematic, he perceives learning English as a right that immigrant students should have in order to successfully assimilate into American culture and sees bilingual education programs as a denial of that right. I think within the education system, these arguments of bilingualism as an impediment has changed, but in our society, I think some of Unz's sentiments regarding how quickly immigrants assimilate into American culture still resonates with many citizens.*

DS: I am never sure that xenophobia or racist are the best way to label the intentions of both the writers of the document and moreover, of the voters in the California elections . . . I believe that even Unz's intentions were noble (although I see them as promoting a racist and xenophobic agenda . . .). However, I believe that some well-intended and uninformed citizens were persuaded to misinterpret the importance of bilingualism/multilingualism as a national resource that can be used in our own benefit and to promote social justice. They were led to believe that in order to promote unity within the country, we should all believe in English-ONLY legislation and goals. However, better-informed citizens in the same area a few years later were able to understand that multilingualism and globalization are important to the promotion of a stronger economy and overall future to the United States!

LANGUAGE AS A RESOURCE

Language-as-a-resource model seeks to alleviate the conflicts between the prior two orientations by emphasizing that language is a valuable resource that should be used by everyone. This model views linguistic skills among citizens and residents as a contribution to the nation as a whole. With increased globalization, Ruiz (1984) states that nations have a great need for linguistic resources for diplomacy, business, espionage, and academic purposes. Consequentially, insisting that bilingual or multilingual students should learn in English exclusively essentially squanders the linguistic resources we can have. Thus, minority language populations are reservoirs of critical skills that can be used to benefit the entire population. This frame of mind introduces the idea that bilingual schools should not only cater to bilingual students, but it should be the curriculum for all Americans, so that both ELLs and native English speakers can practice their native languages while acquiring new languages.

MSK: *I found it very interesting how Proposition 58 emphasized the importance of multilingualism in order to work globally, in direct contrast with the arguments posited by Proposition 227 about English being the only language you need to know when working on a global scale. It is evident here that English is no longer perceived as the most important language in the world, instead multilingualism is both a valuable resource and basic right, which needs to be fostered and protected. The legislation reflects that not only does multilingualism benefit the individual speaker and opens them to more opportunities in the job market, but it also asserts the national value multilingualism has in America's economic trade and diplomatic efforts. It is dubbed as a 21st-century skill required for all students.*

DS: This is the first legislation I am aware of in the United States in which multilingualism and globalization are perceived as the goal of our education system—no more monolingual English speakers and U.S.-centered citizens is our goal. I believe that striving to promote citizens of the world that can connect and communicate with others in different languages and with more sophisticated views of culture is what this law proposes. I am wondering how novice teachers like yourself relate to these changes . . .

MSK: *As a future teacher one of my goals is to prepare students for the real world after they graduate and to equip them with skills they need to be citizens in the community. With the rapid growth of globalization, now more than ever are cultural awareness and multilingualism valuable skills. Thus, it is teachers' responsibility to meet these growing demands and facilitate cultural awareness in their students. Not only should an educator continue to foster the multilingual advantage some students may have, but also encourage students who are monolingual to embrace multilingualism and different cultures.*

DS: As much as I would like to think that teachers all over this country are looking at multilingual classrooms as a great resource to be useful for their teaching, I believe that it is very rare to have such an ideology. Monolingual, White, middle-class teachers are still the norm in the United States, while the student body racial and linguistic composition has changed dramatically during the last 50 years . . . Many of those well-intended teachers may state that having a linguistically diverse classroom is a great resource for their teaching. However, they seldom have research-based and proven techniques and methods to teach their content area expertise for such a diverse population. I hope that chapters like this one and books like the one we are completing right now will serve as guiding forces in this journey!

MSK: *Are there schools which try to incorporate multilingual curriculums? I understand that there aren't too many research-based strategies established about fostering multilingualism in certain subjects, but have there been case studies or examples of teachers trying?*

We have decided to end this dialogical textual analysis section with two open-ended sections to encourage YOU as a novice teacher to research in your own communities to find out how linguistic policies are enforced and enacted in your own community. Understanding how language policies are impacting TODAY our public school experiences is a very important part of the reflection this chapter is hoping to create.

CONCLUSION

FUTURE TRENDS

While there are documents addressed in the dialogue referred to students' bilingualism currently, there is an even greater shift in terminology from bilingualism/multilingualism to translingualism. According to Huang (2010):

> Translingualism is a term from Steven G. Kellman (2000) and David Schwarzer et al. (2006), who see teaching an L2 as bridge building between languages that allow one to retain a unified mind and not be cloven into two for the sake of being multilingual. Thus, in contrast to multilingualism, translingualism stresses the process and not the goal. (p. 44)

Kellman (2000) coined the term without clear explanations of the theoretical differences between bilingual/multilingual, and translingual. We have used in this chapter the conceptualization of translingualism used by Schwarzer, Petron, and Luke (2009)

> The development of several languages and literacies in a dynamic and fluid way across the life span while moving back and forth between real and imagined "glocalized" borders and transacting with different cultural identities within a unified self. (p. 210)

The development of several languages and literacies at the same time could be viewed both as biliteracy development or multiliteracy development. However, both terms elicit the idea of two languages or multiple languages competing and compacted in one "head." Much of the biliteracy research compares bilingual children's literacy development to monolingual children's development in two different languages—which implies the above-mentioned misconception. Transliteracy better encapsulates the dynamic and fluid movements of "back and forth" between the different languages, registers, and dialect variations as a daily occurrence.

Furthermore, the concept of language development as something that happens only in early childhood should also be expanded. We now conceptualize this phenomenon as a developmental process that happens across the life span. It may better explain how young adults, adults, and senior citizens may learn how to use Hebrew as a foreign language while also using e-mail (in Hebrew) to communicate with the instructor. That is why the word "literacies" (in plural) is part of this definition to signal both different languages and different modalities. Finally, the idea and concept of translingual education draws from two bodies of research: transnational education (as opposed to binational or multinational education) and transaction models of language and literacy development.

Moreover, this shift in terminology may significantly change YOUR perception of language study and language teaching. Within the education field, there is a gradual shift toward facilitating translingualism in the classroom. Instead of simply solving the "issue" of students who are unable to speak English through transitional bilingual programs, practioners are encouraged to facilitate learning not only in English but in students' native language as well. The goal of the translingual classroom is to allow bilingual students to further stimulate their skills in their native language while learning English, giving them a multilingual/translingual advantage. With increasing globalization, having proficiency in multiple languages is a desirable resource for our youth in the current century. Thus, in order to prepare our students for the future it is becoming increasingly important to harness and promote the linguistic advantage and fluidity that multilingual/translingual students already have.

Consequentially, the goal of promoting translingualism in your classroom is likely to expand not only as an accommodation for English language learners, but also as a component imbedded in the curriculum for all students. Recognizing multilingualism and translingualism as a valuable resource has shifted the perception of multilingualism as an advantageous skill, especially with the increasing need of global diplomacy and cultural sensitivity. Thus, in order to prepare students for the needs of the future, translingualism in general and transliteracy in particular should be incorporated into the academic curriculum to teach all students (especially native English speakers) about linguistic diversity. Consequentially, the role of facilitating a translingual classroom education will not be exclusive to ESL teachers, but to all teachers regardless of the discipline they teach, promoting transtiliteracy in various fields. Then all students will benefit from having a multilingual curriculum and learning from their multilingual peers. Establishing positive translingual classrooms in which multiple languages are developed simultaneously by monolingual English-speaking teachers are our challenge for educators in the 21st century. Emergent bilingual students will not feel isolated because of their multilingualism, rather they will be valuable members in their translingual learning community.

Finally, we are asking you to re-conceptualize the "American Dream" entirely. Our nation's need for global diplomacy and the glocal forces that are part of the 21st century reality are crucial to this endeavor. Instead of asking emergent bilingual students to abandon their cultures and languages, in order to assimilate into an exclusively American culture, transnational students can comfortably help us all become translingual and transliterate individuals as part of our American identity for the new millennium.

PRACTICAL IMPLICATIONS FOR TEACHERS

As a novice teacher entering the field, it is important to be aware of the changing needs of students to prepare them for the 21st century. It is important for educators to recognize the value of bilingualism/multilingualism and translingualism to their practice. Moreover, we need to remember not to dismiss students' use of their native language in a classroom context (Schwarzer, Haywood, & Lorenzen, 2003). Translingualism is becoming an increasingly important component of the classroom not only for accommodating ELLs but also for fostering language diversity among all students to increase both language proficiency and cultural sensitivity. It is important to understand that monolingual teachers can orchestrate a translingual learning community by encouraging students to use their native language in the classroom and promoting the value of speaking multiple languages (Schwarzer et al., 2003). In doing so, YOU can foster a positive translingual learning community where students can learn from each other.

As a start, teachers can make strides toward these practices in the following three concrete ways:

1. Changing the definition of the phenomenon of study;
2. Becoming a linguistic anthropologist in your students' communities; and
3. Using the linguistic landscape of your community as a resource in your classroom.

Following is a brief description of each one of those concrete ideas that could impact your practice.

1. Changing the definition of the phenomenon of study:

As advocates for all of our students, it is our job to actively keep ourselves informed about shifting terminology in education, especially with how we refer to our students. As evidenced in our discussion about the language used to describe English language learners, it is clear that terminology can have significant implications about not only how we perceive our students but also how they can be internalized by our students. When choosing the appropriate terminology to refer to our multilingual students, it is important that we emphasize the value in their multilingualism as an advantage, not a detriment.

2. Becoming a linguistic anthropologist in your students' communities:

When designing curriculum, teachers should evaluate their students' background and needs, planning instruction accordingly. Likewise, when planning a multilingual curriculum, teachers should evaluate the linguistic culture students come from. For example, how many ELLs do you have in your class? Do your students speak a different language at home? What kind of heritage languages are your students familiar with? These questions can be answered by analyzing your local school district's linguistic demographics data. You can access this information through the school district report card and evaluate the date from the specific school you are tailoring your curriculum to. By familiarizing yourself with the linguistic culture of your classroom, teachers can more effectively arrange classroom instruction, which would be more meaningful for multilingual students.

3. Using the linguistic landscape of your community as a resource in your classroom:

In addition to being familiar with the linguistic demographics within your classroom, it is also important to consider the school's community and the linguistic resources it could supply for classroom instruction. One way of doing this is creating a **linguistic landscape**, which is observing the linguistic variety that is used in a community. Examples include street or store front-signs being written multilingually or national flags on display, all of which would indicate who the members of the community are and to what audiences the community caters to (for examples of students' reports on communities in New Jersey, please visit: https://sites.google.com/site/translingualism305/linguistic-landscapes).

After noting these observations, consider the implications of how having such linguistic diversity impacts the community. For example, which audiences do multilingual signs appeal to? Does use of the languages promote inclusivity or exclusion of certain community members? More importantly, consider how to use these elements in the community and translingual experiences as funds of knowledge for your students. Addressing elements in the classroom can promote meaningful conversations about cultural diversity by connecting it to the relevancy of their own communities. Not only would students, who participate in a given culture, appreciate the opportunity of sharing their insight but also students unfamiliar with a certain culture can learn from their peers, further expanding their cultural sensitivity. Translingual contexts are something that many students encounter in their daily lives and something that most monolingual schools do not take into account. However, incorporating these experiences into the classroom environment has the potentiality for making material more relevant and accessible to all students.

EXTENSION QUESTIONS

1. Have you ever encountered the term "translingualism"? How can this term modify your teaching practice?

2. What are your district policies for speaking English in the classroom? Are the policies still dominantly English or do they encourage facilitating multilingualism?

3. How could you foster and promote multilingualism in the classroom if you are a monolingual teacher?

4. Have you considered incorporating multilingual materials in your classroom (i.e., bilingual word wall, multilingual children's book, authentic texts that mix different languages) or coteaching with a teacher who speaks a different language? How would these change the dynamics of your classroom?

5. What are the benefits of having students use their native language in the classroom? Would this only be a modification for English language learners or could this benefit other students as well?

GLOSSARY OF TERMS

Emergent bilingual—students who are developing bilinguals. This term positions both languages as resources, where students can be in developing stages of the native language and/or the second language. This term is used to reject the deficit-oriented terminology of LEP, ELLs, or ESL students.

English language learners (ELLs)—students who are unable to communicate fluently or learn effectively in English, who often come from non-English-speaking homes and backgrounds, and who typically require specialized or modified instruction in both the English language and in their academic courses.

English-only movement—a movement that began in California in the 1990s that sparked a trend in legislating against bilingual education programs. The initiative sought to make English-only instruction the default program for English language learners, arguing that this immersion was the best way to teach Spanish speakers English.

Language ideology—a set of philosophical assumptions and beliefs related to the development of language in general and bilingual/multilingual development in particular. Most school districts have both an explicit (for example in their mission statement) and a hidden (for example in their language practices) language ideology. They may write that multilingualism is celebrated while their linguistic landscape is clearly in English only.

Limited English proficient (LEP)—refers to a person who is not fluent in the English language because it is not their native language. This is a dated term for English language learners and is discouraged from being used due to its negative connotations that a student is intellectually lacking because they are not proficient in English.

Linguistic landscapes—the linguistic variety and dynamics used in the community (i.e., translingual writing on signs, displaying national flags, etc.). Observations of these dynamics can provide interesting implications for teachers and researchers about the community.

Multilingualism—the use of more than one language by either an individual speaker or by a community of speakers.

Translingualism: The use of several languages in a dynamic and fluid way—moving back and forth between the languages. A common practice for transnational/translingual populations.

REFERENCES

Bilingual Education Act, Pub. L. No. (90–247), 81 Stat. 816 (1968). Retrieved from: https://www.gpo.gov/fdsys/pkg/STATUTE-81/pdf/STATUTE-81-Pg783.pdf

Education for All Handicapped Children, Pub. L. No. (94–142), 89 Stat. 773 (1975). Retrieved from: https://www.gpo.gov/fdsys/pkg/STATUTE-89/pdf/STATUTE-89-Pg773.pdf

English Language in Public Schools. California Proposition 227 (1998). Retrieved from: https://repository.uchastings.edu/cgi/viewcontent.cgi?article=2150&context= ca_ballot_props

Elementary and Secondary Education Act, Pub. L. No. (89–10), 79 Stat. (1965). Retrieved from: https://www.gpo.gov/fdsys/pkg/STATUTE-79/pdf/STATUTE-79-Pg27.pdf

Every Student Succeeds Act. S.1177. (2015). Retrieved from: https://www.gpo.gov/fdsys/pkg/BILLS-114s1177enr/pdf/BILLS-114s1177enr.pdf

Huang, T.C. (2010). The application of translingualism to language revitalization in Taiwan. *Asian Social Science*, 6(2), 44–59.

Grutter v. Bollinger, 539 U.S. 306 (2003).

Immigration and Naturalization Act, Pub. L. No. (89–236), 79 Stat. (1965). Retrieved from: https://www.gpo.gov/fdsys/pkg/STATUTE-79/pdf/STATUTE-79-Pg911.pdf

Individuals with Disability Education Act Amendments of 1997 [IDEA], Pub. L. No. (105–17), 111 Stat. 37 (1997). Retrieved from https://www.congress.gov/105/plaws/publ17/PLAW- 105publ17.pdf

Kellman, Steven. (2000). *The translingual imagination*. Lincoln, NE: University of Nebraska Press.

Lau v. Nichols, 414 U.S. 563 (1974).

No Child Left Behind Act of 2001, Pub. L. No. (107–110), 115 Stat. 1425 (2002). Retrieved from: https://www2.ed.gov/policy/elsec/leg/esea02/107-110.pdf

Non-English Languages Allowed in Public Education Act. California Proposition 58, S. 1174, 113th Cong. § 753 (2016). Retrieved from: https://leginfo.legislature.ca.gov/faces/billNavClient.xhtml?bill_id=201320140SB1174

Ruiz, R. (1984). Orientations in language planning. *NABE Journal*, 7(2), 15–34.

Schwarzer, D., Haywood, A., & Lorenzen, C. (2003). Fostering multiliteracy in a linguistically diverse classroom. *Language Arts, 80*(6), 453–460.

Schwarzer, D. (2006). Monolingual TESOL Teachers Fostering Students' Native Literacies. *Bilingual Basics, 8*(2), 35–36.

Schwarzer, D., Petron, M., & Luke, C. (2009). Conclusion. In D. Schwarzer, M. Petron, & C. Luke (Eds.), *Research informing practice—practice informing research; Innovative teaching methodologies for world language teachers*. Charlotte, NC: Information Age Publishing.

Unz, R. (1997, October 19). Bilingual is a Damaging Myth. *Los Angeles Times*. Retrieved January 24, 2018, from http://articles.latimes.com/1997/oct/19/opinion/op-44399

4

FLEXING OUR DEMOCRATIC MUSCLES: HOW LOCAL AND GLOBAL CONTEXTS SHAPE EDUCATION FOR DEMOCRATIC CITIZENSHIP

EVAN MOONEY
DEBRA H. CHO

INTRODUCTION

"The vigilant protection of Constitutional freedoms is nowhere more vital than in the community of American schools. The classroom is peculiarly the marketplace of ideas."

—*Justice William J. Brennan, Keyishian v. Board of Regents, 1967*

What is being a teacher all about? Is it about being an expert in a subject area and passing that knowledge about history, or science, or math, along to students? Is it about helping students learn and develop as children? Is it about helping students develop as citizens in a democratic society? Or is it about a steady paycheck, convenient hours, and pensions? All of these things and more? None? These are questions that many students grapple with when thinking about entering the teaching profession. Surely, there are no easy answers. As with all professions that are, at their foundation, social acts of service and caring for others (doctors, lawyers, and all forms of public service to name a few), teaching is a complex and demanding undertaking that comes with solemn responsibilities. We believe that in addition to being an act of service to students, there is another foundational responsibility that teachers assume when they enter classrooms: to assist students in being and becoming active citizens in a democratic society. Inspired by the words of Justice Brennan quoted above, we hold that it is the duty of teachers to create, foster, and preserve classrooms that are "the marketplace of ideas," spaces which serve to protect and promote the Constitutional freedoms of our unique democratic society.

It is beneficial to talk briefly about what we, and other scholars, mean when we say, education for "**democratic citizenship.**" From the beginnings of American public education in the 19th century (until quite recently as we discuss below), there was a consistent belief among educators and the public that one of the core purposes of education was to equip students with the understandings necessary to actively participate as citizens in a democracy. Educational scholars such as John Dewey and George S. Counts emphasized the importance of educating students for citizenship in our distinct American democracy (Counts, 1932, 1939; Dewey, 1916, 1937, 1938). Scholars have also had an ongoing dialogue about the role that education should play in supporting democratic society (Kahne & Westheimer, 2003; Newmann, 1975; Parker, 2001, 2003; Westheimer & Kahne, 2004). The essence of these discussions and debates suggests that educating students about democracy as a political system, and importantly, their role within that system as protectors and promoters of the system is one of the central duties of public education. In short, democracy requires citizens to participate, and it is the responsibility of schools to help students develop the knowledge and skills that they need to effectively do so.

As teachers, how do we help students develop into active citizens in a democratic society? For those of you who are just beginning to think about being a teacher, this may seem like a distant and daunting idea. "I don't even know how to lead a class discussion, how in the world am I supposed to help students be democratic citizens?" you may be asking yourself. This chapter provides you with an introduction to the relationship between democracy and education in American society via an exploration and discussion of two documents. These documents illustrate how education impacts democracy and how democracy influences education. In making these relationships visible, we are hopeful that you will see how vital teachers are to our society and how you can begin to envision yourself as an educator for democratic citizenship.

THE DOCUMENTS

We chose to explore and discuss two documents that serve as powerful examples of the relationship between education and democratic citizenship. The first document we examined was the Supreme Court case, *Tinker v. Des Moines* (1969). This case involved several students who protested the Vietnam War by wearing black armbands to school in Des Moines, Iowa. The students were suspended by the school district and appealed the action taken against them to the U.S. Supreme Court. The school board claimed that they suspended the students because they were disrupting school discipline, yet the Court found that the actual reason was a desire to avoid the controversial subject of the Vietnam War. The Court ruled in a 7–2 decision that the suspension of the students for silent protest of the Vietnam War was unconstitutional, as it violated the students' First Amendment right to freedom of speech. Further, the Court ruled that students' First Amendment rights do not stop at the school doors and just as schools cannot compel students to salute the flag, they cannot limit students' freedom of speech, as long as that speech does not interfere with others' rights to learn. The Court found that the students' protest did not "materially and substantially interfere with the requirements of appropriate discipline in the operation of the school . . ." Thus, their speech was protected. The Justices recognized that school is more than the practice of "supervised and ordained discussion which takes place in the classroom." They noted that student communication within the nonclassroom spaces of school was an "important part of the educational process."

This case affirmed the idea of schools as laboratories for democracy and protected places for the free and open exchange of ideas about citizenship. This supports the historical and Constitutional stance that schools serve as the engines for democracy and democratic citizenship as well as the main argument of the second document we examined, *The Century Foundation Report* (2016). This case laid the foundation for *The Century Foundation Report's* call to inject democratic education into public schools.

The Century Foundation Report was published in the fall of 2016 by The Century Foundation, a progressive, nonpartisan think tank. The motivating question for the report was "how can our public schools do a better job of educating children for our pluralistic democracy?" The authors suggest that teaching students to be democratic citizens has two distinct elements: first, providing students with the analytical and critical thinking skills necessary to be well informed and make sound decisions in elections; and second, instilling in students an appreciation for the benefits of liberal democracy as a system of governance, thereby guarding against demagogues who would undermine democratic principles. The authors argue that the focus of education has shifted from preparing students for democratic citizenship to a focus on "marketplace preparation" (i.e. preparing students to work in the economy). They believe that the public currently places greater importance on the economic value of education than the civic value of education. They then offer recommendations at the state and local level for putting democracy back into public education. Some of their suggestions focus on school curriculums while others suggest making democracy and democratic behavior part of the classroom, modeling democracy, and making teacher participation in the democratic process of schooling visible to students.

While the level of focus on education for democratic citizenship may rise and fall periodically in relation to other social purposes of education, such as acquiring a core body of knowledge and preparing students for work in the economy, there has been a significant decline in the emphasis on this goal in the last 30 years. The standardized test movement, in conjunction with a belief that democracy is secure, therefore unnecessary to prepare students to enact democratic citizenship, has led to less emphasis on education for democratic citizenship (Evans, 2011, 2015; Hawley, Hostetler, & Mooney, 2016). This diminishment of civics and democratic education in schools, and the threats to public education that arose from private schools, charter schools, and for-profit schools, is the central argument of *The Century Foundation Report*. Additionally, they recommend:

> (1) Federal and state accountability measures should include civic knowledge alongside math, reading and science; (2) schools should be rewarded when adults model democratic practices for students; and (3) federal charter school programs should encourage those schools that promote democratic practices.

They conclude with a strong statement about the importance of schools modeling democratic behavior: "We cannot expect public schools to do a good job of teaching students to be thoughtful citizens who embrace democracy if the schools do not themselves reflect democratic values and norms."

CONCEPT CHART

The following chart illustrates the global and national forces that influenced the creation of the documents. It also shows an understanding of the phenomenon and some of the educational policies that connect to the documents. The realities of the global struggle between communism and democracy, as well as National civil and student unrest in response to the Vietnam War, shaped the environment within which the Supreme Court ruled in *Tinker v. Des Moines* (1969). Their decision affirmed the First Amendment rights of students and reaffirmed education for democratic citizenship as essential to American society. Similarly, the global retreat of democratic norms and the national retreat of education for democratic citizenship, combined with the advance of education for economic demands, constituted important elements of the environment within which the authors wrote *The Century Foundation Report* (2016). In an effort to counter the advance of education for economic demands, the authors reaffirmed the ideas of education for democratic citizenship.

	Global Forces	National Forces	Educational Policies	Understanding of Phenomenon
Text 1 *Tinker v. Des Moines (1969)*	Cold War; communism v. democracy; Vietnam War	Civil unrest; democratic protest; role of student protest	First Amendment rights of students	Education for citizenship in a democracy is inviolable and essential
Text 2 *Century Foundation Report (2016)*	Retreat of democracy	Retreat of education for democratic citizenship	Curriculum shifts to meet market demands	Education for citizenship in a democracy is inviolable and essential

DOCUMENT DIALOGUE

The following is a discussion we had following our exploration of the two primary documents. This conversation took place via email and we purposefully preserved the structure of the conversation for you here. Through our discussion of the two documents, we hope to illustrate the connection between education and democratic citizenship.

Evan: I'd like to begin our conversation by reacting to the *Tinker v. Des Moines* (1969) decision. As I read the Supreme Court's decision I was struck by several ideas the Justices raised in their consensus, as well as Justice Black's dissenting opinion. Perhaps the most important idea to me was the notion that schools have a responsibility to protect the rights of students. If schools are to foster and promote democratic citizens, they must be places where students' rights are observed and honored. The Justices who affirmed the decision worried that if students' rights stopped at the school doors, they might begin to believe that their rights were "mere platitudes." I saw this as an expression of democracy acting upon schools. Consequently, if we are to maintain schools as places that educate students for citizenship, we as teachers must create classrooms that honor students' rights. And further, we must not succumb to the desire for discipline and control that limits students' rights and freedoms.

These are just two of the ideas from the case that struck me as central to education for democratic citizenship. I am wondering what ideas were most powerful to you?

Debra: *One of the powerful ideas from the case is "hazardous freedom." The very nature of our right to freedom of expression and ultimately democracy comes at a cost. In fact, it is this cost of that lays the foundation of our "vigor of Americans." Thus, the fear of disturbance and controversy, which were the primary concerns from the school administration, should have been embraced and expected. As teachers, this is a hard concept to accept because disturbance and controversy doesn't exactly conjure up the most positive classroom culture and climate. But if we were to create a space for democracy, in both learning it and practicing it, teachers can anticipate and leverage whatever occurs in the classroom. After all, we both agree that it is not enough just to teach democracy—we must create a space where they can practice it and see it in action.*

Evan: I am intrigued by your idea of "hazardous freedom" as an expression of democratic behavior in the classroom. I couldn't agree more that if our responsibility as schools, administrators, and teachers is to promote democratic citizenship among our students, we should embrace and "leverage" opportunities for them to act as citizens in schools, rather than suppress them in the interests of avoiding "disturbance and controversy." As I reviewed the case, one of the ideas that stood out to me was the conception that not only do schools serve as spaces where we grow our democracy but they also serve that goal in another manner, by thwarting tendencies toward authoritarian or totalitarian impulses on the part of the state. In this way, education serves as both a sword for democracy and a shield against authoritarianism. Teachers have the awesome responsibility to take up that sword and shield with their students.

I think there is a clear connection to *The Century Foundation Report* on this point. This document offers an interpretation of the consequences of neglecting our responsibility to democratic citizenship education in favor of educating to meet market demands. In the authors' view, "civic preparation" of students has diminished, as "market preparation" has become the paramount goal of education. This has led students to enter civic life ill-prepared to participate in a democracy and ignorant of the dangers of antidemocratic forces in our social, economic, and political realms. Their report offers extensive policy suggestions for bringing democratic education back into public schools thereby combating this trend.

The most important point of *The Century Foundation Report* in my estimation is this emphasis on education for democratic, *rather than economic*, citizenship. What are your thoughts on any of this, as well as the report in general?

Debra: *I struggle with education for **democratic citizenship** vs **economic citizenship**. While I agree that the absence of democracy in the classroom has led to a series of negative consequences, I wonder what our founding fathers would have said about public education if they were forming their policies in today's world. Would they have felt the same way about building public education with the focus on democratic citizenship? We are an economically driven nation and in some ways, we need it to survive globally.*

Also, to throw in a question that I get asked all the time, can ideas feed people? Is the fact that we teach students about democratic citizenship going to eventually get them a job that will feed them? Furthermore, what about students who are immigrants or second-generation Americans? To this population, the lesson on civics might hold less value than education that could lead them to higher test scores to get better jobs. Is education for democratic citizenship more important that education for economic citizenship? What are your thoughts?

Evan: These are important questions that have been part of the conversation about the purposes of education in America since its inception as a formal institution in the late 19th and early 20th centuries. Educational philosophers, such as John Dewey and George Counts, as well as social studies education scholars more narrowly (Evans, 2011, 2015; Parker, 2003; Stanley, 2005), have debated and questioned whether education should seek to serve citizenship and democratic goals first and foremost, or primarily prepare students to respond to the needs of a capitalist market economy. Many have argued for a balanced approach to both goals in efforts to reinforce the democracy through the economy and vice versa. However, the question of primacy, that is, what is the most important objective of education, has remained in dispute among educators, teachers, and the citizenry alike.

From my perspective, one that admittedly views capitalism as an inherently undemocratic economic system that is destructive to deep democracy, there can be no balance between these goals. Rather, education must act as a check on capitalism if democracy is to survive. Thus, we as teachers must constantly negotiate the tensions between democratic life and a capitalist economy with our students. We must aid them in making the duality of our society transparent. And we are charged with helping them develop the skills to not only negotiate these competing systems, but also to refine and maintain the systems to "keep the ship sailing."

Debra: *So much responsibility for the teachers! This made me reflect on my education up until this point and I'm not quite sure where during my teacher education I was "given" this responsibility. If anything, my motivation for training my students to flex their democratic muscles* *comes from my background as an activist, feminist, and a child of an immigrant. In fact, the identities I have as a person greatly influences the way democracy lives in my classroom. Ideally, we give students the tools to be democratic citizens and they go forth in the world and become the citizens the founders of education envisioned. But the reality is the very definition of being American is different for every person. So, in this diverse society we are part of, do we need to diversify how we teach our students? Maybe we don't—maybe as teachers we can plant the idea and let the students determine how it grows. What are your thoughts?*

Evan: I couldn't agree more. Your thoughts remind us that teaching as a profession is far more complex than simply imparting content knowledge to students. And who we are as people, our experiences, beliefs, and attitudes, contribute significantly to who we become as teachers. Your comments sparked a powerful and complicated question to me: does being an American automatically make one democratic in their thinking and behavior? I think the function of teaching and education is to explore this question with students in attempts to invigorate our fragile democracy.

CONCLUSION

The documents we examined in this chapter emerged within the context of social, political, and international events (the Vietnam War and the 2016 Presidential election) that challenged democracy and democratic norms. From our analysis and conversations about them, we concluded that it is when democracy is challenged that it grows and expands its scope within society. Conversely, when democracy lies dormant, unchallenged, and overlooked, it atrophies and generally recedes from the citizen mind. It is in these moments that teachers play an integral role in educating for democratic citizenship. We hope that your reading of this chapter leads you to see the intrinsic importance of teaching within a democratic society. Your future classrooms will be the "marketplace of ideas" where our society grows and deepens as a democracy that represents all citizens. As the leaders in these spaces, it will be you who works with students to enrich and advance our unique American democracy.

But what does teaching for democratic citizenship *actually* look like? The following implications for teachers, discussion strategies, questions, and terms provide a picture of education for democratic citizenship.

PRACTICAL IMPLICATIONS FOR TEACHERS

With the endless list of standards to address and content to explore, the classroom can easily become a place where the democratic muscle atrophies instead of being a place where it flourishes. A teacher must actively try to incorporate democracy through educating themselves, diligently exploring new ideas, and getting into the right mindset. The following two ideas will help lay a foundation for you as a teacher who fosters democratic classrooms and active democratic citizens.

BEING COMFORTABLE WITH BEING UNCOMFORTABLE

The nature of democracy translates to empowering students in the classroom to take control of their education in some aspect. While it is easy for the teacher to be the one in control, relinquishing that control of the classroom and giving it back to the students is essential for incorporating democracy. What this can translate to is the teacher being comfortable with being uncomfortable. Open discussions can lead to topics where a teacher might have limited knowledge that would otherwise never have been discussed in the classroom. There might also be times when students get involved in a heated debate that may seem chaotic. But this is a display of true engagement by the students. Teachers need to embrace this, put aside their fleeting moment of discomfort and enjoy the passions of the students.

UNDERSTANDING DIVERSITY IN OUR OWN CLASSROOMS

Students come from many walks of life and experiences. This is a major asset to the classroom because this means a plethora of ideas and perspectives. At the same time, teachers need to be purposeful about how their voices are heard in the classroom. Some students may never voice their opinion due to fear of how their classmates might react. Other students may not recognize their biases and privileges in their perspectives. It is a teacher's responsibility to acknowledge and address these moments effectively to keep the conversation going. Perhaps the most important piece of this conversation is that teachers themselves reflect on their own prejudices and check them before engaging in conversation. Institutionalized racism, sexism, and all other "-isms" are inescapable even to the most educated individual. Years of social conditioning take years to deconstruct. But we must recognize it and address it properly.

EXTENSION QUESTIONS

The typical image of a classroom places the teacher at the front of the classroom and students sitting in neat rows of chairs eager to listen and take notes. However, giving the voice back to our students and empowering them to take charge of their education must be a foundational practice in classrooms. Doing so forms an essential component of our effort to enact education for democratic citizenship in public education. The following discussion questions can be used to help students think critically and engage democratically with the curriculum under exploration in the classroom. The questions should be tailored to you as a teacher. Always strive to be authentic in your discussions!

1. *Unspoken perspective*: Students who might hold a less popular perspective might be discouraged from speaking. Ask, "I'm wondering if someone can give me another perspective on this issue?" Take it a step further by having a controlled discussion where the unspoken perspective can be put on the table and students can spend anywhere from 2–3 minutes on the merits of it followed by 1–2 minutes of raising questions about the perspective.

2. *Sparking the fire*: If there is a student who is passionate about a particular topic, encourage them to speak up by asking, "*I noticed you are passionate about this topic, can you tell us why this is important to you?*" This is not meant to single a student out, but rather to acknowledge and support the student's passion.

3. *Gallery of ideas*: Sometimes with controversial topics, all student perspectives can be shared by having them write their perspective on a piece of paper to be displayed anonymously around the classroom. Be sure to instruct students to *justify* what they write. Then, have the students walk around and read each idea. They can write their initials in green if they agree, red if they disagree, and yellow if they are unsure. The gallery can be used to start a classroom discussion or just to introduce new ideas.

4. *Opposing views*: If there is a debate on fire in the classroom, challenge the students to dissect and reflect on their stance. *What led you to this view? Can you rephrase that in another way? Have your views changed during your life? What we heard was this, is that what you meant?* These questions, along with others, can be given to students at the start of a discussion so that they can use them to ask questions of each other rather than the teacher asking them.

GLOSSARY OF TERMS

American—a person who resides in the United States of America who *accepts a common set of values and beliefs and shares a culture of those living in the country.*

Democracy—a type of government where the power comes from the people who choose leaders through fair elections and those who hold the power do so temporarily and work toward protecting the rights of all people; the people have the right to criticize leaders who fail to uphold these values.

Democratic citizen—a person who participates in the decision-making process of the government ensuring that each person's humans rights are protected and laws equally apply to everyone.

Economic Citizenship—the attitudes and behaviors that citizens exhibit in response to the needs of the marketplace.

Democratic Citizenship—the attitudes and behaviors that citizens exhibit in response to the demands of a democratic society. While difficult to define, these behaviors are individually enacted and community minded. Democratic citizenship is always active in pursuit of the maximum equality between and among citizens.

Diversity—understanding that individuals comes from a broad spectrum of experiences, beliefs, and cultures; respecting the differences and acknowledging that institutionalized discrimination leads to privilege for some and disadvantages for others.

REFERENCES

Counts, G. S. (1932). *Dare the school build a new social order?* New York, NY: John Day.

Counts, G. S. (1939). *The schools can teach democracy.* New York, NY: John Day.

Dewey, J. (1916). *Democracy and education.* New York, NY: Free Press.

Dewey, J. (1937). Education and social change. *Social Frontier, 3*(26), 235–238.

Dewey, J. (1938). *Experience and education.* New York, NY: Macmillan.

Evans, R. W. (2011). *The tragedy of American school reform: How curriculum politics and entrenched dilemmas have diverted us from democracy.* New York, NY: Macmillan.

Evans, R. W. (2015). *Schooling corporate citizens: How accountability reform has damaged civic education and undermined democracy.* New York, NY: Routledge.

Hawley, T.S., Hostetler, A.L., & Mooney, E. (2016). Reconstruction of the fables: The myth of education for democracy, social reconstruction and education for democratic citizenship. *Critical Education, 7*(4).

Kahne, J. & Westheimer, J. (2003). Teaching democracy: What schools need to do. *Phi Delta Kapan, 85*(1), 34–66. New York: Peter Lang.

Newmann, F. M. (1975). *Education for citizen action: Challenge for secondary curriculum.* Berkeley, CA: McCutchan Publishing Company.

Parker, W. C. (2001). Educating democratic citizens: A broad view. *Theory into Practice, 40*(1), 6–13.

Parker, W. C. (2003). *Teaching democracy: Unity and diversity in public life.* New York, NY: Teachers College Press.

Stanley, W. B. (2005). Social studies and the social order: Transmission or transformation? *Social Education, 69*(5), 282–286.

Tractenberg, P., Roda A., & Coughlan R. (2016). Remedying school segregation: How New Jersey's Morris School District chose to make diversity work. *The Century Foundation.* https://tcf.org/content/report/remedying-school-segregation/

Westheimer, J. & Kahne, J. (2004). What kind of citizen? The politics of educating for democracy. *American Educational Research Journal, 41*(2), 237–269.

5

ADDRESSING TRANSNATIONALITY AND GLOCALITY IN TEACHING AND TEACHER EDUCATION

ALISON PRICE ROM
HANAN ATIYAT

This chapter will review two documents relating to the use of transnational and "glocal" approaches to teaching as represented in two documents, each written during a different era. Although they are 41 years apart, the similarity between these two documents is striking. The first document was written by James Becker in 1969 on behalf of the Foreign Policy Association, while the second document is a transcript of a speech given by Kenneth Zeichner in 2010 on behalf of the National Association of Foreign Student Advisors. The earlier document by Becker is an excerpt from a 1969 report by the Foreign Policy Association on behalf of the U.S. Department of Health, Education, and Welfare entitled "An Examination of the Goals, Needs and Priorities in International Education in US Secondary and Elementary Schools." Becker's report explores the need for internationalization of school and teacher training program curricula to meet the needs of a "shrinking" globe and the "knowledge explosion" produced by technological advancement of the late 1960s. It demonstrates that the importance of making transnationality and glocality a part of teaching and teacher preparation was realized over 40 years ago, under different circumstances, yet with a rationale that continues to be used today. The more recent primary source, Kenneth Zeichner's address to the NAFSA (National Association of Foreign Student Advisors) Association of International Educators in 2010 makes it clear that transnationality and glocal understanding continues to be absent from the teacher education curriculum and new teacher induction. As a result, graduating teachers begin their careers with minimal understanding of transnational and global cultures, and hence with little understanding of the "glocality" of the communities in which they teach. The FPA report, which was written at the height of the Cold War, the civil rights movement, and Vietnam War protests, and called for increased understanding of global and local human rights, and an increased focus on using a transnational approach and perspective, rather than the traditional nation state and nationalism, seems surprisingly relevant to 21st-century concerns. A comparison of the two documents as they relate to their respective contextual backgrounds will reveal how approaches to globalization, transnationality, and "glocality" have changed over time, as well as how and why the need for globalization in schools and teacher education programs have not been adequately addressed. In addition, the chapter will review and assimilate recommendations from the two reports through a dialogic text analysis, with some reflection and suggestions as to how best to incorporate transnationality and glocality into today's public-school classrooms and teacher education programs.

DEFINING TRANSNATIONALITY AND GLOCALITY

UNESCO (United Nations Educational, Scientific and Cultural Organization) defines transnationality as the principle of carrying out an action across national borders, in order to have effects at a more general level (Vertovec, 1999). It refers to multiple ties and interactions linking people and institutions across the borders of nation-states to form communities. It centers on the exchanges, connections, and practices across borders that may be economic, political, social, or cultural. Transnationality undermines the means of controlling difference based on territoriality, thereby challenging and perhaps undermining the traditional notion of the nation-state (Castles, 2000).

Transnationality in education refers to the cross-border connections generated by international exchange programs for scholars and students and international development projects. Such programs generate transnational communities of scholars and students who share common interests and scholarly pursuits. It may also refer to the borrowing and lending of practices in education across borders (Steiner-Khamsi, 2004), forming transnational communities in education that adhere to the same set of best practices in teaching and learning. The increase in international standardized testing such as OECD's PISA, PIRLS, and TIMSS have influenced the domestic debates about education reform and have bolstered transnational communities of educators, researchers, and policy makers, who seek to prepare their students for such exams by adopting the best practices of those nations whose students have performed well on them. The teaching field in the United States is now part of the global conversation and has evolved into what Kenneth Zeichner refers to as "a vision of teaching that aspires to be world class." (2012, p. 572). How can teachers become more competitive on a global level and include teaching and teacher education in the global conversation when teacher education programs themselves tend to be focused on domestic and local concerns? How can we make teaching in the United States a more integral part of the transnational community?

The local global or "glocal" in education refers to those features of the education context that connect students and teachers with the outside world through the local or near abroad.

Educators may capitalize on the "glocal" and diverse elements of their surrounding communities and members of the school community to help connect students to the outside world. Schools and teacher education programs in particular have long been considered the most insular of academic programs, seeing little need to connect classroom teaching with the rest of the globe. This is a departure from the globalization trend taking place in other fields of study as diverse as engineering and social work. Public schools offer few courses in global or international studies, and those that are available are usually confined to the study of "World History."

Educational efforts that seek ways to connect local schools and teacher education programs with global concerns is by definition "glocal." There are a handful of teacher education programs that offer their students the opportunity to travel abroad as part of their teaching practicum; however not every pre-service or in-service teacher is able to afford to travel abroad, nor do they have the time. Both schools and teacher education programs need to explore a variety of ways to increase the global competencies of teachers who cannot travel abroad by taking advantage of the "near abroad" or "glocal" at home. Teachers can provide their students with exposure to bilingual or language immersion programs, can require them to become involved in communities where residents speak Spanish or Arabic, or can involve them in supporting local social justice causes that are global in nature, such as aiding newly arrived refugees or sending supplies to schools overseas. As Becker's report suggests, schools can rely upon faculty who have participated in international programs such as the Peace Corps, or who have worked as education consultants for overseas development projects. They can also seek out visiting scholars and teachers at district schools or on nearby university campuses and engage them in discussions of differences in values and perspective.

SOCIAL AND CULTURAL RELEVANCE

The concepts of transnationality and glocality are of great importance in the United States as well as globally given the recent rise in intolerance and xenophobia among the general public, as well as new policies barring immigrants and refugees from our shores. This trend in the United States seems to be part of worldwide increases in xenophobia and ignorance of human rights. If teachers lack global awareness, this might mean that the students they teach will leave school with a minimal understanding of cultural awareness, social justice, and human rights in the United States and abroad, and are therefore susceptible to these forces of bias, discrimination, and social injustice. They may demonstrate insensitivity to students in their own classes who represent diverse cultures and pass such attitudes on to other students in the class.

Because teachers affect the quality of education, it is of the utmost importance that they develop global competencies, including tolerance and understanding of the world around them. In order to develop their own cultural awareness, as well as that of their own students, it is important for teachers to develop "perspective consciousness." This is the notion that individuals must come to realize that others in the world do not necessarily share their perspective and beliefs, and that one's own perspective is dependent on a variety of markers, including class, race, gender, ethnicity, religion, and sexual orientation. Villegas and Lucas define this term "socio-cultural competence of the global self" (2002).

In his 2010 address to NAFSA, Kenneth Zeichner points out not only the need to develop global awareness among teachers, but comments that few have sought to understand why it is important. Teachers and their students must "broaden the context of their self-awareness beyond their nation's borders—otherwise they will not be able to cross the us/them boundary that impedes the development of a global consciousness among many Americans and prevents meaningful connections among the world's peoples" (Zeichner, 2010, p. 13).

Previous generations have demonstrated understanding of the need for teachers to develop global competencies as early as the 1960s. In the late 1960s, the Cold War and competition with the USSR abroad, coupled with the civil rights movement at home and the Vietnam War highlighted teachers' lack of awareness of transnational and "glocal" issues.

Although the terminology is different, James Becker's 1969 report for the Foreign Policy Association discusses the need to develop global awareness in teacher education programs (Ch. V). The report bears many similarities to the Zeichner address of 2010. Becker points out that schooling in the United States is "traditionally insular and insulated, circumscribed by narrow vision and protected by tradition and circumstance" (1969, p. 233) He notes that education leaders have promulgated "the other," and that such practices are no longer adequate to deal with the world's problems. The report uses language and phrases that sound surprisingly current, mentioning a "shrinking world" and "knowledge expansion," "technology," and "increased interaction on a global scale" brought about by unprecedented conditions for global human interaction. It is surprising to note that this was written long before the internet and today's "knowledge society." Becker points out that international education must encompass those learning experiences in which the decision-making processes are conceived in global terms, that is, experiences in which individuals have "the opportunity to realize their selfhood and express it within a world system composed of other individuals with the same rights" (1969, p. 234).

The report contends that the education of teachers is the focal point around which major efforts must be concentrated if a change in educational objectives is to find its way into the content and structure of American education and points out that the American Association of Colleges for Teacher Education has spent two decades maintaining an active interest in pushing back the "parochial frontier of American teacher education" (p. 234). There is a need to make sure that teachers' knowledge and attitudes are in tune with the demands of world society.

CONCEPTUAL FRAMEWORK

The contextual framework below analyzes two texts that discuss that issue of globalization and teacher education. Although they come from two different contexts and were shaped by different national and global forces, they have many features in common, and will form the basis of a dialogue in the next sections.

THE GLOBAL CONTEXT OF TEXT 1

In 1968, the year before Becker completed his report for the Foreign Policy Association, the United States and the world in general were in turmoil. In the United States, 1968 represents the height of the Vietnam War protests, ending in police violence against protesters during the 1968 Democratic convention in Chicago. The year also brought the tragic assassinations of presidential candidate Robert Kennedy and civil rights leader Martin Luther King Jr. Much progress had been made in a peaceful civil rights movement, culminating in President Johnson signing the 1964 Civil Rights Act. The assassination of Martin Luther King Jr. brought about widespread protests throughout the United States and a crack-down in which 39 people were killed. Outside of the United States, youth-driven uprisings due to a population surge after WWII were common worldwide, from peaceful protests of the Prague Spring in Czechoslovakia to the more violent protests of radical workers and students in France and guerilla warfare against military dictatorship in Brazil. In the education reform sphere, the United States sought to compete with the Soviet Union in math and science education, as part of the ongoing Cold War rivalry between the two superpowers. In the 1969, the U.S. space program's efforts culminated in Neil Armstrong's moon walk, demonstrating a successful outcome to investments in math and science.

THE GLOBAL CONTEXT OF TEXT 2

The year 2010 was certainly less tumultuous for the United States. Barack Obama was a year into his two-term presidency and signed the Affordable Care Act into law. Internationally, 2010 marked the official end of the war in Iraq as well as the end of the Great Recession. Although ISIS had not yet made its appearance, the tragedy of September 11 had initiated years of xenophobia and fear of terrorism in the United States that had not diminished by 2010. This year also represented increased global connectivity and economic globalization. Of particular note was the growth of social media giant Facebook. In the education sphere, the No Child Left Behind program was in its eighth year of implementation, and its impact on education in the United States was profound. Although the well-intentioned measure sought to make schools accountable for the educational achievement of all students, the program also narrowed the school curriculum, caused school teachers and administrators to spend an inordinate amount of time preparing children to take tests, and left no time for the development of creativity and critical thinking skills. Because assessments focused on math and language arts, there was little room for social studies curricula, including courses in world history and global studies. Thus, opportunities for teaching global studies or in other ways developing a perspective consciousness of the global self in the public-school classroom were very limited. The table below summarizes the concept in terms of global forces during each period.

Table 5.1 Conceptual Framework

Primary Source Text	Global Forces	National Forces	Educational Policies	Understanding of Phenomena
Text 1 Becker Report, Chapter V. (1969)	Cold War, Vietnam War, youth culture, technological advancement. Emerging idea of international citizenship.	Civil rights and student protests, arms race, technological advancement and increased urbanization.	International Education Act of 1966 and increased emphasis on math and science education.	Teacher and student understanding of transnational context is essential.
Text 2 Zeichner address to NAFSA (2010)	Global economic competition, technological advancement. Terrorism and immigration, xenophobia. Increasing competition on international tests: PISA in particular.	The end of the Great Recession, Iraq War. Signing of ACA. Increases in international economic cooperation and connectivity. Feared loss of economic competitiveness.	NCLB and standardized testing. Common Core Curriculum launched 2009. Emphasis on standards and accountability. Weak scores on international tests: PISA.	Teachers and students need to understand both transnational and glocal contexts more than ever. Need for "perspective consciousness," and less emphasis on state standardized tests.

DIALOGICAL TEXT ANALYSIS

The Zeichner address of 2010 and the Becker Report of 1969 help frame our understanding of transnational and global contexts in education. The following text is a dialogue between a teacher educator and practicing teacher, both of whom are globally focused professionals. In the dialogue the interlocutors explore the practical implications of the two documents, and ways to make transnationality and glocality an inherent part of our nation's schools and teacher education programs. In the dialogue below, each individual's point of view is represented by a different font. The initials PT stand for practicing teacher, while the initials TT stand for teacher trainer. The dialogue was recorded and later transcribed:

GLOBALIZATION AND THE CURRICULUM

PT: Growing up as a first-generation American in the early 1990s was an experience that will always be in the back of my mind. Even though we lived in a seemingly diverse New Jersey neighborhood, I still felt some noticeable differences between my American friends and myself, especially the ways our households were shaped. I remember being asked "where I was from" or "what are you" giving me the distinct feeling that I was different, and even more so different when I would say my name. I don't recall in elementary school of being culturally engaged in the classroom. I remember in sixth grade during my history class I became so excited when I noticed that an upcoming chapter was going to cover the history of the Middle East. However, days later, I was terribly disappointed when the teacher actually skipped the chapter in its entirety. I would have felt more included in the class and would have been able to contribute my own knowledge and perspective of my culture if given the chance.

At home my parents are very much involved in shaping our identity and talking to us about culture and diversity. We talk about what it truly means to be an Arab here versus at home. Middle Easterners are portrayed in the media differently than what we believe is a true representation of our people and region. My parents were born in the Middle East and lived through some of the wars and tensions and have seen borders change and refugee crises emerge. My parents have that background experience and it's been in my consciousness so that when I go to work or school I hear what people have to say and I hear their ideas and their perspective. Years ago, I would have not had the courage to speak up or share my perspective, but now as an adult, I do share my ideas, which are often accepted. However, there are people who won't accept your perspective and will be closed minded no matter what.

TT: *I think that is important in terms of the curriculum that we try to set standards so that regions of the globe won't be skipped, such as the chapter on the Middle East you referred to. It's a shame that your history teacher skipped the chapter. Teachers need to know who their students are and be culturally responsive to their students and should also teach about non-Western cultures in general. When I was a beginning teacher I found that my mentor teacher was teaching about Western Europe, yet calling it "World History." This is the kind of Eurocentric approach we have been trying to move away from, but we haven't succeeded. In our schools we also have a tendency to teach U.S. history as if it were in a vacuum, separate from the rest of the world. This is what we do in our teaching of social studies and in our teacher education programs—very little focus on the outside world. Even in teaching civil rights, as Becker points out, we look at the U.S. perspective primarily, and seem to forget that there were similar struggles going on the rest of the world. There is also a dangerous new tendency to ignore the effects of slavery in U.S. history classes, to down play it, or even refer to it as immigration.*

PT: Yes, the Becker Report mentions that there is a lack of focus on the marginalized populations. There seems to be a shortage of truth and sense of reality in history lessons about the "New World" and colonization, for example. Situations and events seem very much glorified. Teachers rarely stir up questions about what happened to the groups that lived here previously? Could they all have lived together to come to a better solution? In middle school, I remember my history teacher went into very little detail about the Native American population. The context of class discussions was mostly a representation of the Pilgrim and Indian interacting over a Thanksgiving Day meal and not so much of a discussion about the violent period of a mass wipeout of people and social injustices.

TT: *That's unfortunate and an approach that hasn't changed since the 1950s and 1960s. Preparing citizens for a democracy is also neglected in our schools. I think some teachers are afraid to have their students debate. Teachers need to try to create a safe environment for discussion, but they shouldn't avoid debate and controversy.*

When you read the Becker report of 1969 it's interesting that even before the internet the idea of a close-knit world and rapidly advancing technology was already emerging, as was the idea of being a citizen of the world. Zeichner's speech mentioned that there is no effort to link teacher education with the current globalization movement, and part of the problem is that teacher education has not institutionalized global competencies and global citizenship. Zeichner points out that many international education NGOs list the essential knowledge, skills, and dispositions teachers need for global competency; however no one asks why global competency is important for teachers and their students.

PT: Both Zeichner's speech and the Becker's report mention that research is disconnected from the actual teaching and some of the assessment standards are very vague when it comes to assessing for understanding of global competencies. Standards are not explicit and that is how content is dealt with in our U.S. school system—controversial topics are briefly and vaguely discussed. Zeichner talks about making content more explicit and making sure teachers are prepared to go out into the field prepared to have realistic discussions and engagements with their students. He believes that the teacher education admissions process and program of preparing teachers should be fused together. Incoming candidates should have prior knowledge of what a democracy is and an understanding of their own power and privilege—reflecting on the self as Becker's report says. Teacher education candidates should be thinking: "What can I do to be a better global citizen myself? How can I help create change and respond to social injustices happening in the world by orchestrating proper classroom discussions?" I mean we've seen this happen before, but more so in higher education institutions. In the 1960s during the Vietnam War, there was a huge outburst of controversy across campuses—college students responded in their own way to social injustices, especially males who refused to be drafted into the military.

TT: *It's unbelievable that the wars in Afghanistan and Iraq have gone on for so long—the destruction of ancient civilizations. Social studies teachers should also teach about these events in the context of world affairs as well as world history. Do teachers point out to their students that in addition to human destruction, war has overrun the cradle of civilization?*

PT: As you have mentioned earlier, teachers mostly discuss the wars and history of Western Europe such as WWI and WWII. The discussions are mostly concentrated around the involvement of the United States as a world power and political hero. There is rarely any mention for example of the Armenian Genocide, Sino-Japanese Wars, or the various armed conflicts in South America, Africa, or Middle East. Many times world powers think they can change history and bring about democracy; however, as we have seen throughout history, there is more damage caused from the aftermath of wars.

TT: *War has rarely succeeded in bringing about democracy.*

GLOBALIZATION AND SOCIAL JUSTICE

PT: From my time spent in the MENA region, I've heard many refugee Iraqis say that their people were better off under Saddam Hussein's regime than the mess they are going through now. They had great universities and a developing society, but that's all gone now. The recent war has caused a complete deconstruction of heritage and culture that existed for thousands of years. This has happened much more often than we think—in Eastern Europe, in India, and Latin America to name a few. But regardless of all the atrocities that have happened around the world, the recent political climate has given many people the entitlement to openly show their bias.

TT: *Yes, they've been given license to say whatever they want without considering others' perspectives. This is why global awareness and perspective consciousness are so vital for our practicing teachers.*

PT: People need to be more globally aware. The IB school where I previously taught was all about internationalizing the curriculum. They encouraged students to be politically correct, internationally minded, but also proud of their heritage and bilingual abilities. For example, there was a large Palestinian student population at the school. When teachers were teaching from the British and American textbooks they had to be aware and address their students' concerns about the geographical terminology that explicitly referred to the students' homeland region. Teachers allowed students to debate controversial events. A specific unit of study that I vividly remember teaching was "Fact vs. Opinion—Can one person's fact be another person's opinion?"

TT: *In the area of social justice and the civil rights movement, we focus on injustices in the United States alone, but as Becker points out this was part of a worldwide movement that reflected the struggle between the global "South" and "North" through colonialism. For the United States, it was the Vietnam War and now there is Iraq and Afghanistan and Syria. In our social studies courses we fail to make the connection between what is going on in the United States and social injustices abroad. We fragment them into separate classes.*

PT: All parts of the world have faced social injustice in one way or another. But Syria in particular is a current issue that our students are very much aware of. The topic of refugees—to help them seek asylum in our country or not is a controversial topic in mainstream media. I think it's important that educators draw students' attention to the historical events that have happened in time, encourage them to draw comparisons to most recent events, and realistically discuss the denial of refugees and disadvantages of that. Educators should point out the refugees in the past that have had a very difficult time seeking asylum—such as our American ancestors, the Jews during WWII and to understand it is not just Middle Eastern refugees who have faced discrimination throughout political power struggles.

TEACHER EDUCATION AND STUDY ABROAD

TT: *So what are the global competencies that teachers need to know to address such issues and what else can we add? How can we change our teacher education programs and make them less focused on the domestic side of things, and develop our students' global awareness and perspective consciousness? What kind of admission standards should we have? During the admissions process, should we screen students for global competencies when the objective of the program is to impart global competencies? In international student exchanges and study abroad programs we screen applicants and look for students who will be able to adapt, be flexible, and open minded and accept different perspectives. I have misgivings about that because those who need it the most are not open minded and adaptable.*

PT: I serve on a committee here at the Center of Pedagogy and we are currently reevaluating our teacher education program and the standards for admissions and completion. You will see that faculty will differ on many topics, but the consensus wants stronger objectives that will help candidates successfully teach in various environments and to vast populations of students. Therefore, that reevaluation in itself is a great start. As for international exchange and study abroad programs, too many times I have seen students treat them as a mini-vacation experience. It is important that our students gain realistic knowledge of the world. We should definitely encourage students to productively interact with people of different cultures, get to understand each other's world views, events, and collaborate on coming up with solutions for social problems. The students who are less open minded and willing to adapt can possibly be encouraged to participate through offering incentives.

TT: *A class that I teach here is designed to prepare students for the application process, and democracy in education is a theme, and this is something they should take away from the course and be prepared to discuss in their interviews. However, with exchange programs and study abroad programs it's different—you don't want to select a student who will then go overseas and be inflexible or offend people, experience culture shock or have difficulty adapting to local conditions. In other words, you have to screen study abroad students to some degree.*

PT: I think you're right. It would defeat the purpose to send students abroad who might just act upon their biases. In the United States, educators are more often concerned about covering a certain amount of content rather than foster conscious and socioculturally competent students. Many students lack effective communication skills and would face immense challenges interacting with others different than them. I think the same goes for our international student exchange programs. I don't think we put enough effort into our international programs. Do international students go back to their home countries and effectively reflect on their experiences here?

TT: *It depends. Having worked with university international programs versus a government-sponsored academic exchange program, the latter is designed to be framed—it is citizen diplomacy. With Fulbright Scholars for example there is a conference and de-briefing program. For the other international students on U.S. campuses there is only an orientation, and little else. I agree that this needs to change. We do the same with U.S. students going overseas for those study abroad programs you mentioned previously. The assumption is that if you are in a different cultural context you will get something out of it just by being there, and that is not the case.*

GLOBALIZATION OF TEACHING AND THE PEACE CORPS

PT: Becker's report talks about Peace Corps educators and our failure to utilize them effectively in our teacher education programs. A very small percentage of Peace Corps veterans are seen in the education system. The majority choose to be international consultants or work for NGOs. Peace Corps educators have previously faced opposition from school administrators who are not concerned about internationalizing the curriculum, and therefore, educators who want to change things get discouraged and eventually leave the school due to the shut down from the community at large.

TT: *Yes, and moreover, the school experience might not be interesting or relevant to those who participated in Peace Corps unless they can somehow use it in their teaching. Becker refers to the International Education Act of 1966—it's interesting that there was a push for global perspective in schools back in the 1960s. We currently have International Education Week at many universities, but I'm not sure this reaches teacher education programs or schools. What other policies might better link schools with globalization and allow teachers who have been in the Peace Corps or overseas in some other capacities to stay in teaching? I think we can set standards for teacher education programs and have a globally focused course that all teacher education students are required to take. Classes could be created or there could be dedicated classes. Students could also be required to earn 2–3 credits in a globally focused activity.*

INCORPORATING "GLOCAL" ELEMENTS IN THE CLASSROOM

PT: At my previous teaching position at the School of Life, Jordan, I remember in 2010 the UN General Assembly passed a policy to advocate for and celebrate a week of World Interfaith Harmony. This initiative was proposed by his majesty King Abdullah and HRH Prince Ghazi in hopes to promote harmony and acceptance between all people regardless of faith. During the first week of February and throughout the academic school year, educators at The School of Life found ways to involve their students in dialogue and social initiatives to celebrate faith and peace. In addition, the following academic year we had a skype talk with students from Russia. That event took away some of the ambiguity and debunked students' stereotypes of one another.

TT: *Do you mean every teacher should go to the classroom and know something about their students' backgrounds? If so, I agree!*

PT: Absolutely! In my methodology course we read the "Ethnographic Eyes," which discussed the journeys of teachers through their students' communities. The discoveries they made throughout the community visits helped the teachers understand their own students, expand their cultural competencies, and effectively reflect on their own teaching practices.

TT: *Teachers can take advantage of the diverse cultures around us in our own communities that represent the rest of the globe. How can kids from diverse cultures contribute to the classroom and their other classmates' understanding. How can we avoid the situation you mentioned in the beginning of our discussion, when your teacher skipped over the Middle East chapter in the history text?*

PT: Students from different backgrounds can learn from one another and promote their different cultures through dialogue about values and beliefs. This helps students understand that humans are humans, worthy of acceptance and equal opportunities regardless of whether they look different or speak differently. This helps debunk bias and fears that people have and promotes tolerance for people's differences.

TT: *Students can also research their own cultural background as Merry Merryfield (1993) suggests through her family tree project, in which they research their own family background and share* *with the rest of the class. A number of schools have an international fair with different foods and traditional clothing. It's a nice tradition but does not get to the different values and beliefs and traditions like the family tree project. International fairs are not a bad thing, but not enough in terms of helping make students globally aware.*

PT: Very true that is not enough. We should want for others what we want for ourselves. If we want to value human rights locally, we should advocate for it globally. If we want to advance ourselves in military power, economic growth, and scientific and technological innovation, then we should be willing to accept that for all people around the world. Zeichner argues in his speech that we have privileges and access to power, which help us advance ourselves but sometimes at the cost of disadvantaging others. It is important that our teachers have a clear understanding of the wider world and take opportunities to prepare the future generations to be better global citizens.

GLOBALIZATION AND TEACHING STANDARDS

TT: *These are all very good ideas but institutionalizing them is another matter. Do we make global competency a standard part of teacher education program accreditation? If we do, the hope is that it will lead to more global competencies in schools. In Becker's day only 3–5% of social studies teachers taught anything about the outside world, and the same is probably true today. Global competencies need to be addressed in curriculum standards in schools so there is specific curricular content for which we can prepare our social studies teachers. However, we don't want to confine it to social studies classes alone, but teach it across the curriculum.*

PT: Many U.S. accreditation councils for teacher education programs fail to provide explicit standards that ensure global competency or understanding of global contexts. However, from my experience, the Council of International Schools in The Hague has a set of standards to improve the outlook of international mindedness and global citizenry. The international baccalaureate school that I previously worked at supported learning in all domains through interdisciplinary units that covered conceptual, contextual, and global contexts. Students in a Design Technology class and students in an English class collaborated with one another to design and create board games for disadvantaged students in their own country. Afterwards the IB educators secured a partnership with small rural schools whose students had the opportunity to play with the games. Some of the students had never seen a board game before or had any opportunities for recreational activity due to their own family circumstances and children having to work in the fields after school.

TT: *This is the sort of international project that our teacher education students could be involved with at the "glocal" as well as global level. This could be a part of community service—why not have a globally focused community service project for teacher education students? The IB project and the Council of International Schools would be excellent models to follow. We do have the IB program in a number of schools—typically private schools or public schools in more affluent districts. However, we need to make sure that our curriculum reaches all kids, not only those who are college bound.*

PT: Community service is an important factor in Jordan—it is important to address the injustices in one's own social structures and work up. There are vast differences between the developed countries and the still developing countries. One example is the distribution of resources. Seeing the way water was used in Jordan and coming back to the United States to see the difference was an eye-opener for me.

TT: *This would be a helpful project for Study Abroad—life in a different culture. Ideally the focus should be non-Western. There is a lack of emphasis on world history in classrooms as well as the opportunity for students to experience other cultures.*

PT: It is important that we expose our students to the various national issues of civil rights, poverty, economy, climate change, and so much more, but we also need our students to learn about the developments, civilizations, and social injustices of the wider world.

TT: *Yes, social justice within our country and beyond. Walter Parker (2018) points out that we teach social justice but it is focused on the United States. There is no effort to take this out of its "multicultural box" and extend it to the rest of the globe.*

PT: Several years ago when I taught Black History Month to my seventh graders, I made the mistake of only exposing my students to Western Black figures of influence. Those such as Martin Luther King, Frederick Douglass, and Susan B. Anthony were the focal point of our discussions. My coordinator at that time commended my efforts, but recommended that I also expose my students to non-Western figures of color that created positive change in the world. Therefore, the following month, which was Women's History Month, I asked my students to research influential female figures from all around the world, including the MENA region. It was so important to my students to include influential women of the Middle East to dispel the stereotype of the Middle Eastern women. It's important for teacher education programs to debunk these myths and stereotypes.

PT and TT: Teachers and Teacher Education Programs need to help their students develop global competencies and perspective consciousness, otherwise future teachers who grow up with these attitudes will then pass intolerance and narrow-mindedness on to their students. Global competencies should become part of teacher education program curricula as well as school curricula, and should become an integral part of pre-service teacher program accreditation standards. Both public school students and teacher education students would benefit from overseas opportunities. However, such opportunities are not available to everyone. If they cannot offer overseas travel, teacher education programs can take advantage of the "glocal" campus community by engaging visiting scholars and former Peace Corps participants in their classrooms. Schools can and should take advantage of global expertise among the teaching staff as well as the diverse "glocal" communities in their neighborhoods and regions and among the students themselves. Including students from diverse ethnic and cultural communities can make teaching more culturally responsive by making those students feel included and valued.

IMPLICATIONS FOR TEACHERS

The incorporation of transnational or "glocal" elements in the public school curriculum is a long-term goal whose discussion dates back to the 1960s. As Zeichner made clear in 2011, the first step in the process is to make global standards a part of the teacher education accreditation process. This is a lengthy process and the results may not "trickle down" to daily classroom interactions for many years. In the meantime, practicing teachers and teacher educators can follow the recommendations discussed in this chapter's text analysis by drawing upon the "near abroad" or "glocal" elements in their school community to help children develop *perspective consciousness*.

Teachers may go about incorporating "glocal" elements in their classrooms through a variety of informal means. These may include making children aware of their own backgrounds and those of others through Merrifield's family tree project. Teachers may also draw upon their own experiences and the global experiences of other students and teachers, administrators, and parents through projects, presentations, discussions, and more. In addition, students may benefit from interactions with the "near abroad" in the community (visiting towns, communities, and schools where a language other than English is spoken, where cultural traditions may differ from those in their own community), or involvement with a social justice related community service project, such as helping refugees in the school community, or reaching out to victims of war and natural disaster in another part of the world. School administrators can help this process along by encouraging school-wide "glocal" and globally focuses activities, and by offering teachers in-service training focused on fostering global awareness in the classroom. For teachers who may feel overburdened by the addition of yet another curriculum or course should be reminded that "glocal" elements are most effective if they are taught across the curriculum, and incorporated in as many topics as possible.

CONCLUSION

Currently K-12 classroom teachers are not deliberately trained to prepare teachers to be world citizens or culturally sensitive citizens of their own communities with broad global perspectives. It has not been an essential element of the teacher education curriculum. In an age of increasing isolationism and xenophobia, where our citizens are suspicious of refugees and where immigrants in the United States face mounting discrimination, the development of global understanding and perspective consciousness is crucial for teachers and their students.

As Zeichner and others have pointed out, teacher education associations must take the lead in developing assessments and accreditation standards that include global competencies, and teacher education programs must make global competencies an inherent and assessed program component across the curriculum, not only for certain social studies teachers, but for teachers of all subjects and age groups. Standards and competencies for schools and students must ensure that every classroom offers elements of global understanding that can be taught across the curriculum. However, there is no need to wait for the lengthy institutionalization process. Teachers can take action on their own by making small, yet impactful changes to the way they teach on a daily basis.

EXTENSION QUESTIONS

1. Are global competencies an inherent part of teacher education programs in other countries? Research teaching standards in one other country and see if you can find any mention of global competencies.

2. Social justice or human rights issues that we learn about at home can have global reach. Can you name two or more social justice issues here in the United States that have overseas implications?

3. We hear more and more about teachers steering away from exploring controversial topics in classrooms in order to avoid extremism debates among students. How can educators help students communicate effectively about varying beliefs, practices, and cultural backgrounds?

4. How can we form partnerships and collaborations to support learning programs that promote glocal focuses for our teachers and students?

5. Should there be global contexts embedded in all content areas for all grade levels? Research some explorations to develop in your specific content area.

GLOSSARY OF TERMS

Accreditation—in education is a quality assurance process in which a program's services and operations are evaluated by an external accrediting organization. It is official recognition that a school, program, or course has met the standards set by the external body.

Assessment (formative)—to monitor students during the learning process and use the feedback to identify areas where students are struggling so that teachers can adjust their teaching and students can adjust their studying.

Culturally responsive teaching—as defined by Ladson-Billings (1994), is a pedagogy that recognizes the importance of including students' cultural references in all aspects of learning.

Global competencies—According to NEA, acquisition of in-depth knowledge and understanding of international issues, an appreciation of and ability to learn and work with people from diverse linguistic and cultural backgrounds, proficiency in a foreign language and skills to function.

Glocal—refers to those features of the education context that connect students and teachers with the outside world through the local or near abroad.

Human rights—The UN defines human rights as being inherent in all human beings, whatever their nationality, place of residence, sex, national or ethnic origin, color, religion, language, or any other status. We are all equally entitled to human rights without discrimination. These rights are universal, interrelated, and indivisible.

Learning standards—concise, written descriptions of what students are expected to know and be able to do (i.e., competencies) at a specific stage in their education. They describe educational objectives for a particular course or grade level.

Perspective consciousness—as defined by Villegas and Lucas, the awareness that a person's world view is not universal but is profoundly influenced by life experiences, as mediated by a variety of factors, including race, ethnicity, gender, and social class.

Social justice—the view that everyone deserves equal treatment under the law: equal economic, political, and social rights and opportunities.

Transnationality—refers to multiple ties and interactions linking people and institutions across the borders of nation states to form communities. It centers on the exchanges, connections, and practices across borders that may be economic, political, social, or cultural (Vertovec, 2009).

REFERENCES

Becker, James. (1969). *An examination of objectives, needs and priorities in international education in U.S. secondary and elementary schools.* Final Report, Project No. 6-2908, Contract No. OEC 1-7-002908-2028. New York: Foreign Policy Association.

Castles, Stephen. (2002). Migration and community formation under conditions of globalization. *International Migration Review, 36*(4), 1143–1168.

Ladson-Billings, G. (1994). The dreamkeepers: Successful teachers of African American children. San Francisco: Jossey Bass Publishing Co.

Merryfield, Merry. (1993). Reflective practice in global education: Strategies for teacher educators. *Theory into Practice, 32*(1), Ohio State University: College of Education, 429–448.

Parker, W. (2008). International education: What's in a name? *Phil Delta Kappan,* 196–202.

Steiner-Khamsi, Gita, ed. (2004). *The Global Politics of Educational Borrowing and Lending.* New York: Teachers College Press.

Vertovec, Steven. (2009). *Transnationalism.* London, New York: Routledge.

Villegas, A.M. & Lucas, T. (2002). Preparing culturally responsive teachers: Rethinking the curriculum. *Journal of Teacher Education, 53*(1). 20–32.

Zeichner, K. (2010). Colloquium on the internationalization of teacher education at NAFSA. Association of International education.

SECTION II SCHOOLS

6

BECOMING AMERICAN THROUGH THE EYES OF PUBLIC EDUCATION: UNDERSTANDING THE CONTEXT OF AMERICANIZATION IN PUBLIC SCHOOLS

JAIME GRINBERG
JACLYN WEISZ

INTRODUCTION

> *"If we do not 'Americanize' our immigrants by luring them to participate in our best civilization . . . they will contribute to the degeneration of our political body and thus de-Americanize and destroy our national life."*[1]

Teaching students to become part of the American experience has been an enduring theme in the mission of public schools. While the above quote refers to immigrants, Americanization as a socializing and enculturating effort has been a goal since the evolution of common schools in the early 19th century to embrace *all* students, regardless of their background, the nationality of their parents, the language they speak at home, their religion, their social class, the level of education of their parents, and other contextual factors that could be identified as potential dividers in a society that was and still is more interested in building a national ethos and common identity. Over the course of this "Americanization" project, there have been multiple instances of forcing the "other" into the American way of living including populations of Native American people and those from Hispanic descent who became Americans as a result of the 1848 Treaty of Guadalupe Hidalgo after the war with Mexico. Additionally, this project also served to groom natural born citizens into the American way of life.

---

[1] William Torrey Harris, first the superintendent of schools in St. Louis, Missouri, 1868–1880, and later the U.S. commissioner of education 1889–1906 (cited in Perelman, 1990, p. 31).

Contributed by Jaime Grinberg and Jaclyn Weisz. © Kendall Hunt Publishing Company.

Hence, beyond the expectation of teaching subject matter and 21st Century life skills, the teaching of social and cultural norms, values, belief systems, duties and rights, and a common national identity has been a reasonable expectation for our public schools and teachers. In the context of the quote above, Americanization meant to civilize the "other" and to develop loyalty to the American system, both politically through the development of democracy and in the homogenization of a cultural commonality in spite of diverse backgrounds. Historically, Americanization became prevalent as an explicit agenda in schools at the turn of the 20th Century and turned into an organized movement geared to assimilate immigrants into the American fabric. Yet, we argue that above and beyond this particular historical time in which Americanization was an explicit project, Americanization has been and continues to be a common practice in American education.

Going forward, we will refer to the process of the initiation of youth into American culture and society as **Americanization**. This involves the use of public schools as the main institution to explicitly teach about national identity and American values, rights and duties, through the use of both the visible and hidden academic curriculum of the school district and the relationships fostered within the classroom. This enduring practice has shifted its meaning and execution over the years, but has continued to be a positive force in the solidification of loyalty to and shared interest in a united nation, above any potential divisions of identity including ethnicity, religion, or social class.

Some common themes of the educational process of Americanization embrace the ideology of incorporating the values and norms of the mainstream, including access and opportunities to be successful, and embracing the values of democracy, freedom, and the rule of law. However, and in spite of the larger ideological purpose of Americanization, not *all* were always integrated into the American fabric at the same time; thus Americanization has been a piecewise process that has focused on various groups of people at different stages throughout American history. Historians argue that this very same process of incorporation also alienated, marginalized, and discriminated against those who were considered the "other." Moreover, some historians also argue that this civilizing project of Americanization served as a platform to sever immigrants from their "country," to "deculturalize," and to perpetrate a social order in which those denaturalized access their social position in conditions of inferiority. Therefore, we argue that the meaning of Americanization is historically contextualized, thus meaning multiple and at times contradicting things to different stakeholders. Grinberg et al. (2005) have asserted that,

> Teachers can open or close possibilities, can reinforce and exacerbate conflicts, or can bridge and integrate differences such as those that derive from assumptions and misconceptions. Teachers can shape learning experiences, make them meaningful, exciting, respectful, relevant, and inclusive, or can teach that who the students are and what they bring with them as cultural beings is of no value. Furthermore troubling, they also can teach that in order to succeed in school students must abandon who they are, their heritages, their language, their behaviors, values, cultural norms, and ways of knowing. (p. 228)

In consequence, Americanization is neither good nor bad, but depends on the particularities of the context of its implementation and its consequences. Americanization has the potential to enable individuals to become part of the larger fabric of a diverse society, it can be empowering, and it can open the doors to achievement and opportunity. Because of this Americanizing process, groups that have been out of the mainstream can gain awareness to claim their rights and demand equal opportunity.

Americanization in the context of teaching refers to teachers providing learning experiences that would foster and result in building communities of learners who learn to live in democratic communities. This includes the teaching for understanding of civics, rights and duties, as well as experiencing democracy as a relational culture focusing on how to relate to each other, who participates, how to resolve conflict, how to negotiate, how to build consensus, how to listen, and how to communicate eloquently, among many other aspects of individual character and community civil harmony (Grinberg, 2009). For this, public school teachers teach students how to discipline their minds through subject matter learning, as well as to discipline their behavior through the enactment of norms, routines, rights, rules and expectations, as well as their dispositions through instilling values and providing experiences that embrace community empathy. Such approach demands that students cannot learn to be Americans if they cannot experience being educated in American in schools.

Furthermore, we argue that three practices of Americanization have been in place in Public schools with more or less influence at different historical times, and that these practices have and will continue to coexist. These three practices that we will discuss are **Deculturalization, Socialization/Enculturation,** and **Multiculturalism**. We will analyze, explain, and discuss these practices by providing historical, cultural, social, and political context; discussing a number of primary documents through a dialogical analysis; and then connecting our analysis with future implications for teachers. But, before we engage with the documents, we will present you with a brief contextual discussion of why Americanization has been such an important construct that permeated our curriculum and teaching in and out of the classroom.

AMERICANIZATION IN PUBLIC SCHOOLS TODAY & WHY TEACHERS PAVE THE WAY

The modern nation state is an evolution from absolutist monarchies and empires into independent self-governing entities, finding some commonality because of geographical, cultural, and economic relations. These entities forge a common national identity in order to establish sovereignty that permits to regiment a local social contract, including a system of laws that rule everyday life in civil, economic, and penal domains. Understanding Americanization is important if we want to learn about public schools and the relationship between curriculum and national agendas. Furthermore, it provides the platform for the analysis of the role that schools have played in the formation of social commonality, national pride, cohesion, and the shared value that public education presents as a common equalizer for all Americans regardless of background. Because public schools are the institution of Americanization and the building of a national identity, the teacher serves as the medium to deliver the invisible curriculum of Americanization.

Post World War II presented America with new educational challenges. At least four large agendas for educational change were embraced that catapulted American education into what we see in classrooms today. First, there was a curricular change toward a more robust and stronger disciplinary based agenda. Secondly, the federal government undertook a more a responsible role regarding educational achievement gaps based on huge differences in social class. Third, desegregation and civil rights movements served to integrate the nation's people and provided opportunities to many who have been relegated due to their ethnicity or religion.

As a result of these reasons, a redefinition of national identity and what it means to be American in this new context—including political disputes and the role of the federal government, foreign wars, the questioning of traditional cultural norms, and youth social movements—reclaiming and redefining democracy constituted a central dimension because it became a symbolizer of American identity as represented by the idealization of freedom, individual and collective rights, and the rule of the law and justice for all. Therefore, in order to incorporate and integrate *all*, a multicultural agenda emerged to redefine the meaning of Americanization in schools and what it meant to be American in the current century. David Tyack (1993) has asserted that the big difference between this movement and others was that at the core it represented a grassroots, bottom up, movement to expand how schools address and represent issues of culture, race, ethnicity, gender, ability, and other qualities that make us who we are. Multicultural education, which we will explain through one of the documents in this chapter, became a competing and relevant approach to Americanizing students in the classroom. The first two documents that will be discussed tell the story of Americanization in the past and the educational the implications that compete with a multicultural point of view of the present.

SUMMARY OF DOCUMENTS

Document #1: Carlisle Indian Industrial School—Three Lakota Boys Picture[2]

----

[2] Three Sioux boys at the Carlisle Indian School in Pennsylvania. The boys were photographed as new arrivals (left) and again six months later (right). (photo: NAA INV 00606600 courtesy National Anthropological Archives, Smithsonian Institution).

The Indian Boarding Schools in the late 19th Century served to educate the children of American Indians who mostly were confined to live in Reservations. During this period of time, many people believed that the only way to save the dwindling Native American population was to rapidly assimilate the population into the American way of life (Utley, 2004). Children and youth were removed from these reservations or from the places of residence of their families and Tribes in order to attend schools. Often, the Boarding Schools were located far away, even hundreds of miles away from their homes. In such schools, students would learn the English language, acquire knowledge and skills that would enable them to function in the larger American society, and would participate a number of recreational and religious activities.

During this process of partaking in an American education, students were forced to abandon who they were before they came to the school. For instance, male students were forced to cut their long hair, which was part of their own identity and a symbol of their heritage. Furthermore, they were forced to reject much of what they brought with themselves in terms of religious and cultural belief and had to participate in mass and embrace Christian rituals and traditions. The food was also strange to their diets, they had to dress in Western clothes, and they were forbidden from speaking their own native languages and could only communicate in English. The photograph we chose as a document to discuss powerfully illustrates these changes that students went through in their Boarding school experience. These changes were a form of **"deculturalization."** These acts of deculturation and assimilation into the American way of life came at a very heavy cost for the students which at times resulted in tragedy as many escaped and did not survive the wilderness in their attempt to get back home. In other cases, some students experienced deep depression. On the other hand, as some American Indian leaders argued, the boarding school experience would enable their young to access the opportunities that the larger society provided for the majority of the white people by giving their youngsters the skills, language, and cultural modes of the dominant society.

In the table following the documents we provide some contextual information about the times of the document, which we will also discuss in our dialogue section after we introduce the other two documents in this chapter. The following document will present a different approach to the concept of becoming American.

Document #2: A 1922 Application for American Citizenship Flyer [3]

"When the school introduces and trains each child of society into membership within such a little community, saturating him with the spirit of service, and providing him with the instruments of effective self-direction, we shall have the deepest and best guarantee of a larger society which is worthy, lovely, and harmonious."

—*(Dewey, 1915, p. 29)*

---

[3] Foreign-Born Friends who are Applicants for American Citizenship; 1922; Publications of the U.S. Government, Record Group 287. [Online Version, https://www.docsteach.org/documents/document/foreignborn-friends-who-are-applicants-for-american-citizenship, January 18, 2017.]

The following document represents another alternative dominant practice of Americanization that was popular a few decades after the birth of Boarding schools. We chose to label it as **enculturation**, following what John Goodlad (1997) described as a purposeful and deliberate practice of schools and teachers to teach students, and by extension their families, to become Americans, which in his argument means the "enculturation of the young into our social and political democracy" (p. 140). Although Goodlad would not have endorsed exactly a practice that ignores what is it that students, their families and their communities can contribute to the cultural fabric of America, he embraced in a Deweyan sense the idea that schools and teachers ought to teach to live in a democratic America similarly to what Dewey's quote above suggested. But, in Goodlad's work, he advances the concept as a process of learning a culture, the culture of democratic life, which also entails the learning of habits, routines, rules, rights, and duties of how to relate to each other, how to learn together and live together in harmony, how to resolve conflicts, and how to develop solidarity and loyalty to each other in spite of differences.

Again, as with deculturalization, enculturation deposits high hopes on what schools and teachers can do in their classrooms. In the case of this flyer, the practice was actually a deliberate educational and political agenda that was labeled Americanization. Furthermore, this also points to schools and teachers not only serving school age children but also addressing the needs of foreign born families, hence teaching adults. We will discuss in more detail in our dialogue section what these times were about, the function of the schools in this process, and the conceptualization of becoming American, as both local and global historic, economic, and political context are very relevant.

Document #3: Sonia Nieto's Definition of "Multiculturalism in Schools" [4,5]

This document is an excerpt from the work of a scholar that represents the redefinition of being American in a multicultural, multiethnic, and multilingual society, which many educators embrace today. While there are several relevant approaches, we chose Nieto's definition of **multiculturalism** because it enables us to better comprehend that multiculturalism and multicultural education are a form of Americanization and that for schools and teachers, there is a central role to play in enculturating students into the principles of American democracy and social justice. While this perspective coexists with some aspects of the traditional perspectives represented in the other two documents, Nieto's definition of

---

[4] Nieto, S. (2000) in Affirming Diversity (Chapter 9, page 305)
[5] For a comparison of these 7 characteristics in a mono-cultural versus multicultural educational setting, refer to Table 10.1 from her book (Chapter 10, pages 342–343).

A SOCIOPOLITICAL DEFINITION OF MULTICULTURAL EDUCATION

Multicultural education is a process of comprehensive school reform and basic education for all students. It challenges and rejects racism and other forms of discrimination in schools and society and accepts and affirms the pluralism (ethnic, racial, linguistic, religious, economic, and gender, among others) that students, their communities, and teachers reflect. Multicultural education permeates the school's curriculum and instructional strategies, as well as the interactions among teachers, students, and families, and the very way that schools conceptualize the nature of teaching and learning. Because it uses critical pedagogy as its underlying philosophy and focuses on knowledge, reflection, and action (*praxis*) as the basis for social change, multicultural education promotes democratic principles of social justice.

The seven basic characteristics of multicultural education in this definition are:

Multicultural education is *antiracist education*.
Multicultural education is *basic education*.
Multicultural education is *important for all students*.
Multicultural education is *pervasive*.
Multicultural education is *education for social justice*.
Multicultural education is a *process*.
Multicultural education is *critical pedagogy*.

multicultural education addresses the needs of a post-civil rights America and at the same time serves as a resource to strengthen the idea of democracy and the historical agenda of opportunity, fairness, and greatness that can emerge from our schools that can ultimately benefit the American way of life.

Glocal Context of Document 1

Historically, since the 1840's and in particular during Reconstruction, the expanding American public school system was tasked with three assignments: (a) to teach content in order to provide students with enough skills to function in the marketplace while providing the sense of equal opportunity (Price & Grinberg, 2009); (b) to educate to live in a democracy in order to warrant the solidification of a nation state with a shared set of values, norms, rules, regulations and rights (Labaree, 2006), and as in the above quote by Harris; (c) attracting the children of immigrants to attend the public school system to instill a cultural project to preserve democracy and the American ways of being (Tyack, 2007), which has been defined through the hegemony of the mainstream society (Kincheloe, 2008).

William Harris, who we quoted above at the beginning of this chapter, was an influential educator who served as superintendent of schools in St. Louis, Missouri from 1868 to 1880, and later U.S. commissioner of education from 1889 to 1906. Harris argued for the imperative need to construct a common American identity and to utilize public schools as the main institution, if not the only one, to carry such an enormous task of integrating all, and in particular immigrants, into the American values and sense of destiny. Harris captured the

CONTEXTUAL TABLE

Document & Year	Global Context	National Context	Educational Context
Before & After Picture of Indian Boys at Boarding School—1880s	Consolidation of modern Nation-state Utopian socialism in Europe Colonial powers control production and trade Large developments in transportation & communications	Post-reconstruction Expansion to and settlement of the West (Manifest Destiny) Industrial revolution Struggle over free markets and the role of state regulation Immigration	Child studies and psychology Land grant colleges Consolidation of a public school system One room schools
American Citizenship Flyer—1920s	Post-WW1 totalitarianism (communism, fascism, Nazism)	Economic crash of 1929 Progressive politics (national parks, schools, increased role of government) Immigration, 19th amendment (womens' right to vote) Settlement Houses	Behaviorism Progressive teaching Great expansion of American high schools
Sonia Nieto's Definition of Multiculturalism—2000s	Globalization 9/11 & terrorism Access to technology (technological divide) Ethnoscapes	NAFTA commerce treaty Service oriented economy in the US Immigration War in Iraq & Afghanistan	Market based reforms No Child Left Behind High stakes testing National standards and the common core

accepted perception of the role of public schools during times of massive immigration to the Midwest of the USA by acknowledging the role of curriculum and teaching as crucial in the project of building the nation-state. Harris recognized that public schools could play a crucial role in inducting students into American national life.

Such vision, desire, and mission of the school systems extended also to the populations of American Indians and Hispanics. For the Indians, Boarding Schools was a solution. Such schools not only will Americanize and in that sense also civilize, but also will eradicate the perceived primitive savage cultural ways of living and belief system of the different American Indians. This was a complex operation which historian Joel Spring (2012) argues meant to deculturalize the Indian from their ancestral traditions and ways of living and believing, a topic we will discuss further in this chapter.

Such educational and sociopolitical practices occur in a time of (1) reconstruction after the civil war thus facing the need to unify and solidify the sense of a common and shared national identity and (2) rapid geographical expansion. Not only the country gain all the Southwest territories (states such as California, Arizona, New Mexico, Colorado, etc.), but also the expansion of communication (think of the telegraph) and transportation of people and merchandise (think railroads), in a time that has been labeled the second industrial revolution because of the modernized systems of production, transportation, and communications. But, in many parts of the world two parallel social phenomena are shaped by such developments: (1) the rapid evolution of ideologies that reject the industrial and capitalist systems as a manifestation of social exploitation to benefit the empowered elites and (2) the rapid counter development of a romantic sense of nationalisms, which manifest in territorial sovereignty, allegiance to the language and culture of an homogenous society above the social class division, and the evolution of the modern nation-state from the fractured empires.

The US was not immune to such global context and Americanizing practices through the benevolent practice of schooling served to solidify a sense of belonging, patriotism, and commonality among very diverse populations (Toheler et al., 2015). And, schooling became more effective because academic fields such as psychology and pedagogy contributed to understand the developmental aspects of the students as well as more effective ways of framing learning experiences. With a consolidated system of schooling across America, with the expansion of schooling to more remote geographical areas, with better access to schools and better school teaching and curriculum, states developed normal schools to prepare teachers, started moving to develop more secondary schools, although its access was selective, and expanded the number of public institutions of higher education, including colleges that will have as a mission to serve and benefit through research and practice the needs of the state (so called land-grant colleges, such as Rutgers in NJ, The University of Wisconsin in WI, or Michigan State University in MI). Would the diverse populations of immigrants, American-Indians, Blacks, and/or Hispanics have access to secondary or higher education?

Glocal Context of Document 2

After the First World War (the one that was supposed to be the last war of humankind), America continued to experience a rapid growth of immigration with waves that came mostly from Europe and Asia, which already started by the end of the 19th Century. Large numbers of diverse immigrants, many of whom did not speak English, and who were occupied in blue collar labor, was common in large cities and industrial areas of the country. Many women were also working blue-collar jobs, while the better educated with some type of degrees might be incorporated into the clerical work force, but with a significant number of them serving in the professions of human improvement (i.e., teachers and nurses). However, not only that society did not pay them similar salaries for equal jobs to these of men in spite of having similar credentials, but women had to fight to obtain voting rights. Some women took on advocacy jobs and developed settlement houses, which were institutions located in houses in neighborhoods with large immigrant populations with the purpose of helping the immigrants settled in America, such as Henry Street settlement House in NYC and Hull House in Chicago. Actually, the main force behind such "houses" who was also an advocate for peace and freedom, was social worker Jane Addams, who won the Nobel Peace Prize in 1931. Settlement houses were a very important agency in providing an enculturating experience into the American culture, particularly for women, who were taught English, art, cooking, and labor skills, among multiple other programs and initiatives, also educational and health services were offered at these places.

In Europe totalitarianism was gaining power in these times. While communism under Stalin was solidifying a tyrannical regime in what was the Soviet Union, fascism, falangism, and nazism were ascending in Italy, Spain, and Germany, respectively. Hence, the educational agenda for Americanization also embraced the purpose of enculturating into a democratic way of leaving, the respect for a system and rule of law and checks and balances, and a clear understanding of rights and obligations in social and political terms. This was relevant because given the European precedent which was coupled with economic challenges, the economic debacle of a crashed market could be a fertile soil for the destruction of a democracy. Americanization sought to instill the values of community, conflict resolution, freedom, and opportunity.

The advancement of human rights, such as women's rights and children's rights, as well as the advancement and strengthening of democracy and democratic values were among the central agendas of the American Progressive Movement. Progressives engaged in social activism and political reform mostly since the 1890s to the 1930s. They attempted to address problems caused by unregulated industrialization, unplanned urbanization, and massive immigration, such as the conditions and context of poverty and depression, by promoting legislation, regulations, social services, and educational changes grounded on scientific knowledge and with a great deal of optimism on individual and collective achievements in every and all fields of human endeavor, from economy to medicine, social work and education among others. For instance, the preservation of natural resources and national parks was a central part of these efforts. In educational terms, progressives advocated for child and student centered practices that will foster inquiry, hands-on activities, and ways of teaching that would nurture student's curiosity and help release the imagination. Learning to live in a democracy was central to the progressive agenda, hence the emphasis on seeing classrooms as learning communities, as John Dewey asserted in the above quote associated with the presentation of this document.

Within this view of the school as an institution responsible for more than engaging in learning content, emerges a new model of the school as a community center was also implemented. These were full service schools that provided social services, health services, an open playgrounds, and athletic facilities to the local neighbors and also offered adult education. English language learning was the center of these adult classes, particularly in the areas where large numbers of immigrants inhabited. These classes not only focused on language acquisition, but fundamentally they served as socializing experiences into the American way of leaving, including behaviors, modes of communication and expression, customs, norms, acceptable and valued behaviors, and the rule of law. This document represents and symbolizes in a visual way the significance and interest in providing immigrants with a structured learning experience, a way of enculturating them, a way of Americanizing them.

However, Progressives such as President Teddy Roosevelt, who advocated for one homogeneous American identity devoid of other ethnic or linguistic identities, chose to ignore the important difference between modern nation states that claimed national identities grounded in the construction of linguistic, geographical borders, cultural, and ethnic commonalities, with that of national identity constructed not on ethnic or linguistic backgrounds, but on loyalty to a system of respect, trust, equality, opportunity, and the rule of law in which difference and diversity are accepted and, furthermore, embraced. The American model of nationhood was distinctively unique since as a nation of immigrants forged a system of norms, rights, and duties, which shaped a democratic culture. Nevertheless, the mastery of the English language has been and continues to be a sine qua non to be able to participate fully in the American experience and to be able to take advantage of educational, social, and economic opportunities. In what follows we contextualize the third document, which call for a different and more complex way of understanding being American with implications to the role of curriculum and that of the teacher.

Context of Document 3

The civil rights reforms of the 1960s and 1970s further defined the role of the teacher as a cultural worker by expecting from them to foster and implement integrated learning communities, thus Americanizing all students regardless of their status, race, gender, or home culture (Spring, 2008, Toheler et al, 2015). The role of education in general, and that of the teacher in particular, continues the practice of purposeful enculturation into the American experience, not only for immigrants or the children of immigrants, but for all the different segments of society. What shifted is not the practice, but the content of how being American is defined. In the post-civil rights movement times, integration, acceptance, and embracement of difference and diversity collide with ethnocentric traditions held by the forging of some essentialist categories of ethnic identity pushing for schools that would be more homogeneous in racial, socioeconomic status, or ethnic characteristics. For instance, the so called practice of "White Flight" that meant either the physical moving out of the older neighborhoods into further away locations, often suburbia, or the abandonment of the public school system in favor of private schools represented in practicality the resistance to desegregation and integration. Similarly, the movement for Afrocentric schools to serve only black students with a curriculum tailored for them by their own civil and educational leaders, served in practical terms, justified or not, to distance from the idea of integration.

Paradoxically, the retreat to ethnic politics and identities, coincides with the explosion of communications at a global level. Technology impacted not only businesses but also everyday life. Cable TV, cellular phones, rapid and enhanced means of transportation throughout the world, opening of global markets, access to goods, access to information, scientific exchange and global research collaborations, and movement of people across borders, characterized a time of global integration at multiple levels, in spite of the huge economic and political differences among and between nations. For instance, markets were open to trade and treaties as NAFTA, which enabled all type of products to be free of taxes to be moved between Canada, Mexico, and the USA, blurred the concept of economic borders into regional economic integrations.

In schools, computers became a fixture in most classrooms and libraries became media centers. Media literacy became an important component of a good education, particularly for the application of critical thinking skills since these would be needed in order to judge the merits of what is being presented through all these new media outlets, from cable TV to websites, to what later evolved into social media. For instance, with almost universal access to media in American schools, learning to differentiate what is fact and what is opinion, or what are the multiple ways in which ideas, stories, or information are represented, for what purposes, by whom, became a challenge in teaching, particularly in a time of competing narratives about identity, experience, scientific trues, and historical facts.

These times have been also influenced by the practices of high stakes testing in schools, meaning that performance of students in standardized test, more than ever before, dictated the opportunities that they would have for further opportunities to access in education. Furthermore, such high-stakes tests also conditioned the evaluation of teachers' performance and that of school effectiveness. In times of market-oriented school reform proposals, performance of schools impacted the chance to stay in operation or being closed. Hence, advocacy for school choice, perceiving education as a product to be consumed, and opening of alternatives within public schools, such as charter schools, became an attempt to address inequalities. Policies such as No Child Left Behind took on a national dimension of school accountability that created a tension between what historically has been the enculturating aspects of school life and that of school function to produce measurable results. Yet, these practices coexist in schools until nowadays as the role of educating the young into becoming fully American are an enduring purpose of our schools, as it has being the role of building a national identity for other modern states around the globe.

DISCUSSION/DIALOGUE

In what follows, we the authors of this chapter, discuss issues related to the three documents presented above. Weisz presents five questions dealing with the role of Americanization, the shifting approaches to it, and the practices of deculturalization, enculturation, and critical multiculturalism represented in the three documents. Grinberg explores the questions provided.

JW: What is the role of Americanization in the context of the Modern Nation State?

JG: *The modern nation state is an evolution from absolutist monarchies and empires into independent self-governing entities, finding some commonality because of geographical, cultural, economic relations forging a national identity in order to establish sovereignty that permits to regiment a local social contract, including a system of laws that rule everyday life in civil, economic, and* *penal domains. For such social contract to function, the modern national state was in need of both a political society and a civil society, which in turn cannot function in harmony without a constructed sense of belonging, of commonality such as common past, common destiny, loyalty based on shared values and shared cultural values. The response of the modern state to impose loyalties has been channelized through educational systems that became public, providing on the one hand possibilities for betterment by enabling individuals to access knowledge and skills that otherwise they would not have had, but also being immersed in the state apparatus which homogenized and hegemonized the messages of values, culture, identity, and loyalty. For example think about the role that certain symbols in school life are forming the discourse of national identity including the American flag, pictures of the founding fathers, and more diverse leaders who can serve as role models (for example, Martin Luther King Jr. and Eleanor Roosevelt, Harriet Tubman, and Rosa Parks).*

In his annual report for the Massachusetts Board of Education in 1948, Horace Mann asserted that the **common school movement** *may become the most effective force of civilization (Mann, 1848). Civilization at the time of Mann's writing about schools meant the familiarity with western cultural classics and the skills needed to be productive. Mann fundamentally meant that schools undertake the task of enculturating children and youth into the ways of living in American society. Furthermore, Catharine Beecher, the great advocate for the development of normal schools, schools that would prepare young women to become well-equipped and well-educated teachers, argued that teachers would have the primordial task of inducting youth into American culture and society.*

JW: Has the concept of Americanization or the function of schools in Americanizing the students being the same through time?

JG: *As the documents and our analysis above suggest, the concept of Americanization, what it means to be America and how schools, the curricula, and teachers go about it has shifted, but elements of the different shifting approaches have an enduring presence, they coexist. Americanization has been redefined as the nation has evolved in demographic, political, economic, social and cultural terms. Americanization has contributed to the development of civil society and democratic institutions. In summary, Americanization continues as an enduring theme throughout the curriculum in multiple forms through multiple experiences; has created tensions and debates over the purposes of public education and who is educated for what ends, but also has enabled access and inclusion; has served as a unifying and socializing agenda, encouraging national identity and, as such, a sense of national ownership, responsibilities, and rights, including an ethos of common interest and destiny; has been redefined as the nation has evolved in demographic, political, economic, social and cultural terms as I have established in my own research (Grinberg, 2009); and it has contributed to the development of civil society and democratic institutions. Presently and in the near future, the task of using public schools as the dominant force to Americanize the youth of this country continues to be relevant in the present political conjuncture vis-à-vis immigration and multiculturalism, hence the play between integration and assimilation with the enhancement of Americanization in the classroom experience by incorporating aspects of tolerance, respect and acceptance of diversity in cultural, religious, and national terms while redefining ethnic/racial conditions in order to embrace the practice of equal opportunity .*

The response of the modern state to impose loyalties based on shared cultural values has been channelized through educational systems that became public, providing on the one hand possibilities for betterment by enabling individuals to access knowledge and skills that otherwise they would not have had, but also being immersed in the state apparatus which homogenizes the messages of values, culture, identity, and loyalty. For example, think about the role that certain symbols in school life that form the discourse of national identity including the American flag and Pledge of Allegiance; pictures of the founding fathers and more diverse leaders who can serve as role models (for example, Martin Luther King Jr., Eleanor Roosevelt, Harriet Tubman, and Rosa Parks).

JW: In the first document, we see a major transformation of young Indian men becoming westernized. Can we expand our conversation here into the meaning of Deculturalization?

JG: *Deculturalization, according to Joel Spring (1998), is the process by which an ethnic group is forced to abandon its language and culture. In spite that the purpose was to enable these students to be fully functional and to give them an opportunity to succeed in an American society, in practice it also meant the rejection of who they were and what could they contribute to America given their own rich ways of knowing and cultural traditions. It is important to notice, however, that there was some level of agreement and compliance with the Boarding school on part of some families and leaders in many reservations (Adams, 1995).*

The modern nation-states did not necessarily abandon the prevailing practice of colonialism, a heritage from the European empires from modern history, hence maintaining an asymmetry of power between the centers (the nation-states) and the peripheria (their exploited colonies). A common tool of the modern-state of the time utilized to maintain such colonial control beyond force, has been the classic imposition of language (such as the Romans and other empires did), and cultural norms of behaviors and belief systems (also classic tools of control). These colonialist practices include deculturalization as an attempt to shift loyalties of the colonized in favor of the colonizer as a desired and convenient regime, hence abandoning resistance. Power was exercised not only through domination by force but also domination by convincing. Hence, educational tools could be effectively utilized to both dismantle resistance and to shift loyalties without using physical repression.

But deculturalization was not necessarily always negative. Take the case of immigrants who embrace a culture in which females are considered property of the males, including the barbaric tradition of honor killing among some groups. In such case, deculturalization meant that not only by law these practices were not permitted, but the need to eradicate the cultural legitimacy of such practices, hence eradicating such set of practices also by changing beliefs. Education, in consequence was as powerful approach to internalize and facilitate a change of belief system, habits of behavior, and ways of building democratic relationships not only because of the imposition of a legal system of rights and duties.

JW: In the second document, we see an effort to engage immigrants. Can we further explore Enculturation as an intentional educational practice?

We prefer enculturation to acculturation. While enculturalization is done with a program, as part of different classroom and school experiences, with a deliberate purpose and a curriculum that can be assessed, acculturation happens through the experience itself, but without a systematic scrutiny and without a pedagogical design. School curricula and classroom teaching require planning and assessment to be effective. Acculturation could or could not be educative and could or could not be effective, but enculturation must be.

Americanization meant to civilize the "other" and to develop loyalty to the American system, both politically through the development of democracy, and in the homogenization of a cultural commonality in spite of diverse backgrounds. Historically, Americanization became prevalent as an explicit agenda in schools at the turn of the 20th Century and turned into an organized movement geared to assimilate immigrants into the American fabric. But Enculturation does not entail per se abandoning one's roots, but rather embrace through a systematic set of purposeful experiences the habits of mind and habits of behavior required for sustaining and improving a democratic way of living, as John Goodlad has argued. The teaching of the English language did not mean forgetting other languages, it meant to open the possibilities for integrating, gaining access, and inserting within the larger cultural fabric. This, was assumed, would enable better opportunities for individual and collective social mobility, better education, skills, jobs, beyond understanding how to live in a democracy.

JW: The third document proposes a radically distinctive and different approach to the role of public education in relation to the glocal context of diversity of the very same American fabric. Can you expand the discussion of the context?

JG: *Since the 1970's, a globalized context, meant also that regional, ethnic, and at times ideological or tribal differences became exacerbated since globalization became a threat to the established power structures and groups with economic, social, ideological, religious, and political control in many parts of the world. As argued by scholar Benjamin Barber, jihad became an appropriated symbolizer of resistance to modernization and change, while globalization represented standardization of cultures into some materialistic superficial commodity. But, globalization also represented the advance of human rights, economic opportunities, democratization, and educational access. Some individuals and groups resisted these globalizing forces to the extreme by engaging in terrorism, which means physical harm and loss of life for anyone, where any civilian of any age, gender, or walk of life became victims of these terrorists, a disgrace we continue to face today. It has led to two intense and long contemporary wars for Americans in the quest to eradicate terrorism far away geographically, in Afghanistan and in Iraq. While terrorism was not new to modern times, the conditions of globalization and global access enabled a more sophisticated and also globalized practice of terrorism. In this context, multicultural education called to celebration of diversity and respect of the other as a form to build civility and a harmonious embracement of democracy not only as a political system but as a way of life, thus learning to live with each other. Interestingly, in times of war, in the battlefield, the military seem to have been effective at integrating diverse populations of Americans, perhaps given the enormous task of having to live and serve together, and at times to defend each others' lives.*

If building a sense of a national identity has been a central task of public schools for more than 150 years, practices of discrimination which privilege some at the expense of others, the construction of others as inferior, or the construction of others who do not belong to my particular group as a problem, as dangerous, or in extreme cases as the enemy, ultimately undermines the sense of commonality and national identity. As discussed above, such identity is grounded not on ethnic shared values, but on the sharing of civic values and the construction of solidarity as members of a society where the rule of law, the principles of equality and opportunity, respect, the sense of common destiny and civility are the glue for such identity above ethnic, racial, religious, or other identity markers. Hence, racism, sexism, discrimination, ableism, ageism, antisemitism, and all other forms of discrimination not only are antithetical to the American experience, but need to be eradicated. However, what Nieto proposes is larger than learning together or embracing anti-racist practices as enculturating aspects. What is being proposed by advocates of multicultural education is normalizing difference as a characteristic of being in America. Such normalization would be possible through the norms, habits of behavior, and habits of mind developed and legitimized as cultural values in classrooms and schools.

PRACTICAL IMPLICATIONS FOR TEACHERS—THE TEACHER AS A "CULTURAL AND POLITICAL WORKER"

As the main institution with the opportunity and ability to reach a significant sector of the population at a formative stage of life, public schools have been in an unique position to play a central role in preparing *all* students to live in a democracy and to value democracy, which also entails advancing civil rights and countering agendas that favor selected interest groups at the expense of the larger public good. Hence, the notion is twofold: (a) it argues that the practices of Americanization in classrooms have served to integrate and assimilate immigrants and natural born citizens into the larger democratic nation, and (b) that Public Schools have played and will continue to play a vital role in preserving the republican character of American democracy. The conclusion is that strengthening the role of Public Schools in the Americanization process and that of teachers as a cultural and political broker is absolutely necessary for the continuation and evolution of a meaningful liberal democracy—contemporary proposals to weaken the American Public School system ultimately would corrupt the democratic fabric of the nation.

Classroom teachers, curriculum, and school experiences have contributed to the building and strengthening of American political and civil society by teaching students to live in a democracy. Teachers, who had a moralizing role in the early development of the common schools, which over time evolved into the public school system, became cultural and political brokers in favor of an Americanizing project by the end of the 19th century. Teachers not only have the responsibility to teach content to students but also teach the development of community, character, and 21st Century skills regardless of the subject matter or grade level taught (Grinberg, 2005). As cultural brokers, teachers mediate between the dominant cultural values of mainstream America, including norms, behaviors, and systems of values and beliefs, and those to which the students were exposed at home or different community instances. As political brokers, teachers have taught students how to learn to live with each other in respectful harmony, accepting the rules of a social contract that manifests not only in individual relationships, but in public relationships of different groups, interests, and affinities under the larger umbrella of a political and civil society with laws, regulations, duties, and rights. Thus as cultural and political brokers, teachers present students the opportunity to learn how to function in such a system by providing tools to be successful in a democratic nation. While a good goal, such tasks are not as easy to foster and implement. To help develop such habits, teachers past and present have to embrace at times practices that would in some circumstances favor a model of American life that would benefit some and disadvantage others. As stated previously, the concept of Americanization shifted depending on the cultural context of the time, going from stripping away any semblance of the mother country to now embracing diversity in the classroom through the use of multicultural teaching practices. Regardless of the ideological ways of defining becoming American, or the practices enacted to Americanize students in schools, the expectation was that teachers would and will continue to carry on such tasks.

CONCLUSION

In spite of tensions and problems, Americanization in schools ultimately provided an opportunity to access the mainstream of society; thus to become part of the system and to move away from marginality (Grinberg, 2009). As such, it has served as a unifying and socializing project, encouraging national identity and a sense of national ownership, responsibilities, and rights, including an ethos of common interest and destiny. Failure to provide such opportunities has been an important reason for educational reforms, including curricular and pedagogical changes (Grinberg, 2009). In turn, Americanization has been redefined as the nation has evolved in demographic, political, economic, social, and cultural terms. Americanization has contributed to the development of civil society and democratic institutions. In summary, Americanization continues as an enduring theme throughout the curriculum in multiple forms through multiple experiences; has created tensions and debates over the purposes of public education and who is educated for what ends, but also has enabled access and inclusion (Grinberg, 2009); has served as a unifying and socializing agenda, encouraging national identity and, as such, a sense of national ownership, responsibilities, and rights, including an ethos of common interest and destiny; has been redefined as the nation has evolved in demographic, political, economic, social, and cultural terms (Grinberg, 2009); and it has contributed to the development of civil society and democratic institutions.

While the meaning of Americanization as an educational policy and school practice has been tied to national trends, we contend that such meaning has shifted over time via the particular historical, social, economic, cultural, and political contexts that have shaped the nation. Throughout this shift, common themes of Americanization through schooling have remained, including:

- Incorporating "all" into the values and norms of the historical mainstream, including access and opportunity to be successful.
- "Acculturation" into the values of democracy, freedom, rule of law, Western traditions, etc. of the dominant culture.
- Americanization as an educational process of socialization, acculturation, and enculturation as a form of "civilizing" through curriculum and pedagogy.

In all cases, Americanization involves the use of Public Schools as the main institution to explicitly teach about national identity and American values, rights, and duties, through both the academic curriculum and the teacher via her/his teaching and the relationships created within the classroom.

EXTENSION QUESTIONS

1. What can you learn that would be relevant to your teaching from the experience of Native Americans at the Boarding School about deculturalization as a practice of Americanization?
2. What could be the particular contextual circumstances that can help you better understand deculturalization, enculturation, and multicultural educational practices?
3. Would teachers who teach homogeneous populations of students with few or no immigrants be engaged in Americanization?
4. How would you approach your role in enculturating the young through your teaching? What would you consider?
5. How the call for a critical multicultural approach, as presented in the third document, can transform your meaning and your practices of teaching?

GLOSSARY OF TERMS

Acculturation—Individuals and groups from other cultural backgrounds are influenced by a dominant culture. The process of acculturation is not intentionally meant to Americanize the student body, but it is done so nonetheless through the different expressions, behaviors, languages, communication styles, values, peer influences, and feedback taking place within the walls of the classroom. Acculturation cannot exist without "assimilation" in which students incorporate new cultural schemata into their already existing prior cultural knowledge.

Cultural Adaptation—Changes made by individuals and groups as a response to a new and/or different environment and social condition. It may involve changes in: behavior, routines, norms, rituals, rules, resources, values/beliefs, language and speech, communication patterns, tastes, dress, etc.

Cultural Hegemony—The cultural norms of those in power become common sense, thus dominated groups and social classes accept their economic condition and social position as natural and unchangeable.

Deculturalization—The destruction of the culture of an ethnic group and its replacement by the culture of the dominating group, including language, belief system, social norms, and customs. Methods of Deculturalization in education include: forceful replacing of language, using the superior culture's curriculum in schools, having instructors from the dominant group, geographical segregation, and avoiding the use of the inferior's culture in the curriculum.

Enculturation—Individuals and groups learn the norms, behaviors, rules, regulations, values, modes of communication, language, and rituals of the culture that influences the local environments. It is an unifying project, encouraging formation of a national identity and an ethos of common interest and destiny. Use of Public Schools as the main institution to teach national identity, rights, and duties; values of democracy; freedom; rule of law; and Western traditions. Enculturation involves a deliberate curriculum for teaching these norms and values. This is an organized learning process with clear purposes and objectives delivered through educational activities, often involving recreational and social activities in addition to formal school environments.

Integration—Integration explains how a society holds together as a functioning entity. Schools serve as an institution that facilitates social integration for the young.

Multiculturalism—Incorporates multiple different cultural backgrounds—accepts and respects their traditions, forms, norms, customs, in as far as they do not have major conflicts with the dominant mainstream civil and political discourse. Tolerates and embraces "difference" as equal and embraces civil rights.

Socialization—Inducting individuals into the norms and ways of being of a society and culture. Students can be socialized in school by teachers, by the institution, or by peers.

REFERENCES

Adams, D. W. (1995). *Education for extinction: American Indians and the Boarding School experience, 1875–1928.* Lawrence: University of Kansas Press.

Dewey, J. (1915). *The School and Society* (2nd ed.). Chicago: University of Chicago Press.

Goodlad, J. (1997). *In praise of education.* NY: Teachers College Press.

Grinberg, J. (2005). *Teaching like that: The beginnings of teacher education at Bank Street.* NY: Peter Lang Publishing.

Grinberg, J. (2009). Playing with ideas: Some notes about learning communities and connected teaching elements. In Tyson Lewis, Jaime Grinberg, & Megan Laverty (Eds.), *Philosophy of Education: Modern and Contemporary Ideas at Play* (pp. 807–817). Dubuque, IA: Kendall & Hunt.

Grinberg, J., Goldfarb, K., & Saavedra, E. (2005). Con coraje y con pasion: The schooling of Latinas/os and their teachers' education. In Pedraza, Pedro & Rivera, Melissa (Eds.), *Latino Education: An Agenda for Community Action Research A Volume of the National Latino/a Education Research and Policy Projects* (pp. 227–254). Mahwah, N.J.: Lawrence Erlbaum Associates.

Kincheloe, J. (2008). *Critical pedagogy.* NY: Peter Lang.

Labaree, D. (2007). *Education, Markets, and the Public Good: The Selected Works of David F. Labaree.* NJ: Routledge.

Nieto, S. (2000). *Affirming diversity: The sociopolitical context of multicultural education (3rd ed.).* NY: Longman.

Price, J., & Grinberg, J. (2009). The foundations of a Public School System. In Jeremy Price and Jaime Grinberg (Eds.), *A brief history of American schools: Selected documents* (pp. 3–9). Dubuque, IA: Kendall-Hunt.

Spring, J. (2012). *Deculturalization and the Struggle for Equality: A Brief History of the Education of Dominated Cultures in the United States.* NY: McGraw-Hill.

Spring, J (2008). *The American school: From the Puritans to No Child Left Behind.* NY: McGraw-Hill.

Tröhler, D., Popkewitz, T., & Labaree, D. (Eds.) (2015). *Schooling and the Making of Citizens in the Long Nineteenth Century: Comparative Visions.* NJ: Routledge.

Tyack, D. (1993). Constructing difference: Historical reflections on schooling and social diversity. *Teachers College Record, 95,* 8–34.

Tyack, D. (2007). *Seeking Common Ground: Public Schools in a Diverse Society.* MA: Harvard.

Utley, R. (Ed.). (2004). *Battlefield & classroom: An autobiography by Richard Henry Pratt. Norman:* University of Oklahoma Press.

7

LOOKING BACK TO UNDERSTAND THE CURRENT CONTEXT OF SCHOOL FUNDING

CAROLINE MURRAY
HEATHER FRANK

INTRODUCTION

Over 6 billion dollars has been spent on K-12 public education in the United States each year in the last decade (National Center for Education Statistics [NCES], 2017). That is over 6 trillion dollars! Where does this money come from and how is it spent? These are central questions that define what we mean by school funding, and they are not simple to answer. For example, if we look more closely at this 6 billion dollar number, we see that 90% of public school funding comes from state and local sources, while only about 9% comes from the federal government (NCES, 2017). This means that funding in each state can—and often does—look very different. In this chapter, we will examine public school funding in the United States by looking back at the history of public education and how it has evolved. We will see how school funding is impacted by issues of race, gender, religion, politics, socioeconomics, and the Constitution, among other factors. How, and how much, schools are funded ultimately determines the kinds of resources schools have for teachers, facilities, materials, special programs, sports programs, and much more.

Contributed by Caroline Murray and Heather Frank. © Kendall Hunt Publishing Company.

SUMMARY OF THE TEXTS

MANN'S TENTH ANNUAL REPORT TO THE MASSACHUSETTS SECRETARY OF THE BOARD OF EDUCATION (1846)

Horace Mann is considered by many to be the Father of Public Schools. In his 10th Annual Address, he seeks to convince the Massachusetts governor and politicians that all citizens have an obligation to fund public education for all children. He does this both by providing arguments in favor of the benefits of universal public education and by arguing against the common reasons citizens gave to avoid supporting public education. Mann provides the minimum standards that he believes should be met through a system of public education.

THE EQUITY AND EXCELLENCE COMMISSION'S REPORT—*FOR EACH AND EVERY CHILD: A STRATEGY FOR EDUCATION EQUITY AND EXCELLENCE* (2013)

The Equity and Excellence Commission is a federal advisory group comprised of top education thinkers and policymakers. About 30 members, representing a wide spectrum of political and philosophical beliefs regarding public education, contributed to this particular report. The report's focus is on how to improve education, and the first area of focus is on school funding. The commission questions the long-standing use of local property taxes to pay for education.

SETTING THE STAGE FOR LOCALLY BASED PUBLIC EDUCATION FUNDING

The seeds of public education in the United States were planted in the late 17th century after Protestant colonists established towns in what is now Massachusetts. Education, and literacy in particular, was valued as a means to understanding Protestant Scripture. This, tied with the need for both men and women to contribute to the economic growth of the new settlements, meant that both boys and girls received informal education in homes and town schools. In 1820, the first public high school—Boston Latin—opened in Boston. Then in 1827, Massachusetts became the first state to make public school free and available to all children. This included girls and Black children; however, neither of these populations was given the same resources and opportunities as White male students (Madigan, 2009; Robinson, 2016).

To create public schools that were available to all children, advocates had to convince lawmakers and citizens that local property tax money—and eventually, state tax money—should be used for education. As you will see in the letter by Horace Mann, this in turn required convincing stakeholders that society as a whole would benefit from the education of all of its citizens. Mann and his contemporaries were influenced by the **Enlightenment** movement, which emphasized concepts such as progress, critical thinking, and the separation of church and state. Education for all was an idea that gained traction during and after the

Enlightenment. This idea was and still is a central focus of debate when it comes to school funding. While most Americans today would argue that free public education should exist, they do not agree about who should pay for it or what funding should include.

The table (*Figure 1*) below shows how our country has changed from an agrarian society and fledgling nation to an industrialized nation, then to a world superpower in a globalized society; Americans' views of the purposes of education have shifted over time, too. Yet, the debate about funding for education that began with educators such as Horace Mann and continues with educators such as those who contributed to the Equity and Excellence Commission report still comes down to several basic ideas that we will discuss now in greater depth, starting with the distinction between state and federal roles in education.

Figure 7.1

	Global Forces	National Forces	Educational Policies	Understanding of the Phenomena
Past Text: Horace Mann, 1846 *Tenth Annual Address to the Secretary of the MA Board of Education*	Industrialization; enlightenment; free education in "model countries" such as Prussia	Pre-Civil War: debate over slavery	Northeast states begin public education; Federal government just starting to get involved in education; debate over federal role	All children should have access to free education, and taxpayers should bear the burden regardless of whether or not they have school-aged children
Current Text: Equity and Excellence Commission, Edley, C. F., & Cuéllar, M. F. (2013). *For each and every child: A strategy for education equity and excellence.*	Globalization; 21st century skills; Age of Technology	Severe budget shortfalls; rise of antiintellectualism; poverty	Accountability movement; debate over federal role in education; support of charter schools	All children should have access to an excellent, free education regardless of their zip code: this requires more equitable funding across districts

STATE VERSUS FEDERAL ROLE IN PUBLIC EDUCATION

It comes as a surprise to many people to learn that education is not addressed directly in the Constitution. Under the Tenth Amendment, topics not addressed elsewhere are deliberately left in the hands of the states. This in part explains why less than 9% of funding for public education comes from the federal government. This percent has varied over the years and generally has represented a higher percentage of the United States' gross national product since the 1950s than before that time in U.S. history. Generally speaking, conservative policymakers seek to limit the federal government's role in areas such as education that the Constitution leaves in the hands of the states. As Chart A shows, in the time of Horace Mann discussions of education were very local and state focused, not federal focused. Mann wrote his letter prior to the Civil War and end of slavery. The country was in no position to think broadly about education for all children. Conversely, liberal policymakers tend to believe that the Constitution allows for a greater federal role both in terms of laws and in terms of funding. For many liberal advocates, the federal role in education is about ensuring that every state has laws that are fair to students regardless of race, religion, economic background, gender, (dis)ability, etc. Part of what makes laws fair involves equitable funding. Here, the Fourteenth Amendment also is frequently invoked. The Fourteenth Amendment requires that citizens receive equal protection under the law. Then there are the concerns that many Americans of all political leanings have today about being competitive on a national level with other countries in terms of education. Based on the most widely used and respected international tests, students in the United States currently are performing at a mediocre level compared to current and up-and-coming economic rivals. If the wealthiest U.S. school districts are compared with other countries, they fare well, but the poorest districts fare poorly (Biddle & Berliner, 2002). This disparity is not seen to this extent in other countries, and many argue that centralized, equitable funding in most modernized countries is a factor. Our national identity in the world in today's global economy is often at odds with our views of the Constitution and the role of the federal government.

To provide funding for education, and for the Department of Education itself, the federal government typically uses the "spending" clause of the Constitution. This clause allows the federal government to use tax money for purposes deemed to be in the best interest of the people. About one-third of the money that public schools receive from the federal government comes in the form of food assistance for students, grants, and other special initiatives under Title I of the Elementary and Secondary Education Act (U.S. Department of Education [USDOE], 2018). Title I money targets low-income students and must be spent specifically on those students unless 40% of more of the students in a school meet Title I qualifications. Over 2 million students receive funding in the form of free and reduced cost lunch and other services and supports. Some of the money is spent on materials and additional teachers. Additional funding comes from Title II of the Elementary and Secondary Act; Title II's focus is on teacher development, and the funding is often used for professional development (USDOE, 2016). However, it is the local and/or state funding that schools receive that pays for the bulk of school costs: staff salaries and benefits, services, and school supplies. One way people compare how much money is spent in different school districts is by dividing all of the funding that is available by the number of students in the district. This provides the *per pupil expenditure* for the district. Let us look at how that expenditure typically is spent.

PUBLIC SCHOOL BUDGETS

As mentioned above, only about 9% of public school district funding comes from the federal government, mostly through Title I and Title II funds. These and other funds began to take shape in the 1950s, when federal education funding—related to the United States's overall funds—began to increase. While states vary greatly, on average, about 47% of funding comes from the school district's state, and the remaining 44% comes from local sources. The sources vary by state, as different states have different tax rules. Some states have income tax, some have property tax, some have sales tax, and some have all three. How specifically is the money spent? As the graph (*Figure 2*) illustrates, about 80% of a district's budget goes toward teachers' salaries and benefits (https://nces.ed.gov/programs/coe/indicator_cmb.asp). Approximately 11% of the budget is spent on purchases, including food, transportation, janitorial services, and teacher professional development. The remaining 9% is spent on supplies.

Figure 2 Percentage of current expenditures per student in fall enrolment in public elementary and secondary schools by type of expenditure: 2003–04, 2008–09, 2013–14

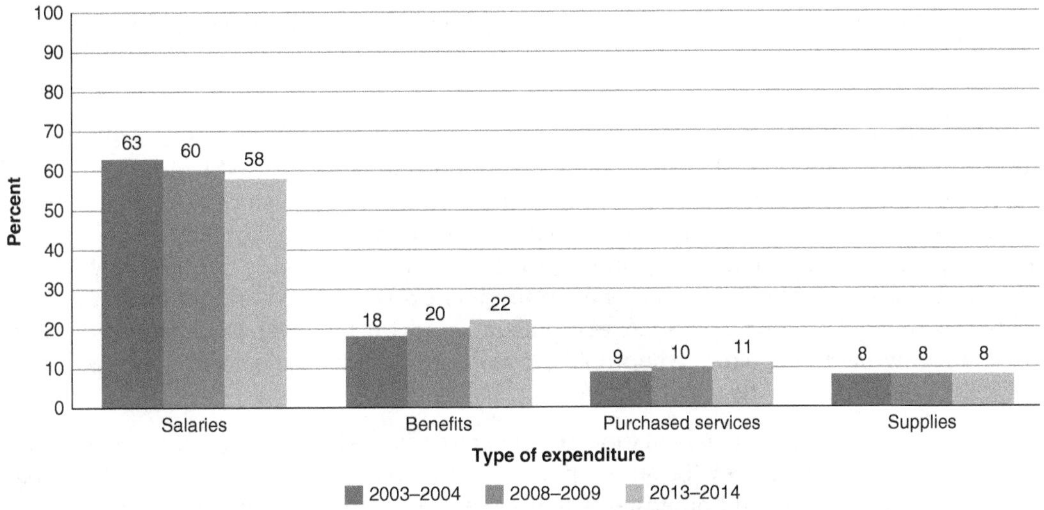

Source: NCES, retrieved from https://nces.ed.gov/programs/coe/indicator_cmb.asp

Districts that have a higher per pupil expenditure typically can have smaller class sizes because they can afford to have more teachers. These districts typically can offer more elective courses at the high school level for the same reason. Further, these districts generally have more funds for classroom supplies, school sports, and special initiatives. Conversely, districts with lower per pupil expenditures typically have larger class sizes, fewer high school elective offerings, and leaner sports programs. Of course, this varies somewhat according to the needs and interests of the district and also based on state laws and mandates. In some states, school budgets are determined at the state level or by local city or town officials. In other states, school budgets are determined by a school board. Teachers, administrators, parents, and other community members often become involved in budget discussions, especially when challenging decisions have to be made about where to allocate funds.

To understand how funding impacts schools, let us compare the budgets of two fictional districts in a state where property taxes are used to fund public education.

District A	District B
Population: 34,000	Population: 55,000
Students in public school system: 6,000	Students in public school system: 8,000
Median household income: $100,000	Median household income: $35,000
Local property taxes for education: $250,000,000	Local property taxes for education: $100,000,000
State aid: $6,000,000	State aid: $10,000,000
Federal aid: $2,000,000	Federal aid: $4,000,000
TOTAL DISTRICT REVENUE: $259,000,000	TOTAL DISTRICT REVENUE: $115,000,000

As you can see, District A has substantially more revenue than District B to apply to the costs of running the district. District A has enough funds in our scenario to add a new world language teacher at the middle school and two new guidance counselors at the high school. District B, meanwhile, determines that it needs to cut a part-time music teacher at one of the elementary schools and eliminate funding for three after-school clubs at the high school. District A finds that it has enough money to fund a new sports field and renovate the high school chemistry labs with up-to-date equipment. District B, however, must reduce funding for its playing field maintenance and hold off until next year to see if there might be funds to fix the leaking roof in the middle school.

This is of course a simplified explanation of a very complicated matter. In reality, districts are required to use certain money for certain purposes, and in most districts there are items that are cut from the budget and other items that are added each year. However, fictional Districts A and B very much mirror the realities of urban, suburban, and rural districts around the country. What is harder to pinpoint is the ability of school administrators to allocate money effectively and efficiently. Dollars and cents may seem matter of fact, but the way money is spent is subjective and subject to questioning from all stakeholders. As a teacher, it will be important for you to be informed about your district's budget and the choices that are made about how to use that budget. To be well informed, it will be necessary to understand the role of larger societal issues such as law and race, which we discuss next. As we continue, consider this question: Why is it that District A and District B have such vastly different resources?

THE IMPORTANCE OF LAW AND RACE

Beginning with the implementation of public education Massachusetts, we see race, class, and legal tensions gain momentum over time that relate to how people interpret the Constitution. It was one thing for voting White men to consent to public education for everyone; it was quite another to consider having Black children being educated side by side with White children. *Plessy v Ferguson* (1896) affirmed the right to **segregate** children. Segregation can be used in different ways, but in education it most often refers to the separation of students by race. This would not be challenged and overturned by the Supreme Court until *Brown v Topeka Board of Education* (1954). What does this have to do with school funding? Segregation allowed for inequitable funding of schools within cities and towns. White schools had more supplies, better buildings, and resources for sports teams. "Colored schools," as they were often referred to, often were housed in crumbling buildings and lacked basic teacher supplies and equipment. Thus, a town's school funding began in one pool, but was allocated disproportionately.

However, desegregation of schools did not and has not ended inequitable funding and legal issues (Howell & Miller, 1997; Robinson, 2016). One result of desegregation was the shift from segregated sections of towns and cities to segregation of whole towns and cities. During the Civil Rights Movement in the 1960s, and as a result of Black riots and other signs of unrest, many White families left cities and towns that were becoming desegregated and moved to communities that were exclusively white. In states where schools were funded primarily by local taxes, this shift meant that there was less tax money available in poorer communities and more money in richer communities. In the 1970s, a number of lawsuits were brought against states claiming that funding was inequitable between municipalities. Among the most well-known was the *Serrano v Priest* case in California, which spawned a number of lawsuits and legislative decisions over the next decade that focused on property tax rates and school funding. Ultimately, these court cases and legislative actions shifted the weight of school funding to the State of California. Lawsuits went in the other direction, as well. In Connecticut and California, landmark lawsuits were brought by taxpayers against the state for taking their money and applying it to lower-income communities. In these and other states, taxpayers worked to have taxes frozen so that there would be less funding for education. As a result, the per pupil expenditure on education went down.

THE CHARTER SCHOOL MOVEMENT

From an economics perspective, scholars disagree on how effective the school funding reforms discussed above have been in the last 60 years (Downes and Shah, 2006). While some argue that state funding reforms have increased per pupil expenditures in lower income districts, others argue that the overall funding for education has typically decreased in states with drastic reform measures. Further, many people maintain that even with reforms, some districts are not showing the academic and structural improvements needed to ensure that students are receiving an equitable education. One reaction to real and perceived lack of change has been the rise of **charter schools** across the country, particularly in low-income communities. Charter school rules vary by state, but in general they can be defined as public schools that operate independently of the district in which they physically reside. They are called charter schools because typically, they must draft a charter that explains the governance and purpose of the school. In many states, charter schools must articulate a specific mission or area of emphasis, such as STEM education, the arts, language immersion, or a particular philosophy. In most states, charter schools draw students from the school district through a lottery process. Beyond these factors, the structures of charter schools, and the controversy that often surrounds them, vary greatly by state because each state has its own education laws (Green, Baker, & Oluwole, 2013).

What makes charter schools controversial if they are providing options for their local community? Since charter schools are public, they receive money from their local school district's budget. When students migrate from district-run schools to charter schools, the money follows them. This means there is less money for the district to use for district-run schools. Many see this as exacerbating the problems that public districts already face. Relatedly, even when there is a lottery for admission, critics point out that there is still a certain amount of self-selection that occurs. By this they mean that students whose parents are more informed/educated are more likely to seek out and apply to a charter school, while the most vulnerable students, whose parents/guardians may not be equipped to apply on their behalf, become more concentrated in district-run schools. In addition, depending on the state, charters often have more freedom and fewer checks and balances than some educators would like despite the fact that research shows that overall, charter schools are neither more or less effective than district-run schools. Further, a growing number of charter schools are run by for-profit agencies. Some critics feel that this is conflicts with the ideals of free public education that is offered by the government. Many teacher unions dislike charter schools because in most states charter school teachers are not unionized, whereas virtually all district-run public school teachers in the United States belong to, or can belong to, a union. Research indicates, in fact, that charter school teachers often suffer from severe burnout and quit teaching because of greater demands in terms of time and expectations.

Proponents of charter schools point to the fact that many charter schools have waiting lists and that often many more students apply for admission than can be accepted, an indication that parents are dissatisfied with local district-run schools. Proponents argue that if there are fewer students in district-run schools, the district should be able to manage operations with a smaller budget. Successful charter schools whose students consistently outperform students in district-run schools make the case that their students achieve at higher levels and have increased life opportunities. Why should it matter, they argue, if their school is run by a for-profit company if the outcomes are good? Perhaps most compelling is the argument that children cannot afford to wait for adults to "fix" traditional public schools. Reforms take time and often face significant roadblocks. Charter schools have offered a way to provide an alternative, sometimes better choice for students and their families and have been able to effect change faster.

Some educators and policy makers fall somewhere in the middle. They believe that charter schools should exist and be supported, but that they should not be seen as solving all of the problems of public education. Again, opinions vary greatly by state since each state has its own rules and regulations for charter schools.

WHAT DO THE ARTICLES SAY? A DIALOGICAL DISCUSSION

CM: Mann argues that public schools should be funded by all taxpayers, regardless of whether they have children in the school system. He takes the position that schools should be funded locally, not federally. Local funding levels for education are still widely contested in towns and cities today. Many people who do not have children in schools do not see why they need to contribute to the school system budget. It is natural, I think, for parents and others with a direct stake in school funding to want to see more money spent on education.

HF: *Yes, but whereas Mann argues for local funding of schools, Edley and Cuéllar recommend that federal and state governments should each play roles in funding public schools. The authors point to inadequacies in the current school funding system, which maintains inequalities in educational opportunities for students. They argue that state and federal governments should reform school funding to ensure that all students, including low-income students, English language learners, students with disabilities, and students in rural districts can meet academic standards.*

CM: I'm glad you mentioned rural districts, which often do not come to people's mind when discussing education funding. If you look in particular at rural districts in poorer states, you see that the inequities in school funding are huge. This is one reason Edley and Cuellar take a different stance from Mann about the federal role in education. Edley and Cuellar's concerns seem to reflect the changes that have happened in our country in the last two hundred years. Mann thought very broadly, but he was living and writing and the beginning of our country's history. The Industrial Revolution had not begun, and the United States was a small and still very agrarian country. Today we have 50 states, but they are all very different, including in their financial status.

HF: *Plus Edley and Cuellar make a compelling argument that everyone should receive a free education. Mann believed likewise, but his definition of "everyone" was every White male, not women or African Americans. He wrote at a time when slavery was still in place and African Americans were not seen as being fully human or having the same rights as White people.*

CM: Yet, we cannot simply say that that was then and this is now. The history of slavery and racism in the United States continues to impact the discussion of school funding and public education.

HF: *It is interesting to consider how Mann's view of "everyone" still permeates the current public school system and education funding in the United States. Edley and Cuéllar emphasize the ways in which per pupil inequities impact the quality of education and achievement for specific students, such as those who attend school in high-poverty districts. This disparity reflects that while scholars may argue that "everyone" is entitled to a free education, not everyone is receiving a high-quality free education.*

CM: This is where the legal issues come in! Many of the legal decisions regarding education funding have centered on issues of race and socioeconomic disparities. Since the fifties, a number of key legal decisions have caused funding shifts toward students of color and students in low socioeconomic areas.

HF: *Let us also consider the legal decisions over the past forty years that have focused on students who receive special education services. The aforementioned decisions and subsequent policies have similarly shifted funding to students with special needs.*

CM: To me, the philosophical question is whether the emphasis is on "United States" or on "America." Are all Americans responsible for the education of all Americans? Is each state responsible for its own children's education? Just as there are differences in wealth and resources within states, there are vast differences in wealth and resources between states. In addition, not all states have demonstrated adequate protections and support for marginalized students. I feel that our country needs to see education as a national imperative, not a state imperative. I also think that a lot of the research points to the fact that countries that do well on international tests have chosen national interests and strengths over state/province rights and interests.

HF: *You raise two important points: (a) the wealth and resources vary from state to state and (b) not all states have adequately protected marginalized students. Considering the funding inequities that exist across and within states, the federal government must incentivize states to adopt more equitable funding systems. To me, it is imperative that the federal government support states in providing a high-quality public education for all students. While I agree that public education should be a priority at the national level, I think it is important that states have some control in determining and implementing effective educational programs.*

CM: What about charter schools?

HF: *I am product of the public school system and an educator in a public elementary school. While I am aware that there are successful charter schools in the United States, I believe they serve as a temporary bandage to a larger systemic problem. Specifically, charter schools do not address the inequities in our public schools or in school funding systems. On the other hand, I can understand a family's desire to send their children to schools where they feel they will receive a high-quality education. Needless to say, the topic of charter schools and vouchers is a complex one.*

CM: I agree. I also attended public school and taught in a public school. Of course, we have to be careful not to take our own personal experience and project it on families and communities that are different from the ones where we grew up. That is a really important thing for a new teacher to keep in mind: Maybe they will be teaching in a school that seems similar to where they attended school, but maybe the school will have more resources, or fewer, than they experienced themselves. When it comes to the charter school debate, it is critical to listen to the members of the communities where the schools exist. Charter schools and voucher programs have evolved in the last twenty years because people have become frustrated with lack of change in school systems.

PRACTICAL IMPLICATIONS FOR TEACHERS

Public schools today in all socioeconomic sectors are facing budget cuts and scrutiny over spending decisions. Preservice teachers need to be aware of the factors that impact school funding. From a social justice perspective, teachers need to understand the various factors that lead to economic disparities in education as well as in society as a whole. In today's society, charter schools and voucher programs are at the forefront of discussions about funding. Teachers need to understand the basic concept of how charter school funding works vis-à-vis regular public school funding in that respective district. Teachers also need to consider the implications of a voucher system. Again, this ties back to the issue of economic disparity. We maintain that racism is an underlying current that runs throughout much of this discussion. Since the inception of public education in the United States, students of color consistently have received less access to education than White students, particularly in terms of funding resources. While some critics argue that the quality of education students' receive is not related to the amount of funding their school receives, the preponderance of research supports the position that funding is related to education outcomes for students (Bracey, 1995). It is worth noting that virtually all developed countries have centralized funding structures for public education and that the United States is the exception in this regard (Biddle & Berliner, 2002).

There are several practical ways for new teachers to build their awareness about funding in their district and beyond. Attending board of education meetings, especially those focused on budget matters, is an important way to gain insight into the priorities of the board itself as well as other constituents. Relatedly, you should read your district's budget report. Districts often create an annual budget report summary that is "user friendly" for the community. Attending parent-led meetings such as a Parent Teacher Organization (PTO) or Parent Teacher Association (PTA), or becoming involved in such an organization, can be highly informative and offer you an opportunity to share your points of view. Within your school, you might see if there are committees in which you can become involved that provide advisement or directives on budgetary matters. Perhaps the most important way to become well informed and to become an advocate for well-designed budgets is to keep an open mind, listen to others' points of views, and consider the political and social structures that influence your district and budget decisions.

CONCLUSION

In 1938, almost at the exact midpoint in time between the writing of Mann's letter and Edley and Cuellar's report, education funding expert John Guy Fowlkes and scholar W.W. Thiesen wrote a comprehensive article about local, state, and federal funding options. They state:

> More and more during recent years local communities suffering from financial distress have turned to their respective states for help. Individual states, and particularly those states in which economic conditions would not allow necessary help to distressed localities, have in turn looked to the federal government for financial assistance necessary to meet the situation. (Fowlkes & Thiesen, 1938, p. 171)

Writing during the Great Depression, it is no surprise that there was increased attention and interest in federal funding for public education. However, the authors go on to say, "The consensus seems to be in favor of no federal control; yet it is an issue far from being settled either as to detail or principle" (p. 173). They could not know how true this still would be 80 years later. If anything, the tension between local, state, and federal funding of public education has grown in this time. There have been many legal battles, particularly since the Civil Rights era of the sixties, that have centered on the inequities in school funding. Many of these battles, at their core, have had to do with race, class, and socioeconomic status. Today, in addition to continued debates about school funding, there are also debates about new structures such as charter schools and vouchers, which seek to use public school funds in different ways than in the past. In short, school funding in the United States is complex and as varied as the states and communities that make up the nation.

EXTENSION QUESTIONS

1. Who should fund public schools and why?
2. Should everyone receive a free education?
3. What role do legal structures in the United States play in determining school funding?
4. How have legal decisions about educational funding impacted funding structures in the United States?
5. What should be the balance between State and Federal responsibility for education funding?
6. What role should charter schools play?
7. Imagine you are in charge of a district's budget and you have been told that you need to cut the budget by 5% for the upcoming year. Where might you make cuts?
8. You would like to purchase $500 in materials for a new program that research has shown to improve student achievement in your discipline. How would you advocate to receive funding for these materials? Who would you speak to? How would you make your argument?

GLOSSARY OF TERMS

Per pupil expenditure—a calculation of school funding based on the total federal, state, and local funds divided by the number of students in the district.

Charter school—a public school that operates independently from other schools in its school district and which receives funding from the public school district in which it resides. Some charter schools are affiliated with nonprofit or for-profit organizations that run charter schools in multiple states. Others are "solo" schools with no outside affiliations.

Segregation—separating students by race or other personal characteristic.

Enlightenment—A philosophical and intellectual movement in the 18th century that emphasized concepts such as progress, critical thinking, and the separation of church and state.

REFERENCES

Biddle, B. J., & Berliner, D. C. (2002). Unequal school funding in the United States. *Educational Leadership, 59*(8), 48–59.

Bracey, G. W. (1995). Debunking the myths about money for schools. *Educational Leadership, 53*(3), 65–69.

Downes, T. A., & Shaw, M. P. (2006). The effect of school finance reforms on the level and growth of per-pupil expenditures. *Peabody Journal of Education, 81*(3), 1–38.

Fowlkes, J. G., & Thiesen, W. W. (1938). The support of education: Federal, state, and local funding. *Review of Educational Research, 8*(2), 171–186.

Green III, P. C., Baker, B. D., & Oluwole, J. O. (2013). Having it both ways: How charter schools try to obtain funding of public schools and the autonomy of private schools. *Emory Law Journal, 63*, 303–337.

Howell, P. L., & Miller, B. B. (1997). Sources of funding for schools. *Financing Schools, 7*(3), 39–50.

Madigan, J. C. (2009). The education of girls and women in the United States: A historical perspective. *Advances in Gender and Education, 1*, 11–13.

National Center for Education Statistics. (2017). *The condition of education 2017*. Retrieved from https://nces.ed.gov/pubs2017/2017144.pdf

Robinson, K. J. (2016). No quick fix for equity and excellence: The virtues of incremental shifts in education federalism. *Stanford Law and Policy Review, 27*, 201–249.

U.S. Department of Education. (2016). U.S. Department of Education Non-Regulatory Guidance Title II, Part A of the Elementary and Secondary Education Act of 1965, as Amended by the Every Student Succeeds Act of 2015 September 27, 2016. Retrieved from https://www2.ed.gov/policy/elsec/leg/essa/essatitleiipartaguidance.pdf

U.S. Department of Education. (2018). Improving basic programs operated by local educational agencies (Title I, Part A). Retrieved from https://www2.ed.gov/programs/titleiparta/index.html

8

THE MATH WARS CONTINUE: HOW GLOCAL EVENTS CAN INFORM MATHEMATICS CURRICULUM, TEACHING, AND LEARNING

TANYA MALONEY
TINA POWELL

INTRODUCTION

A curriculum defines what students have the opportunity to learn in schools. These opportunities can be *written*, or overt, as they can be located in curricular materials, such as texts and classroom activities or lectures. Curriculum can also be *unwritten*, or hidden, in that students may learn from the messages they receive from their teachers, administrators, and other school personnel. Both written and unwritten curriculum is shaped based on educators' ideologies, values, and beliefs as well as societal goals and expectations. In this chapter, we consider how glocal events influence decisions made about written curriculum. We argue that in a democratic society, alignment between the authors and the audience of curriculum matters. More specifically, we consider how beliefs and values have affected math education for students differently, based on their social location. Our focus on science, technology, engineering, and mathematics (STEM) is due to our former roles as mathematics teachers as well as our current roles as STEM educators in the university and local school contexts.

Mathematics education is considered neutral and culture-free in that it is assumed all students work toward a common set of goals with fair access to the same materials and instruction. However, the policies, curriculum, and practices surrounding the teaching and learning of mathematics have been so contentious that the situation has been referred to as a war. Klein (2003) described the "math wars" as "a protracted struggle between content and pedagogy" dating as far back as the early 1900s (p. 177). Debates focused on whether

Contributed by Tanya Maloney and Tina Powell. © Kendall Hunt Publishing Company.

students needed to learn mathematics for mental dexterity or for practical application; as progressive philosophies tugged mathematics curriculum in one direction, beliefs about the need for all students to develop a set of common basic skills pulled it in the other. Progressivists and educational reformers questioned the need for all students to learn topics in algebra and geometry as they were highly theoretical subjects and considered to have little value for individuals not intending to pursue a career in a STEM-related field. Mathematicians and many mathematics teachers purported all educated people should develop their ability to engage in algebraic thinking. These dueling viewpoints suggest that mathematics curriculum is much more contentious than many may believe.

By the late 1980s, the standards reform movement gained momentum as educators worked to determine precisely what students needed to know and by what age. The movement was fueled by *A Nation at Risk*, a 1983 report that suggested American students were not only performing poorly in many international comparisons, but that there was a steady decline in science and mathematics achievement. The report also highlighted how Black and Latinx students and those living in poverty suffered limited access to quality education. The educational standards intended to raise expectations and ensure that all students, regardless of where they were born, received a quality education. The standards were revised numerous times before a set of "common core standards" were adopted by most states across the nation. The mathematicians and mathematics teachers seemingly won the math wars as these standards intended to "[foster] college and career readiness and [set] a globally competitive standard" for all students (Zimba, 2014, p. 1). The more recent *STEM education* reform movement took on a more interdisciplinary approach to the teaching and learning of science, technology, engineering, and mathematics. We discuss this progression by analyzing two documents published in the 1940s and one published in 2016. In a dialogical text analysis, we reveal the ways in which curricular decisions are made and who those decisions can affect. The end of the chapter lists extension questions for new teachers and educators to consider in any field of study.

THE SOCIAL AND CULTURAL CONTEXT

The call for *all* students to receive an adequate education is not a modern imperative, but the social and cultural context often defines who is considered *all*. Though all students are expected to be mathematically and technologically savvy, schools in the United States do not provide every student the necessary tools to reach this goal. Black and Latinx students and students living in low-income neighborhoods continue to experience limited opportunities to attend schools with rich curricular options, up-to-date materials and technology, and/ or highly effective teachers. During the most recent movement toward providing students with an excellent STEM education, by and large, Black and Latinx students as well as those living in low-income communities are attending schools that are not preparing them to be competitive in today's market.

In an effort to further understand this situation, we first provide the global and national context for the two sets of documents under analysis (see summary in Table 1). The first set of texts, penned by the National Council of Teachers of Mathematics' (NCTM) Commission on Post War Plans, were written in the mid-1940s, on the heels of World War II. During this time, the nation was still experiencing *de jure* segregation, known as Jim Crow Laws, excluding Black Americans from social opportunities including modern educational facilities and materials. In their discussion about the state of mathematics teaching and learning, the NCTM Commission did not mention the debilitating effects of *de jure* segregation on the educational outcomes for U.S. students. However, the vestiges of *de jure* segregation and the inequities in educational access were at the forefront in second text under analysis.

STEM 2026: A vision for innovation in STEM education (STEM 2026) was written in 2016 after international comparison tests, such as the Third International Mathematics and Science Study (TIMSS), revealed students in a number of other countries outperformed their American counterparts. In 2015, for example, U.S. fourth-graders' average scores in mathematics was higher than the average scores of students in 34 education systems, but lower than the average scores of students in 10 education systems (USDOE-IES, 2015). U.S. rankings can be attributed, in part, to the nation's inability to effectively educate all of its citizens. Presently, the United States suffers from *de facto* segregation maintained through racially motivated redlining practices; the percentage of K-12 public schools with racial or socio-economic isolation grew from the 2000–2001 to the 2013–2014 school year (Government Accountability Office, 2016). While both texts intended to innovate curriculum for at least the subsequent

Table 8.1 *The Forces and Policies Informing the Texts under Analysis*

Text	Global Forces	National Forces	Education Policies	Understanding of Phenomenon
Text 1 Reports of the Commission on Post-War Plans (1944 and 1945)	World War II	*De jure* segregation, Jim Crow Laws	Separate but equal schools	A call for a core curriculum to provide a functional competence in mathematics sufficient enough to properly educate future army recruits
Text 2 STEM 2026: A vision for innovation in STEM education	International comparisons (i.e., TIMMS); technological advances	*De facto* segregation, market demands	Common core curriculum; maintenance of segregated schools	A call for a culturally relevant and interdisciplinary approach for the learning of mathematics and science that would provide a model of real world experiences

decade, *STEM 2026* explicitly suggested educating all of the nation's children in ways that are also interdisciplinary and culturally relevant. This shift signals the increasing consideration of issues of context as well as racial equity in curriculum development.

Text 1: The reports of the Commission on Post-War Plans (1944 and 1945)

Before the mid-1900s, mathematics teachers simply taught what they knew, using textbooks written by mathematicians. World War II, ranging from 1939 to 1945, exposed a problem when, in large numbers, army recruits coming from public schools knew so little math that the army began to offer classes to teach recruits the arithmetic needed for basic bookkeeping and gunnery (Raimi, 2000). "The need for simple computations and for control of certain basic mathematical concepts is well-nigh universal. The war has demonstrated in a dramatic way what is nonetheless true, but not so readily discernible in peace time, that a boy lacking these competencies is a pathetic victim of a ruthless system" (Commission on Post-War Plans, 1944, p. 227). Entire public schools systems were implicated in what was considered somewhat of a national scandal (Klien, 2003). It was understood that if Americans, mainly White men, could be stronger in their mathematics knowledge, they would be better prepared to fight wars and maintain national security. This was a particularly urgent matter during a war that utilized major technological advances such as atomic bombs.

In response to growing concerns about students' attainment of mathematical knowledge and skills, NCTM's Commission on Post-War Plans wrote a series of reports detailing their recommendations for the future of mathematics curriculum. This chapter includes analysis of the first two of the three reports, as they offered the most explicit recommendations for mathematics curriculum. The authors of the *First Report*—all men and, presumably, all White—consisted of six mathematics educators at the public school and university levels working in major cities across New York, Michigan, Massachusetts, and Tennessee. The 11-member commission who authored the *Second Report* included nine men and two women, presumably all White, and working across a more diverse set of locations including urban, suburban, and somewhat rural areas. In the *First Report*, the commission members propose the following:

1. The school should insure mathematical literacy to all who can possibly achieve it.
2. We should differentiate on the basis of needs, without stigmatizing any group, and we should provide new and better courses for a high fraction of the schools' population whose mathematical needs are not well met in the traditional sequential courses.
3. We need a completely new approach to the problem of the so called slow learning student.
4. The teaching of arithmetic can be and should be improved.
5. The sequential courses should be greatly improved.

(Commission on Post-War Plans, 1944)

Written one year later, the *Second Report* offered a set of 34 theses to guide the improvement of mathematics instruction from elementary through junior college as well as suggestions for the education of teachers of mathematics. The first of these theses was intended for all grades:

"the schools should guarantee functional competence in mathematics to all who can possibly achieve it" (Commission on Post-War Plans, 1945, p. 196). The series of reports was NCTM's first attempt at reforming mathematics curriculum by contesting the progressivist doctrine of the time that insisted school curriculum be determined by the needs and interests of children (Klien, 2003). The Commission's reports did not have an immediate, measurable impact on mathematics education, but NCTM would later develop a set of standards for mathematics teaching and learning that would inform curriculum in schools across the country.

Text 2: STEM 2026: A vision for innovation in STEM education (2016)

In his 2009 Inaugural Address, President Barack Obama pledged to "restore science to its rightful place" (Obama, 2009). Throughout his tenure, the Obama Administration formed multiple initiatives to actualize this call to action. During one such initiative, the U.S. Department of Education, in collaboration with American Institutes for Research, invited a diverse group of 30 experts and thought leaders in STEM teaching and learning to share their ideas and recommendations for an innovative future of STEM education. The resulting document, *STEM 2026: A Vision for Innovation in STEM Education*, outlines an "aspirational vision" for the future of STEM education in the P-12 setting (USDOE-OII, 2016, p. ii). The *STEM 2026* vision emphasized the need for schools to provide culturally relevant education that addresses the needs of all students, regardless of race, gender, class, ability, or otherwise and includes six interconnected components as follows:

1. Engaged and networked communities of practice
2. Accessible learning activities that invite intentional play and risk
3. Educational experiences that include interdisciplinary approaches to solving "grand challenges"
4. Flexible and inclusive learning spaces supported by innovated technologies
5. Innovative and accessible measures of learning
6. Societal and cultural images and environments that promote diversity and opportunity in STEM

(USDOE-OII, 2016).

First, the committee recommended key stakeholders in education, business, and local organizations form communities of practice to develop a stronger evidence base for effective STEM teaching and learning experiences. Among these teaching and learning experiences, the authors emphasized the benefits of providing P-12 students greater opportunities to engage in intentional, STEM-themed play with low barriers to entry, allowing a diverse group of students to be able to share their ideas. The third component suggested offering students authentic, local and global problems or "grand challenges," that require interdisciplinary solutions including, for example, improving water quality. Such work would necessitate learning spaces that offer flexibility in structure, equipment, materials, and technology in order to be able to adapt to the learning activity and to inspire creativity and collaboration. Measuring achievement would also require more formative assessments of academic outcomes including evaluations of student portfolios, demonstrations, and presentations. Finally, the committee boldly called on popular media, toy developers, and retailers to consider issues of racial, cultural, and gender diversity in their images of STEM professionals and their STEM-themed toys and games. In laying out these six components, the authors of *STEM 2026* intended to provide an action-oriented framework that was not prescriptive, but instead provided a starting point from which others could build.

DIALOGICAL TEXT ANALYSIS

In this section, we discuss how the two sets of documents inform our understanding of curriculum development and enactment in a democracy. Our analysis considers four main ideas presented in the documents: (1) curriculum is influenced by the authors' perceptions of global and national imperatives, (2) curriculum is shaped based on the authors' ideas about teaching, learning, and the purpose of education, (3) (in)equity plays a role in the design and enactment of curriculum, and (4) context matters in the design and enactment of curriculum. These overlapping themes are taken up in the dialogue below and will later inform the implications for teachers.

CURRICULUM IS INFLUENCED BY THE AUTHORS' PERCEPTIONS OF GLOBAL AND NATIONAL IMPERATIVES

Maloney: *Each of these sets of documents set a vision for what the authors believe should define mathematics curriculum for the next ten years. I am intrigued by what each group of authors felt should drive these decisions. In the 1940s, they felt the curriculum development and enactment should be guided by what was necessary for war times. It's important to remember that at the end of World War II the country entered the Cold War and the development of the atomic bomb, so people were scared. I image they believed that if they did not have national security, then the nation might perish. In order to protect democracy, they likely believed citizens needed to be mathematically literate.*

Powell: That aligns with NCTM's attempt to define competence—functional competence, for example. In the 1940s documents, NCTM advised moving away from arithmetic development, which also makes clear their position within the math wars. In the third of their 34 theses, they state, "we must conceive of arithmetic as having both a mathematical aim and a social aim." NCTM did not just want students learning how to count, add, subtract, or measure in order to do so, but in order to complete tasks; they wanted citizens to be capable of utilizing math in their career, no matter what they chose to do. They recognized there are career choices that may not need as much mathematics knowledge and that there may be "slow learners," as they wrote. Therefore, they suggest three approaches, which seem to be learning tracks, as we know them today. They write, "The goal of a strong mathematics department should be to have every pupil in the appropriate course" (NCTM, 1945, p. 207). In their postwar plans, they're not looking just at the potential workers in the military, but those who will not enter the military, as well.

CURRICULUM IS SHAPED BASED ON THE AUTHORS' IDEAS ABOUT TEACHING, LEARNING AND THE PURPOSE OF EDUCATION

Maloney: *As I read each of the three documents, I wondered about the authors' perceptions of the purpose of education. One's purpose of education informs decisions about curriculum as well as its enactment. There is a sense in both documents that the purpose of education is to protect democracy. In the 1940s, mathematical literacy was seen as necessary to protect democracy in that such skills were necessary for soldiers to effectively win wars against the country's enemies. The idea of protecting democracy shifts in the more modern document from ensuring soldiers are ready for combat to preparing all citizens to be ready to engage in problem solving in any sector. Instead of focusing on a discrete set of skills, there is more of an emphasis on drawing on multiple, interdisciplinary skills to solve actual problems. In this way, there is not as much of a focus on what could be considered a core curriculum, but instead the curriculum could be defined by the local problems that teachers and students consider in the classroom.*

Powell: In both sets of documents, I observe a struggle to define literacy. The STEM piece spoke specifically to the idea that literacy is not just acquiring skills. The authors write:

> *The complexities of today's world require all people to be equipped with a new set of core knowledge and skills to solve difficult problems, gather and evaluate evidence, and make sense of information they receive from varied print and, increasingly, digital media. The learning and doing of STEM helps develop these skills and prepare students for a workforce where success results not just from what one knows, but what one is able to do with that knowledge.*

> *—(USDOE-OII, 2016, p. i)*

The authors seem to believe that students would find themselves in environments where they would face problems and would need to engage in a specific thought process. In the 1940s, NCTM did not seem to be okay with students learning mathematics for the sake of knowing mathematics, necessarily. However, there was an emphasis on developing a core curriculum and that different students would receive different mathematics instruction based on their aptitude for mathematics.

Maloney: *I agree that there is more of focus on content in the 1940s, whereas now there is a focus on problem solving and engineering. In the 1940s, folks in lower strands were expected to be able do something with the math more explicitly while students with greater aptitude were to learn more abstract mathematics. There was also an underlying belief that when it comes to the study of mathematics, there is one correct way of knowing. Technology in* *the 1940s was much more linear in that there was one input for one output. The first computer was created in the mid-40s, and it was only able to make simple computations. Now technology is more spatial. STEM 2026 is trying to undo the ways in which teaching and learning is still very linear. It makes sense, then, that the STEM 2026 vision embraces a little more ambiguity in what students learn*

Powell: How much is this needs to be a conversation about teacher preparation and development? We are, unfortunately, in a vicious cycle. The same inadequate educational system we are talking about is the same system that prepared our teachers. I see many new teachers come to our schools that are certified to teach mathematics, but do not have a strong grasp of the core concepts. They just contribute to this terrible cycle of inadequacy.

The Commission acknowledged the teacher's capacity impacts what students learn. They suggested teachers will default to how they learned. In the First Report, they wrote,

In the last generation, professional courses for teachers dealing with the teaching of arithmetic have practically disappeared from our teachers colleges, with the result that most beginning teachers do not know how to teach arithmetic. In fact, some actually fear it and escape the task by excessive attention to other activities in which they feel more confident. To make matters worse, many are tempted to teach the little they do teach by the incidental method—presumably the ideal method, but also the most difficult which only a few per hundred could manage even if they had good training.

—(NCTM, 1944, p. 231).

I took that incidental method to mean teachers are often pulling from their immediate knowledge base, no matter how insufficient it may be. I see that all the time in our classrooms. The other part to this is that teachers default to presenting their students with algorithms without discussing underlying concepts. They teach the most expedient approach.

Maloney: *I think it's problematic that teachers see certain rote methods as expedient. Is it still expedient if students are unable to recall what they learned? We need to go back to what it means to learn. I am not sure the answer to this question is influencing curricular decisions. The generations of math wars have brought us numerous different types of curriculum—some that focus heavily on conceptual understanding. However, we often see teachers return to how they understand how to approach a particular problem. I think that in order for students to engage in deep learning, their teachers must do so first.*

Powell: Deeper learning in the 1940s seemingly showed up in exploring *the why* of the concept. You're actually using compasses in the math class. You're actually using the maps. Deeper learning in newer contexts is a lot more comprehensive. It's the idea of being collaborative and using resources beyond the teacher and classmates, using digital resources. Deeper learning is about preparing for the presentation. It's not enough that I just got an answer. I now have to present this in a way that is compelling. It comes from trustworthy, reliable resources. The STEM 2026 article is very open-ended and experiential in nature. The quality of your answer is only limited by how much you work your network. Your product will only be limited by if you are not exploring other careers. We are just going beyond the four walls of the classroom. One of the most powerful approaches to learning is learning to learn. If you know how to tap resources, you're not confined to how much your teacher knows or what programs or curriculum your school offers.

CONTEXT MATTERS IN THE DESIGN AND ENACTMENT OF CURRICULUM

Powell: If we are to embrace ambiguity, though, I wonder about the importance of context. Is *context* supposed to be what determines what is taught?

Maloney: *Certainly the contexts within which our students learn can either limit or bolster their capacity to learn. The STEM 2026 document suggests the context define the curriculum in two different ways. First, they encourage educators to develop "grand challenges" that are problems that are not yet solved at the local community, national, or global levels. In that case, the very questions students would ask would be quite context-specific. Next, the authors of the document encourage the promotion of diversity in societal and cultural images from children's books, toys and games to popular media. It is evident in this document that educators are learning about the importance of a child's surroundings in both their understanding of who they can be in the world as well as the problems and solutions they have the opportunity to explore.*

Here we are in an era where you cannot readily predict the career paths of students or what employment opportunities will be available, so how do you safely prepare students for the unknown? When you talk about universal education and preparing all students, how do you make something universal? In NCTM's First Report, the Commission's way of addressing the context was to look at what would get students ready for professional study, then they looked at what would prepare them for industry, commerce, and military, and then they looked at what were the general needs of students. I interpreted that the students who would work blue-collar jobs would at least need financial literacy. When setting out academic tracks for studying mathematics, are you unintentionally giving advantage to certain students because we do have those students that are taking calculus by year 12? Are we giving unfair advantage to those students?

(IN)EQUITY PLAYS A ROLE IN THE DESIGN AND ENACTMENT OF CURRICULUM

Maloney: *History shows us that certain students are quite intentionally given advantages over others. That suggests a particular purpose of education—education to prepare certain students for certain careers. Is there a more holistic curriculum that we could create that all citizens would need? Once we determine that curriculum, how are we making decisions about who should get certain curriculum beyond the "general curriculum"? When we slate students in "lower" mathematics tracks, I fear that those decisions are based on* *the poor math experiences the student had in earlier years. I see it as the responsibility of mathematics teachers to push students to their own limits.*

Powell: In the STEM 2026 document, the authors were concerned about the inequities in STEM education "along racial and ethnic, linguistic, cultural, socioeconomic, gender, disability, and geographic lines" and the authors recognized "the gaps are so pronounced in STEM" (USDOE-OII, 2016, p. 1). Over 70 years since NCTM's Post-War plans, there is a shift from thinking some students are just not going to be strong at math. The STEM conversation is a lot more unifying.

Maloney: *Yes, there is more discussion about equity in the modern document. However, I often wonder if the concern for equity is about the people or about America's need to be competitive globally. If there is a population of citizens whose talent is not cultivated, then there are greater consequences for the nation's global competitiveness.*

CONCLUSION

In this chapter, we focused on how the glocal context has informed recommendations for mathematics curriculum over the last 60 years. As discussed in the dialogic analysis above, the historical, local, and global context informs authors' ideas about equity, teaching, learning, and the purpose of education. We conclude here with our predictions for curriculum development over the next 50 years and suggest implications for teachers in all content areas to consider.

THE NEXT FIFTY YEARS

As we look to the future, we believe global forces including climate change as well as major technological advances such as artificial intelligence has the potential to influence future curriculum change in the STEM fields and beyond. Unfortunately, national forces including *de facto* segregation and the educational inequity it produces will likely continue to plague the United States, preventing our nation from truly being able to tap into our most valuable natural resource: our children. Though we have experienced some important changes in school curriculum over the last 50 years, as educators we are not certain of our nation's commitment to creating educational policies quickly enough for school curriculum to reflect the urgency of our global and national forces. While the *STEM 2026* document leaves us optimistic about the possible future of STEM curriculum, it will likely take the next fifty years to even start to realize the goals enclosed.

Over the past 40 years, the NCTM has developed guidelines intended to steer mathematics teachers toward teaching deeper, more conceptual mathematics but the implementation of such curriculum is not uniform across all U.S. schools. Teachers teach to the standardized tests that continue to assess students on rote, abstract problems similar to those that were assigned to students attending public schools in the 1940s. More innovative mathematics curriculum is often reserved for special STEM schools usually serving a primarily White and Asian American population of students. Black and Latinx students are still affected by *de facto* segregation and experience inequitable access to the type of curriculum NCTM or *STEM 2026* recommends.

The major feature of STEM curriculum is its interdisciplinary approach, which is not a new concept in curriculum development. Some independent schools utilize the child-centered Montessori Method that espouses the same self-directed activity, hands-on learning and collaborative play associated with interdisciplinary curriculum. The compartmentalized nature of secondary public schools limits the possibility for the interdisciplinary approach that STEM education requires. A shift from the content-driven subjects of mathematics and science to the process-driven approach that STEM education demands would require teachers with different expertise to collaborate in ways that requires preparation and ongoing school-based support. To truly bring interdisciplinary curriculum to the public school context would necessitate nationwide changes in K-12 school and classroom spaces, standardized assessment practices and possibly even approaches to teacher preparation.

A shift to the problem-based approach suggested in *STEM 2026* would also require someone choosing the challenges the students would explore. While we may believe climate change is an urgent global concern worthy of students exploring in school, teachers and families in other communities might not agree. There is a long history of political debates in the humanities around the inclusion of ethnic studies, and there is a growing list of banned books. The analogous "math wars" were about how much mathematics knowledge a child ought to develop, by what age and how practical or conceptual the problems. Moving to a problem-based, interdisciplinary approach to involving students in discussions about local, national, and global issues could serve to embolden the math wars.

PRACTICAL IMPLICATIONS FOR TEACHERS

Outside of the mathematics discipline, educators engage in debates about what ought to be taught, when, and to whom in U.S. public schools. For example, in the field of history, teachers and policymakers have considered whether or not to require or exclude ethnic studies courses such as Mexican American Studies or African American History. Science teachers need to make decisions about if or how to teach the study of evolution versus creationism. English teachers choose the authors whose stories will be told and analyzed in their classroom. In health and physical education, administrators in school districts across the country need to decide whether or not to offer sexual education as well as what will be discussed in such a course and at what age to offer the curriculum. Educators across disciplines have a great responsibility in making appropriate curricular decisions for their students based on their students' needs, goals and interests.

This conversation leads us to three main implications for teachers of all subject areas: (1) School curriculum is influenced by glocal events and is thus never politically or culturally neutral. It is important for teachers to be informed of the political and cultural influences acting on their curriculum; (2) Changes to curriculum take a long time to be enacted and often affect different groups of students differently based on a child's social location and access to schooling; and (3) Teachers' ideas about the purpose and promise of education will serve to guide their practice. The following extension questions are to help new and developing teachers to explore their underlying ideas about curriculum in an effort to engage in a reflective process about its design and implementation.

EXTENSION QUESTIONS

1. What is the *written* and *unwritten* curriculum in your classroom? In your school?
2. How does your glocal context influence teaching and learning?
3. Who should inform curriculum and its enactment? Why do you think so?
4. In what ways does curriculum differ from school to school and even classroom to classroom within one school? Who benefits from these differences? Who is limited by these differences?
5. How does an expressed purpose of education determine the curriculum and its enactment?
6. How do you think the future of your glocal context will inform curriculum development in your subject area?

GLOSSARY OF TERMS

Curriculum—broadly defined as the totality of student experiences that occur in the educational process and is described by a planned set of learning goals.

Interdisciplinary—relating to more than one branch of knowledge or field of study.

STEM—a now common abbreviation for the four interrelated areas of study, science, technology, engineering and mathematics.

Jim Crow Laws—a formal system of state and local laws that enforced racial segregation in restaurants, buses, railroad cars, schools, and other public facilities across the Southern United States from the end of Reconstruction in 1877 to the beginning of the civil rights movement in the 1950s.

Educational equity—comprises a variety of educational models, programs, and strategies intended to provide fair opportunities and access to learning for all students regardless of race, gender, ability, sexual orientation, socioeconomics, language, or country of origin.

Education reform—intended changes in the ways a school or school system functions, from teaching pedagogy and curriculum to administrative processes. Reform *movements* have taken on different forms based on the motivations of the reformers. Reforms focused on increasing equity can include increasing funding levels, redesigning school programs, pedagogical changes, or providing comparatively more educational services and academic support to students with greater needs.

REFERENCES

Commission on Post-War Plans of the NCTM. (1944). First Report of the Commission on Post-War Plans. *The Mathematics Teacher, 37*, 225–232.

Commission on Post-War Plans of the NCTM. (1945). Second Report of the Commission of Post-War Plans. *The Mathematics Teacher, 38*, 195–221.

Government Accountability Office. (2016). *K-12 education: Better use of information could help agencies identify disparities and address racial discrimination (GAO Publication No. 16-345).* Washington, DC: U.S. Government Printing Office.

Klein, D. (2003). A brief history of American K–12 mathematics education in the 20th century. In J. M. Royer (Ed.). *Mathematical cognition* (pp. 175–225). Greenwich, CT: Information Age Publishing.

Obama, B. (2009). "President Barack Obama's inaugural address." *The White House*, The United States Government, 21, Jan. 2009. https://obamawhitehouse.archives.gov/blog/2009/01/21/president-barack-obamas-inaugural-address.

Raimi, R. A. (2000). Judging state standards for K-12 mathematics education. In S. Stotsky (Ed.), *What's at stake in the K-12 standards wars* (pp. 33–58). New York, NY: Peter Lang.

U.S. Department of Education. Institute of Education Sciences [USDOE-IES], National Center for Education Statistics [USDOE-IES]. Selected Findings from TIMSS 2015. Washington, DC. Retrieved August 4, 2016 from https://nces.ed.gov/timss/timss2015/findings.asp.

U.S. Department of Education, Office of Innovation and Improvement [USDOE-OII]. (2016). STEM 2026: A Vision for Innovation in STEM Education. Washington, DC. Retrieved from https://innovation.ed.gov/files/2016/09/AIR-STEM2026_Report_2016.pdf.

Zimba, J. (2014). The development and design of the common core state standards for mathematics, *New England Journal of Public Policy, 26*(1), 1–11. Retrieved from http://scholarworks.umb.edu/nejpp/vol26/iss1/10.

9

PROGRESSIVE EDUCATION

JAIME GRINBERG
JACQUELINE WELLS

INTRODUCTION

The Progressive Era (1890–1920) defined various aspects of American society. Historically speaking, urban communities were industrially flourishing, yet becoming increasingly crowded with the vast amounts of immigrants entering the United States. This posed a conflict for American society. How does America educate the various cultural groups entering the country? This thought as many other thoughts pertaining to the **Americanization** of these populations of these new citizens came to mind. Spiraling out of these thoughts arrived concepts of educational approaches. A diverse and unfamiliar student population required a fresh approach to the educational system. Thoughts emerged about how the youth of these immigrants would fit into the vast and rapidly changing America. Out of these thoughts birthed the modern context for **Progressive Education**. Ultimately, how to teach all children in ways that will connect them with the larger opportunities that American life can provide. Concurrently, how to teach them in ways that will stimulate their healthy growth, nurturing and awakening their curiosity? These are enduring questions that progressive teachers, educators, and policy makers have pondered about and act upon at different times, including the present.

In this chapter, we will discuss two different documents that represent a dominant tradition within the progressive community, which have implications for teaching and learning then and now. The documents are: (1) *Growing Minds: On Becoming a Teacher* by Herbert Kohl

121

(1984)[1], and (2) "On Learning Communities" by Jaime Grinberg (in Lewis et al. "Playing With Ideas," 2009)[2]. The two documents represent an enduring pattern of progressive teaching, that of student-centered practices and the types of environments and relationships that teachers construct to enable meaningful and engaged learning.

Progressive education is defined as a pedagogical practice in which students are valued and educated through **student-centered learning** and community-based teaching concepts. This concept grew out of four major traditions of progressive education: social efficiency, child-centered practices, learning communities, and social reconstructionism. While the first dealt mostly with administrative and organizational matters, including policies and curriculum, it also advanced the concept of serving the needs of each student with the understanding that different students have different characteristics and needs. Hence, the need to create programs and practices that will address those needs and for this to happen these progressives grounded their decisions on what was conceived to be scientific knowledge, including batteries of tests to learn about each student's capacities and propensities. Child-centered practices were fostered by numerous progressives who connected with the tradition of modernity. To these progressives, childhood was defined as a particular distinctive stage of life in need of very neutral environments. It was believed that educators would build a stimulating classroom with many materials that stimulate imagination and creativity, but with as little guidance as possible in order to not hinder that natural inclinations and motivations of children.

In a way these were educators that followed the **romantic ideas** of **Rousseau** (1762/2017) and **Tolstoy** (1967) among others. While educators such as John **Dewey** advocated for student-centeredness, he as well as his disciples were deeply concerned with the need to interact in communities without leaving the student solely to experience what could not be defined necessarily as educative. Furthermore, these progressives embraced the idea that student needs ought to be met by placing the child at the center of learning, while emphasizing the power of community as a means for socially constructed collective learning experiences. In this type of climate, the teacher has to go well beyond facilitating the environment by intervening, challenging, guiding, and monitoring educational experiences.

Social reconstructionism was a response to troubled times of economic depression in the 1930s and as a response to the almost narcissistic and indulgent practices of some progressive teachers who did not connect classroom life with the larger context in which children and older students were living.

George **Counts** (1932/1978) criticized the lack of social and political activism on part of many progressive educators. Concurrently, he was critical of an individualistic pedagogy that was disregarding the need of the individual to learn to be part of a group or a community. This was similar to Dewey's position, who wanted students to learn to live in a democracy by learning to live in a classroom where they interact and learn about themselves and others,

---

[1] This link enables you to see in which libraries the book is available https://montclair.on.worldcat.org/oclc/19507600
[2] Please see Appendix for a version of this document.

about rights and responsibilities and duties. To be a progressive teacher, social reconstructionists argued, educators must also engage outside the classroom in order to alter what they believed to be an unjust social order.

You will notice throughout the chapter that the documents we will discuss are not neatly fitted within the traditions discussed above. While there are some elements that overlap with the four traditions, we would identify the practices proposed in the documents at the center of the learning communities tradition. While honoring and focusing on the individual, both documents propose concepts and practices in which students are not in isolation, but rather as part of an environment of collective and purposeful learning activities. This certainly does not imply that individualities and personal propensities are not recognized and engaged.

This topic is significant to the construction of ideologies; how teachers taught, how teachers teach, and how teachers ought to teach, provide or not opportunities for students. Decisions of what to teach to whom, why, how, and when, are made by teachers on a daily basis. Very often, teachers rely on their own experiences and/or a limited repertoire of practices to make many of such decisions unaware that there are alternative ways, which might create great learning opportunities for students. Student-centered practices and progressive teaching mean different things to different people. At times, these terms have been overused to the extent of becoming a slogan more than a thoughtful discourse or practice. We will unpack their meaning by briefly exploring their roots and by analyzing the two documents.

HISTORICAL BACKGROUND

THE DEVELOPMENT OF PROGRESSIVISM

The progressive movement was about fostering economic, political, and social reform in the United States, which began during the 1880s and lasted until about World War I (Church & Sedlak, 1976). Industry grew significantly during the past century causing several social tensions, such as business monopolies, city slums, marginalization, and inhumane conditions in factories and mines. During the 19th century, the effects of industrialism were threatening the fabric of a democratic nation. Despite the accelerated economic growth, the differences between those who had and those who had not were growing in ways that exacerbated social class differences, hence undermining the fabric of democratic America by not enabling equal opportunity to those who didn't have access to an education. By the end of the 19th century, the technology derived from the uses of electric and steam energy translated into massive production of goods. This development created a new industrial class among the owners of the means of production, and an industrial underclass of workers employed in the production circle. Artisans were displaced and many had to migrate to urban centers in search of labor (Cremin, 1988).

Urbanization was also increased not just with internal migration but also with massive immigration. Immigration came from East and South Europe, which was very different from prior immigration waves from Central and Western Europe. The differences were not only languages, but also customs, traditions, and perspectives (Cremin, 1988). Schooling could provide an opportunity to socialize immigrants into the life, habits, conventions, and practices of a democratic community. Measures that aimed to ameliorate these conditions were furthered by the progressives who demanded a greater role for the government to regulate and take responsibility in controlling social and economic relations. Progressives came to the realization that conditions in cities were becoming increasingly harsh. They shared this sense of social and political commitment, which could be threatened if some form of social intervention did not occur. Schooling provided an opportunity to provide for human improvement (Cohen, 1988). Therefore, schooling became a tool for progressives who aimed to reform societal standards and city conditions. Paraphrasing Hofstadter, Cremin asserts that the progressive mind "was ultimately an educator's mind, and that its characteristic contribution was that of a socially responsible reformist pedagogue." Not only did progressives see school as an improvement of city conditions, but they saw it as a vehicle for social and political improvement.

It may seem as if progressives had one stream of thought, but progressivism did not represent one homogenous agenda. According to Westbrook (1991) to define progressivism is difficult since there are conflicting views on what progressivism means. One view argues that this was a movement that aimed to maintain the power and status of the old middle classes, which wanted to use the state as a mean to neutralize the ascending power of big industry and business, while aiming to control the working-class immigrants. Another view agrees with the idea that progressivism as a movement represented middle-class interests, but it was really a new technocratic and professional class seeking to position themselves in power through the use of the state in the name of efficiency and expertise. Yet another perspective sees progressive reforms as a "conservative movement led by big business, rationalized by 'corporate liberal' intellectuals, and designed to create a 'political capitalism' friendly to the giant corporation" (Westbrook, 1991, p. 182).

Although it is not the purpose here to analyze social progressivism, it is also important to clarify the generic meaning of the word "progressivism" as it is used in the educational context. As some scholars already argued, there are many educational progressives (Cremin, 1961; Church & Sedlak, 1976; Kliebard, 2004). It should be noted that educational progressivism was not directly connected with American progressivism as a social movement, although both perceived democracy as a way of improving social conditions and equity (Church & Sedlak, 1976). During this time, there was an enormous amount of optimism attached to the industrial prosperity, along with the individual and scientific advancements made. In educational terms, this meant to search for meaningful ways in which the individual powers and capacities could be advanced, schools being the primordial institution for the fostering of such agenda.

EDUCATIONAL PROGRESSIVISM

Cremin (1964) argued that progressivism in education meant an effort to use schools as a way of improving the lives of individuals. Progressivism in education built upon scientific research in psychology and social sciences to address the needs of all the learners, which implied a need to better understand differences and to develop appropriate methods. Progressive educators perceived that scientific, rational, and practical methods could help to provide opportunities to all children and youth. Within this large framework of ideas and proposals, there were different perspectives and approaches coming together or separating from each other according to the specific issues to address and to the political contingencies (Kliebard, 2004).

Some dominant perspectives within educational progressivism were influenced by John Dewey (1902, 1904, 1938), who argued that educative experiences lead into learning when these were properly designed, organized, framed, and scrutinized to advance growth, "The difference between civilization and savagery, to take an example on a large scale, is found in the degree in which previous experiences have changed the objective conditions under which subsequent experiences take place" (p. 39). According to Cremin (1964), the progressive education movement developed into three distinctive and sometimes oppositional directions during the 1920s. One direction was the search for scientific answers with a focus on measurement, evaluation, and efficiency. The second direction was rather experiential with some psychoanalytic influences. The third direction represented that of the radical critique of the reconstructing society.

A different angle in progressive practices was behaviorist (Cremin, 1961). The belief of these progressives was that schools can condition and change human behavior to improve human relations. Teaching in this view had to be informed by the results of research in human nature and human behavior. For instance, the curriculum had to provide experiences that will prepare students to function in society and to be productive. A consequence of this perspective within progressivism was that of student selection by ability or talents, which meant to classify students to fit in determined social roles. Science could help determine the needs and capabilities of individuals, and the school could tailor a curriculum for different needs and expectations, becoming efficient as a sorting machine.

These were times of optimistic scientific advancement and certainty that science would help advance social organization and justice. Scientific knowledge informed policy and was to be supported and accessed by all. The Progressive Education Association supported strong scientific research on learning, policy, child development, testing and evaluation, among many fields of educational studies. However, critiques of the Progressive Education Association, which was founded on April 4, 1919, after the progressive movement started to decline from American politics, suggested that this organization focused more on methods and practices of teaching, but it did not advance social or economic ideas (Cremin, 1964). George S. Counts, in his address to the Progressive Education Association in 1932, presented a sharp critique of the movement that was entitled "Dare progressive education be progressive?" in which he spoke to the fallacies of the assumptions of neutrality of schooling, to the fallacies of child-centered practices disconnected from a social context, and to the fallacies of the technocratic and efficiency views. He argued that progressive educators should educate to advance a social agenda of justice. In its beginnings, the Association was on the fringes and its influence started to assert during the 1930s when the organization grew in number to about 6,000 members, and its leadership was enhanced with several prominent educators (Cremin, 1964). One of reasons for its growth was the publication of "Progressive

Education," which was a journal founded in 1924, and by the end of this decade was a quarterly publication. Annual meetings, national committees for the study of educational problems, and the journal as an arena for debate and for dissemination of ideas, helped to promote the movement as a central space for the progressive conversation in education.

PROGRESSIVE TEACHING: STUDENT-CENTERED PRACTICES

According to Antler (1987), "During the Depression, the search for a redefinition of the relationship between individuals and society brought fresh support to progressive educators who believed that the classroom could become the model for a new collectivism, integrating self-expression with larger social goals" (p. 307). We argue that such view of society in classroom terms meant the refocusing of the educational activity on the student, hence the embracement of student-centered practices.

Many teaching practices of progressive schools and progressive teachers during the effervescence of progressive teaching in the 1930s translated student-centered pedagogy. Studies on child development influenced the perspective that schools should tailor the curriculum to the stages of development of the child. In the United States, G. Stanley Hall was an influential researcher in the study of children's stages of growth and in the shaping of school curriculum that attempted to meet the needs of the development of the child (Kliebard, 2004). This child-centered curriculum called for a more individualized instruction and to attend to the needs and interests of the child. These are to be properly nurtured by designing activities and materials that fit the child's developmental stage. In contrast to pure behaviorist and efficiency models, John Dewey (1899/1991, 1938) presented a perspective that advocated for active learning that stems from student's interests and needs. This concept happens in a learning community, in a social setting, thus enhancing student-centered practices by incorporating the individual within a classroom context with social interactions. Teaching should occur through educative experiences, should advance expression and cultivation of individuality, free activity, understanding and engagement in a changing world, and should be relevant for the present life of students. Gordon (1988) argues that many of these views were not entirely new, since European ideas about pedagogy like those influenced by Rousseau, Pestalozzi (1801/2012), Froebel (1895/2017), Tolstoy, and others, had an impact on many American educators. Educators like Francis Parker or the same John Dewey practiced some of these ideas in schools (Semel & Sadovnik, 1999). Therefore, classrooms should be communities where students live and learn to live in communities, democratic communities.

In this student-centered tradition, the teacher creates the environment and has to be a curriculum developer connecting subject matter with students. The teacher guides and facilitates experiences instead of being the only source of all knowledge. This teaching is inquiry oriented with eliciting questions, with individual and group projects, and with field trips. Dewey (1903/64) asserted that "The transition from an ordinary to a scientific attitude of mind coincides with ceasing to take certain things for granted and assuming a critical or inquiring and testing attitude" (p. 24). In this perspective, the world, the community, and the life outside the school are not separate from the classroom. On the contrary, the world is a classroom. This type of teaching expected the active participation of the learner. Authority was not exercised in authoritarian ways by teachers, it was promoted through internalization, understanding possible implications of different behaviors, and by enhancing senses of respect, trust, and self-discipline.

By the 1930s several schools, mostly private, adventured into fostering this type of experiential–developmentalist community and student-centered approach to teaching. However, with few exceptions, teaching in this century remained teacher-centered, with traditional exercise of authority in terms of conception of knowledge as a body of facts and procedures, and in terms of teachers and books as the only sources for such knowledge to be transmitted (Cohen, 1988; Cuban, 1993; Tyack et al., 1984). Progressivism as an educational movement attempted to shift away from teacher-centered practices. Ideas such as reflection, thoughtfulness, inquiry, constructive critique, and life-long learning, were advanced by Dewey (1904) as imperative dispositions to be fostered by prospective teachers to be able to move beyond the necessary technical skills in teaching. The implication is that teaching should happen in an intellectually open and challenging environment, which furthers systematic, scientific, inquiry, where ". . .'scientific' means regular methods of controlling the formation of judgments regarding some subject matter" (Dewey, 1903, p. 24).

While the PEA ceased to function by 1955 as progressive practices and ideas were in total decline (Cremin, 1964), some teaching practices endured (Cohen, 1988). Since then, many educators have maintained their interest and preference for a more inquiry-oriented and student-centered teaching approach, which engages in a dialogical practices of teaching and learning. These practices can occur in different teaching contexts; however, an enduring element in this tradition is that students have the power to initiate, suggest, facilitate, and lead. It is an empowering experience that provides students an opportunity to be validated and legitimized while gaining ownership of the content and of the class community (Grinberg et al. 2017). The two documents we present and discuss in this chapter illustrate multiple facets and aspects of the enduring progressive tradition of student-centered teaching concepts and practices. These two provide insights to what contemporary student-centered practices could be when an inquiry-oriented learning community environment is created to nurture all of the student capacities, propensities, and interests, many of which ought to be stimulated through careful, rigorous, purposeful, and relevant teacher planning. Novice teachers can experiment with some of these practices in order to enhance the teaching repertoire and to gain a sense of comfort and safety, while giving some space for uncertainty (Floden and Clark, 1988).

DOCUMENTS

DOCUMENT 1: *GROWING MINDS ON BECOMING A TEACHER BY HERBERT KOHL*

The first document this chapter we will be delving into is titled *Growing Minds on Becoming a Teacher* by Herbert Kohl. Published in 1984, this book exemplifies the core concepts of Progressive Education. Kohl illustrates personal narratives and discusses his teaching background. Born to a family of construction workers, Kohl believes that humans are similar to construction projects, meaning, people grow outward from their foundations. He notes that like a construction worker, a teacher must understand a child before developing a plan for building.

Throughout the course of Kohl's work, it is evident that several key principles exist within his work. Many of these principles deeply coincide with the concepts that have been interwoven into the fabric of modern progressive education. Several of Kohl's key concepts will be highlighted in this section. The first of these principles is this concept of support from teachers and peers. Kohl believes that in order for students to open up and inquire in a classroom, teachers must aim to create an environment that fosters this release of judgment so that students can learn, share, and grow.

The second principle that will be discussed is this concept of creating an environment of positivity and focused energy on learning. As mentioned previously, Kohl believes that it is crucial for students to feel comfortable. Along with this, Kohl notes that the teacher must also create an environment that is inspiring and intriguing. This is executed when teachers take note of student interests and strengths. Once a teacher capitalizes on these two aspects of student life, he believes that learning becomes even more natural to students.

The third idea that will be analyzed is this concept of free thought and Sprache, also known as thoughtful speech. Sprache fosters free thought by allowing students to practice thoughtful speech. Kohl notes that there is a lack of discussion and reflection within classrooms. He believes this is mostly due to the lack of time that teachers are given for these forms of course work. Kohl exemplifies his use of this concept of free thought when he discusses the use of Pink Floyd's "Another Brick in the Wall" in one of his junior high classrooms. Several of his students in this class voted for this song to be their graduation song. Building off of this, Kohl decided that it was important for students to truly understand the song if they wanted it to be their graduation song. He constructed a lesson surrounding this song, which eventually led the class to discussing biases present in school textbooks. From here, the class was able to use the context of the song and analyze a much deeper rooted, educational concept. Kohl's use of this lesson not only inspired free thought and discovery, but also taught students a deep lesson while connecting to their interests.

DOCUMENT 2: SOME NOTES ABOUT LEARNING COMMUNITIES AND CONNECTED TEACHING ELEMENTS BY JAIME GRINBERG

The second document that we will be discussing throughout the course of this chapter is titled "Postscript: Playing with Ideas: Some Notes About Learning Communities and Connected Teaching Elements" (2009) by Jaime Grinberg. This document contemplates the various roles that learning communities play within a classroom. Simultaneously, Grinberg highlights the importance of learning communities in relation to seeing the "whole student" and developing child-centered approaches within these groups. Along with this, these communities challenge the dichotomies that have developed in the classroom regarding both teachers and student.

Grinberg notes that there are three dimensions to the impacts of learning communities. The three dimensions being: learning together as group, learning the community itself, and learning to live in a community. The classroom becomes a microcosm for the world around it. One might question why learning communities are essential to the development of child-centered approaches, however, Grinberg notes that these communities provide students with systematic inquiry, relationship building, and conflict resolution experiences. Learning as a group allows for students to understand others, while reflecting upon their own behaviors, viewpoints, and knowledge.

Throughout this reflection, it is crucial that the teacher is discussing his/her classroom experiences with other teachers. Similar to students discussing their experiences with one another, teachers are expected to do the same, fostering this sense of collaboration and self-reflection. Coinciding with this, it develops relationships between teachers much like the relationships built between students in the classroom. Concurrently, Grinberg notes that teachers are expected to see the whole student and understand the perspectives, wants, needs, and individuals within the learning community. This creates interest and connection within the community of learners. The teacher is not only expected to reflect on himself/herself and foster these concepts of connection and reflection, but they are expected to challenge the ideas surrounding teaching as a whole. They must challenge dichotomies that live within the classroom. Meaning, teachers must understand that they are not only instructors, but they are artists, intellects, and citizens, who are expected to express these aspects of themselves to learning communities.

Another set of coinciding themes present in Document 2 is this connection between inquiry and experience. Learning communities provide an epicenter for inquiry, which ultimately fuels classroom experiences. It is expected that teachers utilize these opportunities to capitalize on student experiences, turning them into teachable moments allowing students to reflect as a group and individuals. This connection between inquiry and experience fit neatly together when discussing student-centered approaches. Students are expected to inquire within their learning communities and fully experience the lesson being learned. Meanwhile, teachers are expected to guide these lessons through forms of human expression and communication, further capitalizing on the various roles that they play in regard to their students.

Document 2 creates a solidified sense of the progressive impacts made in classroom during the 2000s. Not only are child-centered practices evident within this text, but also concepts of community and learning together. More specifically, it becomes evident that the goal of this approach is to not only develop intelligent students, but well-rounded citizens who know how to live in a community of diverse, rivaling opinions.

TIME TABLE AND EXPLANATION OF CONTEXT

The following table aims to aid in understanding the driving forces and historical context surrounding Document 1 and Document 2 described above.

	Global Forces	National Forces	Educational Policies	Understanding of Phenomena
1980s	• Economic interdependence • Berlin Wall Falls (Cold War) • China opens • Rebirth of democracies in S. America • Cable TV (MTV/pop culture) • Open markets • Growth of transportation network (movement of people)	• Reagan Presidency (opens markets) • Market-oriented growth of corporations • Market competition with Japan and other markets • Star wars • War on drugs • GM, Ford, Chrysler	• School choice (vouchers and Charter Schools) • A Nation at Risk (1983) • Tomorrow's Schools • Tomorrow's Teachers • "Quality," "Accountability," "Excellence" • Closing of the American Mind • Cultural Literacy (conservatism) • Standards movement • Horace's Compromise (1984) • Shopping Mall High School (1985) • Central Park East (Harlem) • Market-oriented school reform	• Teacher's voice trying to provide solution to challenges using student-centered approaches
2000s	• War on terror • 9/11 and terrorism • Globalization • Access to technology (technological divide) • Ethnoscapes	• NAFTA commerce treaty • Service-oriented economy in United States • Immigration • War in Iraq and Afghanistan	• No Child Left Behind (2001) • Market-based reforms • High stakes testing • National standards and the common core	• Call back to the principles of a student-centered learning community and the role of inquiry

HISTORICAL CONTEXT OF DOCUMENTS

The civil rights reforms of the 1960s and 1970s further defined the role of the teacher as a cultural worker. The teacher was by expected to foster and implement integrated learning communities, thus enculturating all students regardless of their status, race, gender, or home culture (Trohler et al., 2015). In the post-civil rights movement times, integration and acceptance of diversity collided with ethnocentric traditions of ethnic identity pushing for schools that would be more homogeneous in racial, socioeconomic status or ethnic characteristics. For instance, the so called practice of "White Flight" that meant either the physical moving out of the older neighborhoods into further away locations, often suburbia, or the abandonment of the public school system in favor of private schools represented in practicality the resistance to desegregation and integration. Similarly, the movement for Afrocentric schools to serve only black students with a curriculum tailored for them by their own civil and educational leaders, served in practical terms, justified or not, to distance from the idea of integration.

Paradoxically, the retreat to ethnic politics, coincides with the explosion of communications at a global level. Technology impacted not only businesses, but also everyday life. Cable TV, cellular phones, and rapid and enhanced means of transportation throughout the world expanded. The opening of global markets, access to goods, access to information, scientific exchange and global research collaborations, and movement of people across borders characterized a time of global integration at multiple levels. This occurred despite huge economic and political differences among and between nations. For instance, markets were open to trade and treaties as NAFTA, which enabled all type of products to be free of taxes to be moved between Canada, Mexico and the United States, blurred the concept of economic borders into regional economic integrations.

In schools, starting in the early 1980s and more so in the 1990s computers became a fixture in most classrooms and libraries became media centers. Media literacy started to become an important component of a good education, particularly for the application of critical thinking skills since these would be needed in order to judge the merits of what is being presented through all these new media outlets, from cable TV to websites, to what later evolved into social media. For instance, with almost universal access to media in American schools, learning to differentiate what is fact and what is opinion, or what are the multiple ways in which ideas, stories, or information are represented, for what purposes, by whom, became a challenge for this "modern" teacher. This was particularly challenging because this was a time of competing narratives about identity, experience, scientific truths, and historical facts.

Such expansion into a globalized context meant also that regional, ethnic, and at times ideological or tribal differences became exacerbated. Globalization became a threat to the established power structures and groups with economic, social, ideological, religious, and political control in many parts of the world. Multicultural education emerged and called to celebrate and respect diversity as a way to build social harmony. This was another way for educators to construct civility, while aiming to embrace democratic ideals as not only a political system, but a way of life. Hence, learning communities and student-centered approaches to teaching and learning were advocated by those who envisioned educational experiences as a tool to build a better society, which connects with the tradition of progressivism discussed in this chapter.

However, these times were also influenced by the practices of high-stakes testing in schools dramatically increased, meaning that performance of students in standardized tests dictated the opportunities that they would have for further access in education. Furthermore, such high-stakes tests also conditioned the evaluation of teachers' performance and that of school effectiveness. "A Nation at Risk" (National Commission on Excellence, 1983) and other similar reports criticized public education stating that the lack of higher standards, the poor preparation of teachers, and a diluted curriculum were risking the prevalence of America as a power with potential negative impacts on the economy. However, not only that many exciting and successful models of schooling and teaching were in place contradicting the statements of this report, such as the case of Central Park East (NYC), but also data collected about students' achievement levels collected from studies conducted by NAEP (National Assessment of Educational Progress) were showing improvement at the national level, not decline as stated in "A Nation at Risk." Hebert Kohl's teaching as described in his short stories, is a powerful example of an alternative approach to creating engaging and stimulating learning opportunities with a focus on the student and the group. But, the times were not receptive of this type of teaching and teachers had to struggle to maintain their integrity and to offer a student-centered practice.

In times of market-oriented school reform proposals, the performance of schools impacted the chance to stay in operation. Advocacy for school choice, perceiving education as a product to be consumed and opening of alternatives within public schools, such as charter schools, became an attempt to address inequalities. Policies such as No Child Left Behind (2001) took on a national dimension of school accountability that created a tension between what historically have been the enculturating aspects of school life and that of school function to produce measurable results.

In addition, a backlash to multicultural education and other progressive practices were destructive. In academia, books such as the Closing of the American Mind (Bloom, 1987) advocated for a traditional curriculum based on the traditions of Western thinking and the rejection of curriculum that was described as superficial and relativistic. Books like this emphasized the need for strong values as represented in the Classics. In school curriculum, this was also manifested by proposals and successful implementation of programs based on core traditional subjects. Every student learns the same thing at the same time and they rely heavily on the teacher's expert knowledge, such as those based on the work of E.D. Hirsch, whose book on Cultural Literacy (1988) became a best-seller.

While these lines of thought and practice continued to be present in the first decade of the 21st century, a more balanced yet rigorous approach to curriculum was in place for those districts and states that adopted standards developed by professional and academic associations with expertise in different disciplinary areas. For example, standards developed by the National Council of Teachers of Mathematics called for teaching approaches that were focusing on mathematical thinking. Within these standards, there would not be rote memorization or steps to follow in problem solving, but on developing understanding of how mathematics functions.

The parallel to push for alternatives, such as with magnet and charter schools, invited teachers to revisit successful practices from the past. This required them to rethink possibilities in the creation of environments that will foster engaging learning communities with a student-centered approach. In times of heavy high-stakes testing and times of so many prescriptive curricula in which teachers and students were following highly crafted scripts, such as Success for All, teachers understood they had to align with what was being tested.

Alternatively, they also understood that real opportunities for students to be successful were being formed. Hence, the call to reclaim the progressive legacies of dialogue, curiosity, imagination, inquiry, and student-centeredness, as discussed in the learning communities document as an alternative to the teaching recipes imposed on schools and teachers if success for all was not a slogan or a title, but an authentic goal.

DIALOGUE

After an analysis of the documents, it is clear that there are progressive themes laced within the context of each of these works. To further this discussion, we have constructed four dialogue questions surrounding both of the documents. For the sake of this chapter, Dr. Jaime Grinberg (JG), a seasoned educator and scholar will converse with novice teacher, Jacqueline Wells (JW). The dialogue is as follows:

1. How do you think learning communities tie into Kohl's concept of construction and tapping into child before developing a plan to build?

JG: *For Kohl to engage in the type of practices he proposes, he has to construct an environment of trust, respect, and caring, which nurtures curiosity and stimulates imagination. For this to happen, there are at least two important components: (a) an inquiry-grounded classroom culture, where questions, challenges, and risk taking, play with concepts, experimentation, and rigor is necessary, and (b) the idea that Lilian Weber advanced, the great scholar of practice, that we must "see" the student. What Kohl's adds is that seeing, understanding, accepting, listening, and embracing the student is not a laissez faire practice—while he argues that we must "love" our students, he clarifies that this means to love them as learners, which incorporates the responsibility of not abdicating responsibilities as teachers, as adults. Furthermore, the need to see and love the student, does not mean let them get away with anything. Learning to live in a community is part of the process and certainly will require from the teacher to construct the right environment. However, to do so a teacher must know as much as possible who their students are, what their motivations and interests are, and who they are as a whole person in order to tailor practice in a relevant, responsive, and challenging way (Grinberg, 2002; Weber, 1997). After all, as teachers we make the road with our students and for our students by walking it together, as Miles Horton and Paulo Freire have suggested.*

JW: I love that Kohl brings up this concept of constructing a nurturing learning environment for students. As a novice teacher, this is an ideology that I plan to follow. I think that it is crucial to create an open environment where students feel comfortable forming opinions and learning to become valued citizens of a community. I like how you brought up this point about how Kohl points out that we must "love" our students. I appreciate how you mention that this does not mean that we allow them to get away with things, rather, we emphasize transforming them into better people and members of a community. Sometimes, we must discipline our students, but this is because we want to see them do better, not because we want to see them punished. This is a crucial life lesson that schools teach. Consequences are a life concept that students need to understand before entering the "real world." If students have no understanding of "good" consequences and "bad" ones, how can we expect them to make sound decisions on a larger scale.

Along with this, this analogy conveying that students are similar to constructing a building plays into this concept that there is a beginning and an end to this process within means of the project timeline. Once a project is started, it is up to the builder to finish it regardless of the time that is taken to finish. Similar to construction, it is the job of teachers to help build on student knowledge and help to form a responsible, productive person. This process is ongoing until the building period is over. It is crucial for teachers to understand this concept of construction as a process. It is not something that happens overnight and most of the time, it is something that happens as a collective experience. Meaning, that the years spent in school and the lessons learned become a cohesive structure.

2. Document 1 discusses this concept of creating an environment of lack of judgment, but does not specifically name using learning communities to foster this, do you believe that the evolution of progressive education is responsible for this concept of learning communities present in Document 2?

JG: *I wouldn't say that the evolution of progressive practices inevitably leads into learning communities and I wouldn't say that Kohl ignores the concept purposely. I think that what Document 2 suggests is that to teach the way Kohl did it, you need to have a learning community. These are not recipes as in baking a cake, but there are elements that must be present as discussed in the document on learning communities in order to teach progressively. The lack of judgment proposed by Kohl is necessary for embracing the potential of the student. It also enables higher expectations about what a student can do and about what a group or a whole class might be able to do. In a sense, by not judging, which does not mean not challenging or not giving feedback, the teacher is better positioned to enable students to go to places they never been before. Judgment could constrain what teachers think students' capacities are and how can they be successful. In turn, this builds both trust and respect because students realize* teachers care for their learning. It requires often to teach against the current, which for me also means that while schools are adult-centric, have been designed to fit students into the structures and organizations adults decided are functional, what transcends in Kohl's stories and in the idea of building learning communities is that schools are to be constructed in ways that fit the students.*

JW: I agree that Kohl does not ignore this concept purposely. After reading Document 1, it becomes evident that Kohl's teaching ideologies align with many of the community development concepts in Document 2. I think that Kohl would resonate with using this concept of community-based learning to hinder judgment by the teacher and fellow peers. Specifically, when thinking about a high school level social studies class, which is what I intend to teach, judgment and citizenship play large roles in lessons learned. What do we learn in social studies? We learn about our roots as citizens of America and the world, we learn from the mistakes of others, and we learn to develop opinions. All of these factors require lack of judgment. Students feel safest opening up when they believe that their teacher is biased to their opinions. When it comes to peers, peers can challenge views of their fellow peers, but must do so in a way that is not demeaning, rather constructive. These concepts of judgment come to light, especially when looking at middle and high school students in a classroom setting.

3. Kohl notes that there is a lack of time for classroom discussion and inquiry, while Document 2 suggests that learning communities provide collaboration along with inquiry. How has this theme of Sprache developed and shaped current concepts of progressive education?

JG: *Kohl is pointing out to the sad realities that condition classroom life and school activities. Too often curriculum is structured in such way that disables dialogue in favor of didactic practices, which just deposit information in the student's brain, but without a process of making the student a knower. School demands often put so much pressure on teachers to cover certain contents and to test students on these, that learning is reduced to transmission to the mimetic mode, about which Phil Jackson (1986) was preoccupied, and not the transformational approach, which Jackson, Weber, Horton, Freire, and Kohl advocated. This is not to dismiss a good lecture that could be fascinating or could open minds to new perspectives and information, but it is also about how to follow up on these "mimetic" moments. Sprache provides a concrete example of how dialogue enables meaningful learning, the type of learning that awakens the imagination, the type of learning that helps to build connections and makes students knowers, they own the knowledge, they explore, they test ideas, they have to develop good arguments, using reasonable premises and questioning each other's propositions, including their own. Sprache is a form of collective inquiry, which I endorsed in Document 2.*

JW: I appreciate how Kohl brings this to light, this fact that there is a lack of time for discussion in the classroom. I think that this is true from my own experiences as a student. Some teachers are so focused on cramming all of the information they can in a student's brain for the pure reason of standardized testing. I am not denouncing testing or advocating for it, but rather speaking on the ways in which students absorb knowledge. You bring up this concept of students becoming "knowers." I love this idea. As a knower, students relate to the content being taught and interact with it, while mimetic learners repeat. Knowers come to formulate their own opinions while mimetic learners are simply told something and are expected to regurgitate that thought. There is no interaction with the content.

As you mentioned, in Document 2, this concept of Sprache emerges. Sprache enables interaction with the content and also with the community around the learner. As a result, the learner can formulate ideas and thoughts about a learning concept and build upon it with the surrounding community of learners. Without the components of following up and reflection, along with community interaction in classrooms, how can we expect students to truly become knowers?

4. Document 1 and Document 2 both speak to the interests of students and understanding students. It is clear that this concept of understanding the "Whole Student" is

present. How does this tie into this concept of student-centered approaches as discussed throughout the historical context of progressive education?

JG: *From the early times of progressive practices in educational settings, teachers understood that the learner, the student, must take the center since knowledge without a knower resides in a vacuum. Furthermore, discussions among progressive educators questioned if knowledge exists without people knowing. If the focus is the books or the teacher, the student could be left out of the meaning-making process. The power of the text resides on the reader's ability to connect. The teacher builds such a connection. But for the student to be able to participate in such a relationship of producing meaning, the teacher needs to know who the students are, as discussed above. Progressive teachers used to refer to this process as relational knowing. This meant that no knowledge is divorced from the students, the context of learning, the classroom experiences, and the environment constructed, and it also meant that knowledge connects and builds a solid foundation for further growth. In addition, progressive educators were concerned with a school culture that perceived students as if they were one dimensional: only a learner of the content designated as relevant to be part of the official curriculum. However, students are multidimensional, as every human being, progressives argued. Paying attention to the whole student, their social growth, their emotional growth, their cognitive growth, their psycho-motor growth, or other aspects of who they are and how they are, enables teachers to better tap into the potential of the student as well as to identify what are their needs and how to stimulate their propensities and address their weaknesses. For example, students could be very inclined to their artistic dispositions and be very good at them, but as progressive teachers have argued, students also need to be exposed to other experiences even when they not always meet with total success (and there were some who also argued that failure sometimes could be a great source of learning). The idea is not to give up and let students just engage in superficial activities, but rather to push the boundaries of their comfort zones enough to challenge them without building up frustration. The learning community can have a positive impact in the sense that the journey does not have to be only individual, but it could be collective, thus building and depending on each other as a way of gaining enough confidence that when facing failure, this could be overcome.*

Progressive teachers knew that seeing the student, the whole student, not only as a student who needs to perform in a particular subject area, renders a more meaningful and relevant learning experience.

JW: Through your response, it is clear that all students are multifaceted, which is a crucial concept for all teachers to understand. Students reside in many other headspaces outside of the world of academia. The classroom should be a microcosm for the world outside of school. This means, that as you mentioned, students need to be considered as having multiple levels of growth, not just academic growth. It is important for teachers to truly know their students to see these layers of the student. Once students see you are invested in who they are as people, they will be more invested in you as their teacher. I believe that things become more seamless once this happens. Learning becomes more fluid because interactions between teachers, students, and peers become more open.

You bring up this idea of pushing comfort zones, which I personally have found to be one of the best qualities of progressive education. This way of teaching allows students to push their comfort zones, while feeling safe within their comfort zone. As you mentioned, learning communities play a role in pushing boundaries. The support provided by the community enables students to feel more comfortable trying new things.

CONCLUSION

We have discussed progressive teaching historically by focusing on two documents that represent the tradition of learning communities, which embrace a student-centered approach to teaching, learning, and schooling. We have seen that this tradition has endured in spite of a social, political, and educational context that focused on productivity as measured by outcomes represented by tests and other criteria where the purposes of teaching were directed to the curriculum and to what the tests cover rather than the centering on who the students were and their needs, propensities, and characteristics in order to design engaging, stimulating, and challenging classroom environments with high standards for learners who should be knowers.

We have also analyzed in some detail the contexts that shaped the practices as well as the roots of these particular progressive teaching legacies. The dialogue attempted to clarify some of these concepts and the implications for practice summarized the type of dispositions a teacher embraces when approaching teaching by centering on the students and building a learning community.

IMPLICATIONS FOR PRACTICE

Learning from the implications pertaining to what the documents suggest and what historically encompasses progressive teaching, teachers who want to foster a progressive student-centered pedagogical approach are lifelong learners of students, lifelong learners of subject matter, lifelong learners of their own practices, lifelong learners of the contexts in which students, families, schools, and communities exist, and ultimately have an experimental and inquiry-oriented disposition. These teachers have skills, but equally or more importantly they have dispositions, attitudes, and approaches that enable them to design, implement, and modify learning environments to fit the needs of the students and their collective and individual characteristics, inclinations, propensities, and motivations. But, these teachers do not abdicate their responsibilities to help students move into places they have never been before. Hence, the obligation of the teacher in terms of creating the right type of environment for learning while building the type of relationships in the classroom among students and between individual students and the teacher that have integrity and are grounded on foundations of trust, respect, and very high standards and expectation.

It is not, then, about following steps or an algorithm of good teaching, but about relational knowing, seeing the student (Weber), seeing the whole person as an individual and in relation to others as well as to subject matter, exploring, interrogating, challenging, testing, and applying what is learned through hands-on and minds-on activities stimulated by curiosity and interest. Here again for the teacher this means that many times there is a need to learn new things in order to better engage in the teaching process. This requires an adventurous disposition because it involves uncertainty, as when Kohl engages in Sprache in which every discussion and every lesson are shaped also by the content of the conversation and discussion where the students are co-constructing the dialogues and inquiries mediated by who they are and how they think. It is not unruly or without protocols, but it is risky because there is a level of unpredictability when experimenting with new elements.

In this student-centered approach teachers need to adapt and modify, change directions, make the road by walking, as Horton and Freire argued (1990), but there could be multiple roads. Thus it is not about losing the north of the compass, it's about finding different ways to get into the journey of learning and this means that there are different routes for different students. If the teacher is authentically interested in centering the classroom around the students, then curriculum, assessment, and instruction are in a constant changing arrangement for creating the right environment that stimulates student growth. It is not about giving exact directions, but rather about the dispositions that are required of a teacher, as mentioned above the teacher becomes a learner with his or her students and the journey provides them with the opportunity for transforming into knowers.

EXTENSION QUESTIONS

1. What would be the first step a novice, first-year teacher, could take to construct a community-based environment within a classroom where he or she has no prior experience?

2. Reflect on your own education. Who were your favorite teachers? Who were your least favorite teachers? Do any of these teachers align with any of the concepts presented in the chapter?

3. It is clear that progressive education has transformed and formed over the years due to technological innovations. Access to technology is growing. How do you see this concept of education changing in a world where the majority of students have access to a plethora of technology?

GLOSSARY OF TERMS

Americanization—the act of making a person American in character or nationality.

Progressive education—a pedagogical practice in which students are valued and educated through student-centered learning and community-based teaching concepts.

Student-centered learning—a learning method in which the student's interests, learning styles, strengths, and weaknesses are considered upon learning

Romantic ideas—the glorification of childhood to the point of sanctification. It is asserting that children are always good by virtue and that society will corrupt a child. It assumes humans are naturally good and that self-reflection, introspection, and intuition could be supported by an education that is tailored to the individual inclinations and instincts of each student.

Rousseau (1712–1778)—Genevan philosopher who developed educational ideas pertaining to citizenship, individualism, and social refinement.

Tolstoy (1828–1910)—author of *War and Peace*, this Russian writer and philosopher is credited for having "modern" views related to exploration-based education and writing.

Dewey (1859–1952)—American philosopher who believed that people learn and develop by approaching education through a "hands-on" method of experiencing their own realities.

Counts (1889–1974)—American educator and theorist who is noted for educational concepts relative to developing a sense of social change through education.

REFERENCES

Antler, J. (1987). *Lucy Sprague Mitchell: The making of a modern women*. New Haven, CT: Yale University Press.

Bloom, A. (1987). *The Closing of the American Mind: How higher education has failed democracy and impoverished the souls of today's students*. NY: Simon & Schuster.

Church, R. L. & Sedlak, M. W. (1976). *Education in the United States: An interpretive history*. New York, NY: The Free Press.

Cohen, D. K. (1988). *Teaching practice: Plus ca change. . . .* East Lansing, MI: National Center for Research on Teacher Education, Michigan State University.

Counts, G. S. (1932/1978). *Dare the school build a new social order?* Carbondale, IL: Southern Illinois University Press.

Cremin, L. (1961/1964). *The transformation of the school: Progressivism in American education, 1876–1957*. New York, NY: Knoff.

Cremin, L. (1988). *American education: The metropolitan experience, 1876–1980*. NY: Harper & Row.

Cuban, L. (1993). *How teachers taught: Constancy and change in American classrooms 1880–1990* (2nd ed.). New York, NY: Teachers College Press.

Dewey, J. (1899/1991). *The School and Society*. Chicago, Il: University of Chicago Press.

Dewey, J. (1902/1964). The child and the curriculum. In R. D. Archambault (Ed.), *John Dewey on education: Selected writings* (pp. 339–358). Chicago, IL: University of Chicago Press.

Dewey, J. (1903/1964). The relation of science and philosophy as a basis for education. In R. D. Archambault (Ed.), *John Dewey on education: Selected writings* (pp. 295–310). Chicago, IL: University of Chicago Press.

Dewey, J. (1904/1964). The relation of theory to practice in education. In R. D. Archambault (Ed.), *John Dewey on education: Selected writings* (pp. 313–338). Chicago, IL: University of Chicago Press.

Dewey, J. (1933/1964). Why reflective thinking must be an educational aim. In R. D. Archambault (Ed.), *John Dewey on education: Selected writings* (pp. 212–228). Chicago, IL: University of Chicago Press.

Dewey, J. (1938/1963). *Experience and education.* New York, NY: Macmillan.

Floden, R. & Clark, C. (1988). Preparing teachers for uncertainty. *Teachers College Record, 89*(4), 505–524.

Froebel, F. (1895/2017). *Pedagogics of the kindergarten.* NY: Andesite Press.

Grinberg, J. (2002). "I had never been exposed to teaching like that": Progressive teacher education at Bank Street during the 1930s. *Teachers College Record, 104*(7), 1422–1460.

Grinberg, J. (2009). Playing with Ideas: Some Notes About Learning Communities and Connected Teaching Elements. In *Philosophy of Education: Modern and Contemporary Ideas at Play* (2nd ed.) (pp. 807–817). Dubuque, IA: Kendall & Hunt.

Grinberg, J., Schwarzer, D., & Molino, M. (2017). Creating a Dialogical Learning Community to promote dialogical teaching and learning. In D. Schwarzer & J. Grinberg, *Successful teaching: What every novice teacher needs to know* (pp. 247–262). Lanham, MD: Rowman & Littlefield.

Gordon, E. L. (1988). *Educating the whole child: Progressive education and Bank Street college of education, 1916–1966.* Unpublished doctoral dissertation, State University of New York: Stony Brook.

Hirsch, E. D. (1987). *Cultural literacy: What every American needs to know.* Boston: Houghton Mifflin.

Horton, M. & Freire, P. (1990). *We make the road by walking: Conversations on education and social change.* Philadelphia, PA: Temple University Press.

Jackson, P. (1986). The mimetic and the transformative. In *The practice of teaching,* (115–145). NY: Teachers College Press.

Kliebard, H. (2004). *The struggle for the American curriculum, 1893–1958.* NY: Routledge.

Kohl, H. R. (1984). *Growing minds: On becoming a teacher.* New York: Harper Torchbook.

Pestalozzi, H. (1801/2012). *How Gertrude teaches her children.* NY: Forgotten Books.

The National Commission on Excellence in Education. (1983). A Nation at Risk: The Imperative for Educational Reform: A Report to the Nation and the Secretary of Education. Washington, DC: United States Department of Education.

Rousseau, J. (1762/2017). *Emile, or On Education.* NY: Basic Books.

Semel, S. & Sadovnik, A. (1999). *"Schools of tomorrow," schools of today: What happened to progressive education.* NY: Peter Lang.

Trohler, D., Popkewitz, T., & Labaree, D. (Eds.) (2015). *Schooling and the making of citizens in the long nineteenth century: Comparative visions.* NY: Routledge.

Tolstoy, L. (1967). Are the peasant children to learn to write from us? Or, are we to learn from the peasant children? In R. Archambault (ed.) *Tolstoy on education* (pp. 191–224). Chicago: The University of Chicago Press.

Tyack, D., Lowe, R., & Hansot, E. (1984). *Public schools in hard times: The great depression and recent years.* Cambridge, MA: Harvard University Press.

Weber, L. (1997). *Looking Back and thinking forward: Reexaminations of teaching and schooling.* NY: Teachers College Press.

Westbrook, R. B. (1991). *John Dewey and American democracy.* Ithaca, NY: Cornell University Press.

APPENDIX

Grinberg, J. (2009). Playing with Ideas: Some Notes About Learning Communities and Connected Teaching Elements. In *Philosophy of Education: Modern and Contemporary Ideas at Play* (2nd ed.), pp. 807–817. Dubuque, IA: Kendall & Hunt.

INTRODUCTION

Learning communities, communities of learners, communities of inquiry, socially constructed learning, or learning in community have been discussed, analyzed, defined, and criticized too many times. However, in contemporary educational environments an overwhelming number of classrooms at different levels and in different school contexts have been using some version of group work, group discussion, group project, group inquiry, or group cooperation with or without modern technologies in varied ways, at least a few times in the course of an academic year. In the following notes, as in the title of this book, I will "play" with some of these ideas.

Although in these notes there are implicit themes related to the larger purposes of education, the reasons for schooling, what constitutes a classroom, what type of institutional organization schools foster, and what knowledge has to be taught (the overt curriculum) and what does not (the null curriculum), the discussion in these notes will not address these issues directly. That is the reason for the title of this postscript; these are only some notes, not a comprehensive essay. In these notes, I will first discuss three prevalent dimensions of learning communities. Then, I will proceed to play and explain some teaching elements within the framework of classrooms that foster a learning community.

LEARNING COMMUNITIES

In general terms, "learning communities" refers to at least three dimensions of group or class-centered practices, which include the individual student within the classroom context by emphasizing some levels of cooperation, exchange, support, dependency, and collective explorations. These dimensions complement each other and often develop simultaneously, but they do not function as taxonomy. In addition, fostering learning communities as a teaching approach does not mean that eventually there is no room for good lectures, direct instruction, or traditional memorization. The teacher is not divorced from the learning community, for the contrary, the teacher is a member and participates actively. However, the teacher is the authority and cannot and should not relinquish such responsibility, for the teacher has experience and expertise in addition to the trust that is inherent in the role. The authority is not only that of the role but also that which emerges from the relationships and environment created to support the learning community; thus, it includes that of expertise and inquiry knowledge. The issue for the teacher is to ask how that authority would be used, for what purposes, and under which circumstances.

The first common dimension is that of learning together as a community. Such a dimension assumes that it is possible to learn not only from each other but also under the right classroom environment and with the right direction from a teacher; this is desirable. The argument is that enough research, such as that within the framework of constructivism, or the analysis of practical experience, for instance, as in the work done by "Philosophy For Children," support the assumption that group learning experience enhances understanding of a subject matter or a concept studied while also facilitating the development of critical thinking skills. For this to happen, the tasks, projects, discussions, or inquiries have to be relevant, connected, engaging, and intellectually stimulating in a way that are challenging enough to demand effort, but are developmentally tailored to avoid frustration.

The focus of the second dimension of learning communities is on learning the communities. While much of it can be related to learning the local environments, the cultural milieu, the organization of social life, the social institutions within a civil and a political society, rules, regulations, or legal rights, all of which tend to resemble much of what is taught in social studies disciplines, it is not limited to that. It is also a process of learning about each other member of the learning community, including cultural traditions, languages, literature, music, art, dance, sports, and media, by looking at similarities and differences, commonalities, and legitimization of diversity but in a unifying experience. This dimension also includes a very important aspect: systematic inquiry. Since this inquiry is about learning the communities, such communities not only are geographic, cultural, or institutional, but also are also disciplinary. Systematic inquiry, ways of exploring, discussing, validating, rejecting, accepting, organizing, and building relationships within a discipline have similarities and differences with each other whether the subject matter is history, literature, geography, music, dance, mathematics, or any other area of study. Learning the ways by which different scholarly communities engage in such systematic activities that ultimately deal with the "nature of knowledge," or epistemologies and some of their politics, is a process, a developing habit of learning to think and understand these ways of disciplinary knowing. This is not to reject the learning of skills and the acquisition of information, but the assumption is that this aspect of learning the community (or a community) is indeed a way of inducting youngsters into the discourses of the discipline, engaging them in tasks that would create, for example, communities of "young geographers," "young artists," or "young biologists."

The third dimension involves learning to live in a community. For the inquiry to happen, for the learning environment that builds on the assumptions that lead into the other dimension of learning communities, this third dimension has to be an ongoing development. Learning to live in a community, to be a member of a community, it is not an easy task and requires much effort, not only from the participants but also fundamentally from the teachers. There is a need to create an inclusive climate of comfort and trust, respect and engagement, tolerance and acceptance, caring and listening, with the ambitious expectation that students will gain ownership over their own experiences, individually and collectively. Procedures for discussion, the right expressions, the language and tone, and the body language and silences have to be moderated in such a way that students feel at ease with others while maintaining their own individuality without imposing on each other. This is not easy to accomplish, it takes time, and it is somehow idyllic.

Conflict emerges from time to time. Teachers who foster this framework of community learning do deal with conflict and often utilize conflict resolution as a learning experience in order to further inquiry into how to live in community, as well as a way of validating multiple and diverse voices. For instance, in a process of inquiry where there has to be argumentation, demonstration, and defense of a proposition or a speculation within a project, an investigation, or problem posing and problem solving, how do students challenge each other, how do they accept or reject each other's alternative perspectives, how do they contemplate the merits of these arguments—and not only within the norms of the subject matter but also in terms of personal styles and emotions? At times, as in Talmudic disputes, members of the community have to learn to accept "teikko," meaning that both or all points of view are equally valid and valued, there is no resolution in favor of one, at least for the time being. Thus, learning to live in community involves the development of a classroom culture that leads beyond the learning of the content into learning about oneself and about others. This educational concept resembles one the established traditions of the Jewish collection of interpretation, the "Talmud," which argues that if one is not for oneself it is not good, but if one is only for oneself, it is not good either, and if it is not now, then when?

These dimensions are particularly difficult, considering that in most schools, and in most classrooms, students have little choice over who are their teachers or their classmates—and teachers often have little or no choice over who the students are. Therefore, the building of these learning communities is a form of necessary imposition on the members. Moreover, individual differences in terms of needs and personalities, cultural backgrounds, and motivations present both a resource and a challenge to teachers and students.

In addition, there is a hidden curriculum of learning communities by the fact that the dynamics of participation in a group forces its members to be exposed to the rest of the group, whether by discussion or by silence, by observation or by documentation, which results in forms of surveillance and control of students and teachers, even when these are unintended consequences. It would be naive not to understand that, even in the best situation, group dynamics involve power dynamics and, under some circumstances, can become oppressive to some members, yet they can provide a stimulating intellectual journey—the power dynamics can become a source of support and mutual dependency for a more sophisticated, vibrant, and exhilarating learning experience. Certainly, this is also challenging for the teacher who did not experience learning communities as a school student, in a non-formal environment, as a student of teaching, or with colleagues in his/her own disciplinary communities. Thus, teacher education programs, as well as professional development opportunities, have to provide experiences in learning communities in order to support teachers who foster or want to foster a framework of learning communities in their own classrooms.

TEACHING ELEMENTS

INQUIRY-BASED PRACTICE

In order to sustain, develop, and enhance a learning community, teachers need to experience the study of their own experiences with others, which is counter-culture in most school environments, where teachers tend to be isolated from their colleagues. Thus, an alternative to this dominant culture is for teachers to engage in systematic inquiry about their own practices. Furthermore, teachers can model their own practice as researchers, they can involve colleagues, and they can also engage their students as researchers vis-à-vis the learning experience in their own particular learning community.

In a sense, the assumption is that, when a teacher makes instructional decisions, they are grounded on a body of knowledge. However, this body of knowledge not always has been tested in the particular conditions of the specific classroom with a particular and distinctive group of students. Thus, in spite of generic understanding of the so-called knowledge base, the application translates into who the teacher and students are and what the situations are. For these decisions to be better informed, an inquiry-based practice means to practice teaching as a form of research, which takes into consideration the complexity of the factors or variables at play, the testing of assumptions, the analysis of information gathered, and the implications for further action. Furthermore, the accumulation of varied evidence, at times in contradiction, serves as a source for learning. In addition, these bodies of accumulated information have to be presented, shared, discussed, dissected, challenged, and reinterpreted in light of new evidence and within a learning community of educators who have similar commitments.

The habit of inquiry, as previously mentioned, is present also within learning communities where students research various subjects, pose and find problems that need to be investigated and converse with the field of study in a way that they do not reinvent the wheel but make the road by walking, as much as the road might have been traveled before. What this means is that the engagement is not only with a problem posed by a teacher or by the field but with questions that emerge as the students immerse themselves in the study of the subject matter. At times, this might be challenging and complex but engaging, because the questions and the inquiry process might require multiple disciplinary lenses and multiple processes. Thus, inquiry is also looking from multiple perspectives including the propensity to analyze, make connections, see relationships and patterns, and provide alternative explanations to the dominant "explanations" of what constitutes "truth," "false," and "fact." For this to happen, these learning communities not only experiment and practice "hands-on" activities but also practice "minds-on" and at times even "emotions-on" activities.

LISTENING TO AND SEEING THE WHOLE STUDENT

Students, and teachers, bring with them a baggage of experiences into these communities. They are more than a good or not good math student, student-athlete, or writer. While for purposes of understanding youngsters, aspects of growth and development are isolated, they do function as a unity. While a student might have a high cognitive development, an appropriate-to-age psychomotor ability, a limited social experience or ability, and/or a "balanced" emotional development stage, the student is not one or the other but all of the above.

Listening is not just hearing the student. It means to actively engage in a dialogical mode, looking at the student's point of view, attending to his or her need, and focusing on the meaning and messages conveyed. This does not mean that all is legitimate and valid, or that there has to be agreement. It means that the student realizes that the teachers, and classmates, understand what they are articulating and engage with them. Seeing the student also adds the element of visibility, seeing the person not just as a presence but also as an individual and as a member of the group. Seeing the whole child includes seeing the strengths and limitations, the needs and potentials—and providing opportunities for growth not only within a subject area, but also as persons.

TEACHING AS A FORM OF BUILDING RELATIONSHIPS

While it is clear that relationships are created between teachers and students and among students, the primary function of these relationships is to enable growth, development, and learning. In any relationship there are ups and downs, tensions and expectations, which are also ethical and incorporate mutual caring, with feelings and emotions not detached from cognitive processes, yet the relationship between individuals, the I-Thou relationship, also includes a context such as the classroom, and the content of the relationship such as a subject matter. This content tends to mediate the relationship in terms of interactions, but not always in terms of quality, as all the other elements of trust, respect, safety, and high expectations of learning are also present.

Creating the classroom climate, the environment for developing, nurturing, and growing relationships without content of study—social, academic, spiritual or emotional—render a vacuum of learning. There is learning about relating to each other and about treating each other, even learning about the self, which is very important, but not enough for a classroom. The inquiry, the project, the problem finding, the problem posing, and the problem solving are sine qua non for a learning community.

This is not to neglect that, while experiencing and growing within a learning community, members develop a sense of self, identities. For instance, students learn to be mathematicians and artists; they build a sense of themselves as such. But this is not the only aspect of their building identities, since in these relationships they also interact with each other and build other aspects of themselves, including many psychological and emotional, at times even spiritual, dimensions of who they are. As they experience multiple opportunities to participate, these can be empowering and/or repressing experiences simultaneously. Teachers who see and listen to the whole student are aware and tune to the issues of relationships with and among students, individually and collectively.

Aesthetic relationships are also included in seeing and listening to the whole child. Aesthetics are a central component of a whole education and a whole person. Furthermore, the incorporation of music, plastic arts, drama, dance, and other forms of human expression and communication—including in my judgment sports—enhances the learning experience both as forms of disciplinary knowledge and as a form of involvement of the body, the feelings, and the sense of beauty. Such experiences open up the whole experience to more complex and sophisticated means of relating, understanding, and critical thinking.

PROBLEMATIZATION

This crucial element is an intellectual tool that enables ways of looking at situations, experiences, information, and arguments by unveiling and challenging underlying assumptions, revising ideas, and thinking of different ways of analyzing, explaining, and interpreting. For example, a way of starting to think about subject matter connections and building relationships is through incorporated explorations and inquiry. However, problematization is more than this. It does involve critical thinking and problem solving, but problems have to be identified, at times created, developed, and framed. The development of the habit of interrogating, to ask questions that were or were not asked before, and of eliciting imagination and scrutiny are also aspects of problematization. There has to be a dimension of discomfort, confusion, and uncertainty about what is known and what is unknown, a daring to ask and to search for more than common sense to further problematization, which is something that scientists in the social sciences or natural sciences do not just because of curiosity but because of understanding the limitations of their own knowledge.

For example, facts and information by themselves without individual and collective problematization are dangerous because they can manipulate and fit the needs of a few at the expense of the rest, a way of maintaining hegemonic dominance. What is important to consider, then, are questions such as how facts and information are used and how facts are judged. Whose facts and whose information are presented? What facts or information is not presented and why? Who can and who cannot benefit from these facts and information? Moreover, for problematizing further, what facts and information need to be investigated?

This not only engages the mind (thinking) but also engages the body (feelings, behaviors, aesthetics dimensions), and even the "spirit." This requires a process gaining awareness, which can be started by questioning the given conditions of our own experience and existence, what we are told are the facts. To problematize implies that we ought to consider multiple possible alternatives; it invites us to play with what counts as facts, truth or false, and to consider possible multiple coexisting realities. In consequence, what starts with questions, with finding the problems, leads into critical habits that also analyze power arrangements, as well as connections with larger contextual issues, such as gender, social class, and race.

IMPORTANCE OF CONTEXTS

As previously discussed, aspects of knowledge are located and shaped by the particularities of place and time. Spaces—physical and metaphysical, virtual and material—are elements that contextualize relationships, cooperation, and even identities. A learning community constitutes such space, but it is not the only space. The classroom is part of a larger institution, which is part of multiple systems—including cultural and political dimensions in a macro sense, and in a micro sense also families, networks, neighborhoods, and listserves.

While a subject matter—say, biology—would be relatively stable regardless of the where it is studied, a number of contextual elements influence and shape the learning community vis-à-vis that subject. One obvious element is resources. What a second-grade or a high-school biology class has in terms of equipment, materials, rooms, teacher expertise, or natural environments to extend the class beyond the school walls depends at least on the geography, economy, and politics of the place. If a school has technological resources and another does not, then, influences the quality of what some students can access to learn. Although a learning community can be resourceful within it, external factors can limit or enable it at times. However, besides some clear conditions that the context provides, there are students and teachers who might be influenced by culture or other factors. For instance, looking at the same cell through a microscope, different students in the same learning community might ask very different questions, or they might be interested in different issues regarding the cell. Furthermore, in some places, given, for instance, the geography, the culture, the environmental experiences, and/or the weather, students might ask very different questions. Thus, external and contextual factors are two-fold in terms of the variation within a group and that between groups, yet in both cases a learning community would center some practices utilizing local resources, the community at large as a place to learn. This also implies that the context can provide opportunities for learning.

TEACHER AS INTELLECTUAL AND ARTIST (AND CITIZEN)

Much has been written and discussed about the elements of teaching in a learning community. Teachers invest a tremendous amount of energy in developing, supporting, sustaining, and enhancing learning communities. They invest intellectual energy, since their work is intellectual by definition. They also display an authentic intellectual respect for students and foster such respect as part of the everyday life in learning communities. However, they also invest emotional, physical, and even spiritual energies. Students, too, invest these energies in a learning community.

The artistry of teaching involves the nuances, the unpredictability, the uncertainty, and the beauty of building meaningful relationships. Often intellectual and artistic are presented as dichotomies; this is a false dichotomy. There is an intellectual aspect to the artistic in teaching and there is an artistic aspect to the intellectual. In this discussion, I prefer to include two dimensions that capture this element in somehow a different way. In the following lines, I will discuss "Passion and Coraje to teach."

These are not only intellectual dispositions but also are feelings and emotions, passion is often associated with an intense emotion, a feeling, and it happens with devotion and dedication, with love, and with physical energy. It also includes a level of risk-taking because it can produce suffering. Oftentimes teachers have been instructed to control their passions and not to be too directive of the students' innate interests, to avoid being intrusive. However, passion is an important element, particularly in communities and with students who learn to value and understand passion and who, themselves, learn to become open about being passionate.

"Coraje" can be translated in a number of ways. Often it means courage, as in the courage to take on unpopular positions, the courage to confront authority, the courage to risk one's own privilege, the courage to accept one's own limitations, the courage to confront injustice, the courage to teach everybody's children, the courage to learn from one's students. Coraje is also anger, even rage, at least indignation. The conditions of schooling in some places—including historical structural inequities, or the expectation that some students will drop out, the perpetuation of discriminating against "others"—provoke coraje. Coraje is also daring; it is in many ways a form of cheerful disrespect toward institutions and toward people who exploit their positions to their own advantage. Coraje is also "hutzpah," a way of both daring and cheerfully disrespecting authority, norms, and power arrangements.

Passion and coraje are elements of the "teacher as citizen" since it develops the expectation of acting, of doing, of involving, beyond the classroom and beyond the school. Eventually, this teacher works to alter difficult conditions, acts to defend the spaces that enable meaningful learning, and negotiates for and with students to control the conditions of their learning. Responsibility and mission fuel their coraje and passion and are fueled in a circular way by courageous and passionate teachers. These teachers, and on occasion their students, learn to make things happen rather than letting things happen to them.

LAST NOTES: BRIDGING FALSE DICHOTOMIES?

An important challenge for learning communities is the bridging of false dichotomies. Throughout these notes, I have addressed that problematization is an important aspect of inquiry and that inquiry is at the center of learning communities' experiences. I have implied that some elements complement each other and that at times we explain dimensions as separate entities, but they are connected and related and as a total are more than the addition. Learning communities provide opportunities to challenge and to bridge these dichotomies. Some of them are mind and body, emotion and cognition, practice and theory, school and home, and virtual and physical communities. They are part of the same. While one might help define the other, maintaining the dichotomy is problematic because it can privilege one over the other or might create the sense that they are separate. This is an open note to play with more ideas.

The potential and limitations of virtual and mediated learning communities were not discussed in these notes. However, technology has presented a tremendous potential for reaching out and broadening the ways in which learning communities can operate. Physical proximity or human warmth is not sine qua non anymore. Although I prefer the energy generated in a direct and constrained physical environment, I recognize that this could also be limiting, and at times oppressive. Virtual learning communities—given time is provided and multiple confluent conversations are taking place—have the potential to add new dimensions of reflectiveness, problematization, alternative points of view, and multiple resources also in terms of access to variety and quality. Nevertheless, virtual learning communities also necessitate many of the elements previously discussed, such as trust, safety, respect, and intellectual curiosity, to name a few. In addition, a virtual learning community is as much or even more surveillant than the traditional classroom where students are just seating at their desks or tables with a group, for it requires, if nothing else, more exposure in writing—what is said and written in most cases is recorded and kept in cyberspace, which can be accessed by many, including non-members of that community. Ultimately, it will also depend on the type of relationships constructed. Playing with ideas is the challenge that these "Notes" attempted to instigate in you, the reader.

SECTION III TEACHERS

10

ON BECOMING A TEACHER: FINDING YOUR VOICE THROUGH DIALOGUE

Maya S. Levanon
Yelena Adelman

INTRODUCTION

In this chapter's written dialogue, we examine the very same construct of "dialogue" as two influential philosophers, Martin Buber and Paulo Freire—and we—deem essential to the process of becoming a whole teacher. At the core we argue that this entails: a process, a way of being that invites you to see yourself and others as truly human, and by that allow you to find and refine your own personal teaching identity/**integrity**. One major feature we examine in this relationship between dialogical engagement and the establishing of one's sense of self is the type of knowledge that is desired and much needed in our current system; we compare and contrast it in relation to the type of knowledge the current system emphasizes and values. While the knowledge we consider as fundamental for the process of becoming a good teacher is **self-knowledge**, that is, knowledge that is intrinsically subjective and relational, and thus un-measurable and incomparable, the existing teacher-education programs reflect the common approach in education regarding knowledge: That although we speak in **constructivist**/progressive terms, practices such as core curriculum and standardized testing reflect the positivist approach toward knowledge, that is knowledge that is supposedly objective and measurable. We stress the importance of self-knowledge as the basis for ethical dialogue, which in turn, is the mainstay of good education, especially one that wishes to remain effective and relevant in the age of information.

In the following pages we will first present you with our premises, which ground our discussion. Second, we will provide a brief chart helping you contextualize the historical times for the two authors' work that we discuss as a way of understanding how ideas and concept both shape and are shaped by social, political, cultural, scientific, and other dimensions that help to unpack ideas. Third, we engage in a long dialogue about these ideas and concepts as they also connect with our present as educators. Throughout the process of joint writing, a process that was new for both of us, we found ourselves constantly challenged, as it is one thing to talk or write about dialogical education, it is even different than practicing it in a designated time-slot in school, than it is to engage in a fashion that encompasses the dialogical way-of-being. This challenge found expression in posing each other with new situations from the field as well as from theoretical frameworks, and while we did not always agree, we found each lived experience as an educator and ideas as a thinker, important to pose and rethink our own. Doing that with genuine respect and curiosity encouraged us to find our separate voices, something we both believe is missing from the current education system, including teacher-education programs.

SUMMARY OF DOCUMENTS

1. Buber's *I-Thou*: The idea of Buber's *I-Thou* (1970) explains two main options for one's relation to the world and specifically to the encounter with other people. He divides these encounters into two types: one is I-It and the other I-Thou. He explains that these types of relations exist in three realms: our life with nature, our life with other people, and our life with spiritual beings, but we will focus on these categories of relation as they relate to the relationship between people. The I-It relationship is primarily to view others as objects and the I-Thou relation is to view others as subjects. Buber writes, "If I face a human being as my thou, and say the primary word I-Thou to him, he is not a thing among things, and does not consist of things." He also claims that there is no I, but rather always either an I-It relation or I-Thou relation and thus, when one relates to things or people as I-It he or she also relates to himself or herself more as an object and when one has an I-Thou relation, they also relate to themselves as a subject. Buber lays out that the I-Thou relationship requires active choice, one's whole being, directness, being in the present, and that the relation must be mutual. These ideas can be understood as a counter reaction toward what Buber witnessed in those years: the rise of fascism and totalitarianism. Distinguishing between two main structures of human relationships, that is I-It and I-Thou is a call to re-frame humanism on its interrelations, seeing persons as persons, subjects, as opposed to objects who serves the regime. Furthermore, reframing human relations in the I-Thou structure in fact distinguishes between equality and equity, and allows us to respect each person's unique contribution without trying to

mold her. In fact, in I-Thou relationships: "My Thou affects me, as I affect it," that is, there is no hierarchy where one serves another, but instead it is mutual and symmetrical. Buber does not view the I-It relationship as evil and explains that people will always relate to parts of the world as I-It, but also demands that we strive to increase our I-Thou relation to the world as this relation is critical to developing the real I. Buber says, "Through the Thou a man becomes I. That which confronts him comes and disappears, relational events condense, then are scattered, and in the change consciousness of the unchanging partner, of the I, grows clear, and each time stronger." While Buber does not use the word dialogue in the book I-Thou, his writing and the I-Thou relation is seen as the basis of Buber's definition of dialogue.

2. Freire's *Pedagogy of the Oppressed*: In *Pedagogy of the Oppressed*, Paulo Freire, an educator who focused on literacy in the slums of Brazil, talks about the creation of a better society based on eliminating oppression and cultivating dialogical practices instead. When reading Freire's ideas within a context: Communism in general, and Maoism in particular (a Communist totalitarian regime, that mixed ideology with personality cult, using violent oppression). These influences were very strong in 20th-century Latin America, where Che Guevara influenced the creation of a new social order. And so portraying teachers as active agents for social change is a counter-response to aggressive, totalitarian practices on the one hand, while at the same time reflects the New Left ideologies, which found a global expression in global students' demonstration who called for social change with regard to equality between different social segments. Freire argues that there should be mutual responsibility of the oppressors and the oppressed and claims that much of our oppression is rooted in the education system, one that is based on the "banking method" where students are seen as vessels to be filled with information. This education system that he criticizes has a very clear hierarchy between the teacher and student such as that the "teacher knows everything and the student knows nothing" and "the teacher acts and the students have the illusion of acting through the action of the teacher". Freire proposes "problem-posing" education where the "students are co-investigators in dialogue with the teacher" and demands that "students see the reality in process, transformation." Further, "problem-posing education affirms men and women as beings in the process of becoming—as unfinished, uncompleted beings in and with a likewise unfinished reality." Freire also presents the condition of dialogue as a necessary praxis for problem-posing education and eradicating oppression. Freire presents a few main points for what is dialogue and the conditions required for such dialogue: (1) It is an encounter between people, mediated by the world surrounding them, so they can understand it; (2) It cannot exist without love (for the world and for people; and (3) It requires a genuine trust in humanity and its ability to create and change, which in turn is what makes us fully human. Finally, Freire talks about the need for this pedagogy to be rooted in theory and action, that one cannot stand without the other and that action and reflection need to be ongoing and simultaneous.

RELEVANCE/PREMISES

The philosophies presented by these texts are relevant to novice teachers because they invite to develop habits of mind and practice in which our own humanity, who we are, who we become, is not only an individualized or self-indulgent experience, but it is a process of engaging also with others in authentic and meaningful ways. Hence, novice teachers benefit from a dialogical approach that integrates, respects, and listens to oneself and to others, colleagues and/or students, as it impacts the very act of teaching. Consider the following:

1. A good teacher integrates the different aspects of her life into a holistic way-of-being, that is, one that overcomes our current tendency of fragmenting our lives into separated roles. This is important because only a whole person can in fact meet uncertainties with dignity and the life of an educator brings plenty of uncertainties. This is also because a good teacher is a teacher who sees her students as people, not as numbers on achievement charts; in order to view others as whole people, one must first consider herself as one.

2. In order to ethically advance the facilitation of a teachers' authentic voice and sense of identity, there is a need for a dialogical ongoing engagement throughout the different processes of the teaching and learning journey. We suggest that it is through dialogical practices and ways-of-being that individuals find their voice.

In what follows, we explain the context of the texts that we will discuss in our own dialogue.

CONTEXTUALIZING THE TEXTS

The following chart provides you with the historical context for the two texts we are discussing. As you will notice, the authors of the texts lived in different places and at different time periods. Buber is writing against the background of rising totalitarianism and Nazism in Europe, while Freire is writing in the context of a global movement for peace and justice in a post-colonial time and more specifically in the Latin American context of the 1960s, which coincides with the civil rights movement in the United States. Both time periods and places were pivotal in imagining and shaping the role of the teacher and the humanization of the students. Hence, thinking of schools as a space that is designed for meaningful, exciting, engaging, respectful, and challenging experiences that could fit the students and teachers as people instead of fitting students and teachers to a structured and fixed institution.

	Global Forces	National Forces	Educational Policies	Understanding of Phenomena
Text 1 *I and Thou,* Martin Buber (1927)	Rise of Communism Post-WWI	Great Depression New Deal under President Roosevelt Increased role of federal government in the economy and social programs (Social Security) View of formal education as a vehicle for social mobility	U.S. Supreme Court ruled that students could attend private schools to comply with state compulsory education laws High schools added sports to their curriculum Beginning of Progressive Education Movement Teachers' professional organization begin to take place in large cities	Dialogical teacher education as a vehicle to teacher's inner **subjectivity**; and vice versa: Teacher's **wholeness** as a condition for dialogical education
Text 2 *Pedagogy of the Oppressed,* Paulo Freire (1968)	Israeli and Arab forces battle: The Six-Day War ends with Israel occupying Gaza Strip and east bank China announces explosion of its first hydrogen bomb Prague Spring Global protests and rebellions Death of Che Guevara	Robert Kennedy is assassinated Martin Luther King, Jr. is assassinated Racial violence across the United States Cuban Missile Crisis Vietnam War North Korea seizes U.S. Navy ship Peace movement Human rights movement Miss America protests (burning bras) *Hippies *Student protests across the country	Administration pushed congress to increase federal aid to education The Human Potential Movement Diversity enters American curriculum Teaching for thinking Bilingual education programs Army-funded education program	

DIALOGICAL TEXT ANALYSIS

In what follows, we analyze the implications and nuances of the two texts. We will discuss dialogue as a process for change, dialogue in relation to spirituality, love, and teaching, dialogue as a way of being, the dialogical teacher, and the authentic teacher.

Maya: Living, learning, and teaching in era of exponential informational knowledge, and reconstructed relationships with it, suggests we need to start a conversation about what it means to be a teacher from an organic perspective, that is, one that invites us to look outside the "pedagogical toolbox," and by that enables us to see teacher's personal development just as important. Arriving at this perspective is a result of three interrelated premises: (1) A teacher is first a person: with needs, fears, interests, and otherwise lived experiences. In order for teachers to approach others as persons (whether peers, administrators, parents, and of course pupils), who bring their own needs, fears, interests, and lived experiences, it is important that teachers will first acknowledge their own. (2a) Since teachers' work includes an ongoing learning, teaching, and caring, it resembles the archetypical spiritual journey (Wexler, 1996). And indeed one important aspect in spiritual journeys is about finding and acknowledging thyself, as the foundation for meaningful relationships with others. (2b) For most teachers with whom I conversed over the years, the reasons to become teachers was what we can consider as "noble" reasons, for example, sharing knowledge with future generations, making an impact on a child's lives, or making a change in the educational system or in the community. Paraphrasing Freire's words, teachers perceive educational practice as a social intervention, an endeavor that concerns with transforming lives, which again, is an expression of spirituality. But it isn't an aloof spirituality, rather it is a form of stewardship (Fenstermacher, 1999; Goodlad, 1991), that is, spirituality that exists within mundane moments of daily interactions. But being stewards doesn't come without a price; teachers often ignore their own needs, fears, and aspirations. Subsequently, they may unconsciously ignore these aspects in others, and by that self-defeating their original motivation. We can break this circle by understand that today, teacher's work calls for meaningful relationships: with knowledge, with others, and with oneself. Enabling, even encouraging teachers, novice, and veterans, to find and construe what they need in order to meet themselves and then others "face to face" (Levinas, 1985). With that said, I suggest that the most urgent understandings we have to bring into our educational discourse concern with: (1) the importance of meaningful interactions with one another as well as with the subject one teaches/learns, and (2) increasing teachers' and learners' agency and autonomy.

Yelena: *I agree with you that in order for education to be a meaningful field, educators need to come to it with a desire to create change and to make a difference. However, many teacher preparation programs fail to give these aspects any importance during the training years. Further, the demands placed on teachers, such as the stress around high performance and test scores, make it difficult to have space to focus on making a difference. If the main praxis of being a teacher* *is preparing students for tests, and if a teacher is measured by their students' test scores, it is hard to keep the drive of making a difference that often led individuals to the field initially, or perhaps even ideologically. With this said, I think strengthening this drive to make a difference and viewing teachers as agents shaping society is the only way to ensure the longevity of the profession (as a teacher who doesn't feel meaningful will likely leave the field). Much of the ability to feel meaningful rests on if teachers succeed in forming meaningful relationships.*

SPIRITUALITY, LOVE, AND TEACHING

Maya: In that aspect, of forming meaningful relationships, being a teacher also resembles a spiritual journey, where I continuously strive to constitute meaningful relationships with the other who is in fact my reflection. And although this endeavor often feels Sisyphean, it doesn't dishearten me to keep going, and what makes me keep going is understanding this type of endeavor as the key to my students' hearts; these meaningful relationships are the key to what it mean to be human.

Yelena: *This reflects Buber's idea of I-Thou. Buber says that only through the interaction with others and creating I-Thou relationships where both individuals are truly present and something new is created in the world through this encounter, can one truly know herself. This may not sound as much, but in reality, most of our daily interactions are not aimed at a deep reflection of who we are as people or a desire to grow and change, and even less at who the other really is or where does she come from. I think this I-Thou type of human interaction demands an active choice. And that is far from being easy.*

Maya: I agree. Meeting others in their otherness is a challenge, and a greater challenge is meeting our inner self, a murky entity that for many became a complete stranger whom we are afraid to meet. Earlier I suggested that we start looking at teachers' education from a more organic perspective, and that includes teachers' personal growth as well. It is important to establish an "arsenal" of daily opportunities for practices that facilitate this much-needed personal growth, for example, journaling, support circles, or meditation.

Yelena: *That reminds me of Freire's ideas, that education is based on love. He writes, "But to the humility with which teachers perform and relate to their students, another quality needs to be added: lovingness, without which their work would lose its meaning. And here I mean lovingness not only toward the students but also toward the very process of teaching. I must confess, not meaning to cavil, that I do not believe educators can survive the negatives of their trade without some sort of 'armed love,' as the poet Tiago de Melo would say. . . . It is indeed necessary, however, that this love be an "armed love," the fighting love of those convinced of the right and the duty to fight, to denounce, and to announce. It is this form of love that is indispensable to the progressive educator and that we must all learn" (Freire, 1998, pp. 40–41). He also adds, "Loving is not enough; one must know how to love" (ibid.). I think what Freire implies here is that teaching is a spiritual journey, as you suggested earlier also. Understanding how to love the students and the profession, to reignite convictions that you have about the world and about teaching. This never-ending journey must constantly be re-chosen.*

Maya: Making an ongoing choice is a result of a healthy ontological autonomy, which in turn is an outcome of conducting an inner dialogue that ties together the different pieces of the self into one. It is once again a question of relationships, this time with yourself. The practices I brought above as means for personal growth are all, essentially, dialogical, if "dialogue" stands for a genuine relationship that brings about a co-creation of something new, like another layer in the ongoing process of construing knowledge. A courageous reflection for example, carries a dialogical quality in that it constitutes a dialogue between the different parts of the self, with the unconscious desire to bring about an integration. In that sense, the idea is not for teachers to understand "dialogue" as another pedagogical tool, but embrace it as a way of life, as an attitude.

DIALOGUE AS A WAY OF BEING

Yelena: *Exactly. Dialogue cannot be just a pedagogy, it ought to be a way of being. This idea is the foundation for the teacher preparation program I participate in which is based on the ideas of Martin Buber and Paulo Freire. While "dialogue" is a word we hear quite often today, the way Buber defines genuine dialogue is as "where each of the participants really has in mind the other or others in their present and particular being and turns to them with the intention of establishing a living mutual relation between himself and them" (Buber, 1967; p. 37). With that said, dialogical education requires the educator to view her students as people who are whole and complex, not vessels teachers need to fill. Through this dialogical deep encounter between people, new knowledge emerges, often inviting us to become better versions of ourselves.*

Maya: "New knowledge" is definitely something I want to pass on. We hear about the transition from "the age of information" to "the age of knowledge" (Drucker, 1992). We can understand this as if "information" pre-existing/expert's propositional knowledge, and "knowledge" as the result of something individuals with a common goal cocreate, based on what they already know and experience, hence, what characterizes "knowledge" is its relevance to its creators, within their context, a relevancy that translates itself to **meaningfulness** (Dewey, 2004; Freire, 2000; Vygotsky, 2002).

Nevertheless, we still find a dissonance between this constructivist position and the practice in most public schools, which is essentially still embedded in a traditional structure that leans on two pillars: centralization and standardization (Toffler, 1984, 2000). Schools who lean on these pillars fail in preparing children for their context, which is ironic given the stated mission of school. And since schools emulate the traditional academic structure that is, "top-down," experts-based, and so on, then contemporary critical epistemologies are ignored. This is not a surprise because of the dissonance between how in academia we tend to teach alternative, progressive, liberal approaches, and how most schools continue to look as they did 50 years ago or more, thus having far more influence on how novice teachers are socialized and how they end up teaching their pupils.

Yelena: *One thing that is unique to the program I participate in is that it creates a model of what we—the participants/learners—believe education should look like and thus allows us to transfer this type of pedagogy as teachers to our own pupils, by creating images of what new paradigms are possible for us to create. At least this is my experience as a young educator simultaneously teaching in a dialogue-based school and participating in a unique teacher preparation program. In the program, we attempt to reconstruct many of the paradigms held in formal education, including the hierarchy and ownership of knowledge. In the age we live in, it is easy to access information and we do not need a teacher for this. So naturally most of our learning is not frontal, it is discussion based, it is active, collective, and based on things that interest us and come back to the question of where this meets us in our lives. This model reflects the idea that through dialogue we can reach deeper understandings of the world and ourselves. We—the learners—participate in the cocreation of knowledge and curriculum in an attempt to develop shared ideas. In fact, we participate in construing all of the educational processes, including pedagogies and evaluations, in many cases even the instructors we want to work with. But all these leave me with questions such as: What does the meeting between students and the professors need to look like? What should the meeting between students studying education look like? How do we prepare teachers to choose to bring themselves, authentically, to the classroom (including allowing themselves to be vulnerable and to be wrong)?*

Maya: The answers to these questions depend on one's educational creed, and what precedes it is one's relationship with herself, which is what **authenticity** is about. One thing we need to promote is the practice of safe space, where practitioners explore and develop their unique educational fingerprint.

Yelena: *One thing the program does indirectly is encouraging us to create a stance of how we see ourselves as people and thus as teachers, in this way, we find ways to bring our values to our praxis, and in turn it enable us an agency and autonomy in it.*

Maya: So if we return to the idea of dialogue as a way of life, then what you describe is a dialogical process that complements your entire educational journey. I guess that is what you mean when you earlier said "deep meeting between people?"

Yelena: *Exactly! In order for education to be dialogical, it cannot just be a tactic used at times. Dialogical education means the educator brings herself as a whole person to the encounter with the students and choosing to see the students in the same way. It means taking an interest in students' lives and not just their academic performance. It's approaching this encounter with a desire to be influenced by the students, and to be willing to change as a result. Dialogical education means approaching every aspect of education differently. For example, if a student does something that is unacceptable, the teacher cannot just decide on a punishment alone.*

A class or school like any other social grouping needs to define rules and norms. Dialogue does not mean each person does what he or she wants. However, usually a school has a set of rules and if a student breaks a rule there is a set punishment. Dialogical education demands that the teacher sees each student as unique and that the problem is resolved mutually between the student and teacher, that the student thinks about how to fix the situation and that they decide on the consequences of the action together.

Maya: So if we understand dialogue as a way of life, an adverb that accompanies my plethora of relationships, including with myself, then when it enters my teaching it challenges me to re-examine my predisposition and preconceptions, so change becomes possible, even desirable. When I, as a teacher allow myself to embrace change, I model to my students that change is a good thing. But unlike in a debate, dialogical approaches change as ongoing, often subtle, as a process that affects all participants. Furthermore, in a dialogue, we perceive change as a symptom of growth and courage, and not as a weakness of one's position. In this sense, living dialogically reflects the natural state of "becoming," which is the authentic human dynamic nature.

Earlier you suggested that dialogue enables us a deeper understanding of ourselves and of others. I think this deeper understanding is possible due to the mirroring effect dialogue has on us (Eagleman, 2015; Levinas, 1985). The moment we become aware of it, we begin seeing others and ourselves as separate yet interrelated beings.

I guess what we, as dialogical educators, are intrigued with, is finding a balance between what we perceive as our traditional role: deliverers of knowledge and decision makers; and being equal members in our community of learning. Clearly, the facilitator is in a different epistemological position from her students, but what is it? For me, it is introducing new ideas to the discussion, and thereby inviting learners to reflect critically on their predispositions and ideological premises. Then, together we create norms and criteria for learning and knowing. This reflects once again a commitment to an ongoing change.

THE DIALOGICAL TEACHER

Yelena: *I think the instructor/teacher, putting aside the educational context/setting, definitely has a special role: She can be part of the learning community, nevertheless, her role is different. Without a doubt, the educator comes with a specific knowledge base, often an actual expertise and a very rich lived experience, and it is important that they bring this perspective to the classroom.*

Maya: So, if we are to accept your notion that indeed a teacher is oftentimes highly knowledgeable, how do we abstain from falling back into the banking structure, how do we to maintain the I-thou dynamic within this asymmetry?

Yelena: *Well, this difference does not mean that there needs to be a hierarchy. There is inevitable asymmetry in almost any relationship. In a teacher-student relationship, there are for example certain responsibilities the teacher has and the student does not, as a result, teachers are the ones who are held legally accountable for things that happen in the classroom. Also, in most schools (with the exception of the Democratic schools and alike), teachers are the ones who ultimately decide what happens on the first day of school; here they can decide whether they leave the processes of shaping the atmosphere in the class or the curriculum completely* *to the students, or they are the ones telling students how things will work. However, this different set of responsibilities does not necessarily mean the teacher is more important than her students, or that the knowledge she holds is more valuable than students'. It also doesn't mean the teacher is single-handedly responsible for the curriculum and evaluation. In terms of evaluation for example, dialogical education presents new codes to the evaluation process—evaluation needs to be in relation to the student himself or herself. There can be no one standard that every student is measured by; evaluation must be in terms of the change, progress, or regression that the student has gone through. Acts like that attempt to break down the power dynamics between students and teachers, which is one of the biggest challenges of dialogical education.*

I think our program at Beit Berl is a model of what relationships between people can and should look like. One of the main relationships is the "teacher–learner" relationship. Enabling the program to operate from a different understanding of this central relationship, one that breaks down the traditional hierarchy, rejecting the banking method, and by offering an example of how an alternative "teacher–student" relationship can look like. Obviously, it cannot be copy-pasted into a school setting as a "teacher–student" relationship will look very different based on the age of the students and the educational institution, but the more images of innovative teaching that a teacher enters the classroom with, the more they will have the means necessary to implement something that is outside the outdated standard practices.

Maya: So in this context, where we deconstruct hierarchies altogether, striving for epistemological equalities while preserving differences, will you be comfortable with the term "(positive) anarchy"?

Yelena: *I am not sure that I would call this anarchy. I think at the end of the day teachers have the ultimate responsibility to facilitate a learning process for the students. The teacher can do this in a nonhierarchical way that encourages and enables students to take ownership and autonomy over their learning, to aim the curriculum to be flexible and meaningful to her students. She can do this by allowing, even encouraging students to bring content to the classroom. She can also change how evaluations look like: for example, she can eliminate grades all together, or having students evaluate themselves or each other, based on criteria they developed.*

However, I think radical, alternative education does require shaping by the teacher (sometimes even more than in a regular school as most students come from at least some lived experience in a school that has different codes and making this switch needs a lot of shaping by the educator) and not just anarchy.

As you suggest earlier, in a dialogical learning process, students' lived experiences and knowledge have a central place, just like the teacher's. In an ideal learning situation, the facilitation of learning will be a rotating shared responsibility of learners as well. For example, in Beit Hamidrash, we as students are just as responsible (if not more responsible) for the learning process as our academic instructors. We plan the overall curriculum of the program and facilitate most of our own classes.

Maya: Freire suggested something along those lines: Since not all lived experiences carry the same quality, they do not have a correlation to one's age. Perhaps understanding that is the key to understand why Freire also suggested that the different educational inherent responsibilities need to be rotated among all participants. In my experience, this is also an accurate rubric to evaluate the progress of a dialogical community of learning. Take for example the role of a facilitator in such a community of learning: leading a discussion doesn't have to be the teacher's exclusive role, if anything this may actually hinder the flow of ideas. Each one has to decide where is a good place for her, as a teacher, to start designating responsibilities to others. Accepting a genuine responsibility is the first step in feeling ownership for your own learning.

So we clarified what we mean by "dialogical education" and the role teacher has within this model, but what it requires from her? So she can operate within this paradigm?

AUTHENTIC TEACHING

Yelena: *In our program we emphasize on authenticity as a characteristic of a good educator, not the one who may carry a well-equipped "tool box." Also, and that is from my own personal experience as a teacher, I believe that one of the most important elements to being a good educator is entering the field with a desire to really meet the students and coworkers and to choose to constantly grow and change from this encounter. While many teachers might find uncertainty a weakness and feel they need to have all the answers, I believe the desire to constantly change is an important strength.*

Maya: And this requires courage. In order to bring your authentic voice to the educational discourse you need courage. Since we are both familiar with two different working and learning cultures, the American and the Israeli, I wonder whether allowing myself to be vulnerable, by making mistakes or not knowing something, for example, is that a matter of cultural codes and social structures. The price of not bringing this voice is the reason why we parent the way we were parented, and as Freire suggested, we teach the way we were taught. Usually it happens unconsciously, thus requires a great amount of personal work to reveal.

Coming full circle, we began this conversation with inviting the teacher to enter an educational interaction as a person, and by that transforming this interaction into a dialogue. I remember I used to refer to this person, on her fears, hopes, and desires, as a "whole person." Today I understand "whole" as an attribute of integrated person, someone whose multiple, supposedly universal aspects (cognitive, emotional, social, etc.), those aspects that constitute personhood, are in balance, and that the good education acknowledges them all equally. But then I started to look at it differently, it's not about one person carries all of these attributes and that they all need to be equally developed and interconnected. Every individual experiences her own life from her own unique perspective, that even if it is universal it can never be experienced as such. The psychoanalytic term "subject" invites me to see the person in front of me as unique, separate individual, who may carry those different aspects, but he may as well not.

It challenges me to see myself as a person in and by itself, not merely as a means to others' hopes or despairs This ability for separation enables me to have hopes for my students that are not about me, instead I strive to equip them with the mechanism that will enable them to make the very decisions that are right for them as subjects themselves. Seeing my students as subjects means I see them as individuals whose lived experiences are unique and complex. Being a subject with other subjects is what turns the shared space into an I-Thou. I want to see teacher education programs that stress this aspect.

Yelena: *A program that allows freedom provides future teachers with a sense of an authentic self. Yet, one of the challenges of dialogical education though is that it cannot be one sided.*

Maya: Like Nodding's circle of reciprocity of care.

Yelena: *Exactly. However, it is the responsibility of the teacher to shape the encounter, provide the students with an alternative image of education, and invite them to this type of learning. Eventually, the students will need to decide if they are interested in this type of relationship with the teacher, because dialogical education cannot be coerced. Similarly, dialogical education demands us to re-examine fundamental organizational structures. Dialogical education cannot happen if students sit passively while facing the instructor, or if there are tests and grades, as this perpetuates the hierarchical structure in education.*

Maya: Right! Because again, this structure does not acknowledge the face, thus it doesn't acknowledge a sense of self, a subjectivity to exist. It is a form of oppressive objectification, as it turns all participants into objects, means in an unhuman system.

But I want to return to something important you just mentioned, that dialogue cannot be coerced. A famous Shaw's maxim said "liberty is responsibility hence so many people dread it." Very quickly in life of very few choices to be made by us (while many choices are made for us) we learn that once we make a decision there is always a ripple effect. The idea of students taking an active, participatory role in their learning, often translates to a larger academic requirements, and so they often end up defaulting back to instructor's assignments. Active choices can only happen if students see their learning as meaningful for their whole life, as yet another layer in the process of improving it. Enabling and encouraging active relationships: among learners, between learners and whatever it is they are learning, how they learn, and how they demonstrate their knowledge—all these make learning meaningful because it builds ownership over one's life.

CONCLUSION

In this chapter, we had a dialogue about the nature of dialogue as a way of living, which necessarily includes one's way of teaching and learning as well. We examined two philosophers we deem essential to the development of the term ("dialogue") within the educational discourse, from merely a pedagogy to a way of teaching, learning, and relating with others. We have argued that dialogue as a pedagogy is not merely enough, and in fact cannot be conducted in isolation, that is, as an "island of subjectivity within an ocean of objectifying acts." Here, we have suggested that perceiving all participants in the educational arena as subjects, that is, as individuals with needs, interests, strengths, and weaknesses, is necessary for both teachers' professional—and personal—well-being, and clearly for learners' healthy development. In order for that to happen, we suggest to critically examine our systematic premises with regards to both teachers and learners positions toward each other and toward oneself, calling for a genuine reconstruction of these relationships, toward a healthier, more democratic and dialogical place.

PRACTICAL IMPLICATIONS FOR TEACHERS

As can be found in some unique teachers' education program, and in some schools, structures from which the more traditional, formal models can borrow and benefit. Structures like that embody a dialogical way of being in general and dialogical interaction in particular. Dialogical interactions emphasize the importance of verbalizing one's thoughts, and the necessity of differences, in opinions, in ways of knowing and learning and otherwise. Subsequently, structures like that, when conducted in safe space, enable participants to find their unique voices and develop it. Some suggestions, practical and conceptual, are, for example, expanding/creating places where learners make an independent choice, whether regarding the curriculum, the pedagogy, the mentor/teacher, where and for how long they are going to learn one topic or another. This can be achieved through project-based learning, peer evaluation, self-evaluation, community of learning, mentors instead of "teachers," outside learning, and more. Another important aspect concerns with bringing educational structures to approach its participants as subjects: Through meditation, sharing personal stories, sharing interest, oral narratives and lived experiences, and of course emphasizing creativity in both teaching and evaluating, creativity increases one's vitality and contentment. Empowered, active teachers and learners create an environment that is more conducive for learning and social change.

EXTENSION QUESTIONS

1. Can we separate the different aspects of our lives when participating in life's different contexts? Should we strive for such separation? What are the implications if we do manage to separate? What are the implications if we don't?

2. What are the benefits as well as the weaknesses of dialogical practices for teachers? And for students?

3. The adage goes: True knowledge is self-knowledge. What does it mean for you? Do you think teacher's self-knowledge is necessary for being a good teacher?

4. What are some potential obstacles for dialogical practices in education?

5. In what ways can you implement dialogical practices in your professional settings as a teacher?

EXTENSION THINKING ACTIVITIES

1. On a Scale of 1–5, where 1 means "not relevant at all" and 5 means "essential:" What do you consider necessary for your identity as a teacher:
    *   Your ideas
    *   Your knowledge
    *   Your creativity
    *   The way you think
    *   Your hobbies
    *   Your friendship circle
    *   The curriculum/subject matter I teach
    *   The evaluation method I use
    *   Your students
    *   Your students' parents
    *   Your principle
    *   Your personal space
    *   Being a parent yourself
    *   Your lived experiences
    *   Your educational creed
    *   Your personal history
    *   Your training in a teacher-education program
    *   Your ambitions
    *   Your institution and its leadership/culture

Now determine which of the above is essential to your overall well-being.

2. Critical and Creative Thinking Activity: Describe a world where all interactions are dialogical. What would this world would look like? (If that feels too overwhelming you can focus for now on the educational realm: If education, for toddlers all the way to andragogy, will be genuinely dialogical, what will the education systems look like?)

3. In this chapter, we suggested that there is a crucial relationship between seeing a person as subject, that is, a person (as opposed to seeing a person as an instrument for my life, i.e., an object). We argued that the first step is practicing listening without judgment. The following exercise demonstrates this acquired ability:
    *   Think quietly about something that happened either in the recent past or in your life in general, it has to be something personal: your first love, a bad breakup, your hopes, your deepest fears, something that really hurt you to the bones. In 5–10 minutes think and write it down.
    *   In couples: In 5–10 minutes, tell your story. Partner's role is listening: No questions/comments/sounds are allowed, also try to reduce as much as possible forms of responsive body language. Eye contact is encouraged, as much as possible.

- Alone: each of you write how did it feel to tell your story to someone who didn't respond/how was it to listen without commenting.
- In couples: switch roles.
- Alone: same as before: write down how it felt.
- In couples: in dialogue, share your feelings during the activity.
- Assembly: Did I learn anything new about myself? How do I feel about the feelings I had during the activity? What was especially challenging for me? Was it an interesting experience?

GLOSSARY OF TERMS

Authenticity—the quality of being genuine, truthful to oneself and to one's personal traits, needs, and beliefs.

Dialogue—literally stands for Through (Dia, Gr.) Words (Logos, Gr.). An interaction that aims at exchanging ideas without the purpose of winning an argument, not changing my interlocutor's views, but rather expanding all participants' knowledge and deepening their understanding.

Constructivism—a theory of knowledge according to which knowledge is given to an ongoing democratic processes, as opposed to knowledge as something static, finite, and absolute.

Integrity—to be a person who possesses the quality of integrity means to be a person who acts with accordance to oneself and one's believes and values. This occurs when the different aspects of one's subjectivity are being integrated,

Meaningfulness—an inner compass that allows us to act with a sense of meaning, or toward creating one, within our different practices and lived experiences

Self-knowledge—the virtue of holding the truth—as opposed to false consciousness that is given to social structures—regarding who I am as human in general, and more importantly, as a concrete individual with specific qualities.

Subjectivity—a perspective toward others as human with subjective lived experiences and self-awareness, thus ends by the virtue of being alive, as opposed to perspective that sees others as means to the observer' end.

Wholeness—an approach that perceives humans as complex beings with different aspects: body, mind, spirit/heart, when each entails different needs. What stands behind seeing persons as whole being is attempting to touch upon these different aspects and needs simultaneously, instead of focusing on developing one aspect (e.g., the mind) while ignoring others (e.g., body and spirit).

REFERENCES

Buber, M. (1967). *Between man and man*. New York: Macmillan. (Original work published 1947)

Buber, M. (1970). *I and thou*. New York: Charles Scribner's Sons. (Original work published 1958)

Dewey, J. (1916). *Democracy and education: An introduction to the philosophy of education*. NY: The Free Press.

Drucker, P. F. (1992). The new society of organizations. *Harvard Business Review*, September-October 1992.

Eagleman, D. (2015). Mirroring Others [Television series episode 5]. In D. Hirmes (Producer), The Secret Life of Brain. PBS.

Fenstermacher, G. D. (1999). Teaching on both sides of the classroom door. In K. A. Sirotnik & R. Soder (Eds.), *The beat of a different drummer: Essays on educational renewal in honor of John I. Goodlad* (pp. 185–196). New York: Peter Lang.

Freire, P. (1998). *Teachers as cultural workers: Letters to those who dare to teach*. Boulder, CO: Westview Press.

Freire, P. (2000). *Pedagogy of the Oppressed* 30th Anniversary Edition. Bloomsbury.

Goodlad, J. I. (1991). *Teachers for our nation's schools*. San Francisco: Jossey-Bass.

Lévinas, E. (1985). *Ethics and infinity*. Pittsburgh, PA: Duquesne university press.

Toffler, A. (1984). *The Third Wave*. Bantam, New York.

Toffler, A. (2000). "Life Matters" (Interview). Interview with Norman Swann. Australian Broadcasting Corporation Radio National. Archived from the original on October 20, 2000. Retrieved May 4, 2016.

Vygotsky, L. (2002). *Thought and language*.Cambridge, MA: The MIT Press.

Wexler, P. (1996). *Holy sparks: social theory, education and religion*. New York: St. Martin Press.

DISABILITY AND INCLUSIVE EDUCATION: CHANGING PERSPECTIVES

Susan Baglieri, Daniel Abuabasa, Ellen H. Cahill, LaChan V. Hannon, Justin Matyas, Erika P. Oliveros, David Schwarzer, and Laurie M. Summer

CENTRAL CONCEPTS

Definitions of disability vary across time, place, and context for meaning. **Social models of disability** examine the interplay of sociocultural contexts in order to understand how it is meaningful in varied times and places and to different individuals. **Disability studies** is a transdisciplinary field that examines public policy, medicine and public health, economies, architecture, art and literature, philosophy, religion, science, gender, race, and sexual identity to understand how disability and disabled persons figure into schools and society. The World Health Organization (WHO) describes:

> Disability is "an evolving concept" . . ."disability results from the interaction between persons with impairments and attitudinal and environmental barriers that hinder their full and effective participation in society on an equal basis with others". Defining disability as an interaction means that "disability" is not an attribute of the person. Progress on improving social participation can be made by addressing the barriers which hinder persons with disabilities in their day to day lives. (WHO, 2011, p. 4)

The influence of a social model of disability is clear in the WHO conceptualization. Disability is perceived as an *interaction* between the individual with impaired function *and*

Contributed by Susan Baglieri, Daniel Abuabasa, Ellen H. Cahill, LaChan V. Hannon, Justin Matyas, Erika P. Oliveros, David Schwarzer, and Laurie M. Summer. © Kendall Hunt Publishing Company.

sociocultural factors. Whether a personal characteristic is a barrier to participation in life activities such as school, work, and community participation is dependent on whether a context is **accessible**. Promoting access means to identify and reduce physical and sociocultural barriers to enable the community participation of people who experience disablement.

The concept forwarded by the WHO contrasts with the way that disability is conceptualized in American schools. The *Individuals with Disabilities Education Improvement Act* (2004) is the most recent reauthorization of the USA's national policy guiding the provision of education for children with disabilities. In this policy, first implemented in 1975, a child with a disability is one:

> Who is experiencing developmental delays, as defined by the State and as measured by appropriate diagnostic instruments and procedures, in one or more of the following areas: Physical development, cognitive development, communication development, social or emotional development, or adaptive development; and, Who, by reason thereof, needs special education and related services. (IDEIA, 2004, §300.8)

While the WHO defines disability as interactional, the IDEIA locates disability as measureable *within* the child. In contrast to a social model of disability, a medical model of disability is expressed in the IDEIA. A **medical model of disability** defines disability as a disorder belonging to an individual. The individual body or mind is evaluated using standardized instruments then labeled according to its divergence from a "normal" standard. A course of treatment or intervention is then prescribed for the individual to enable them to achieve more "normal" appearance or function.

The heart of the distinction between social models of disability and medical models of disability is how each informs the response of schools and societies to people with disabilities. Social models aim to reduce physical and sociocultural barriers to create more inclusive societies in which people with disabilities can more easily learn, work, and live within their broader communities. Medical models seek to improve the function of the individual. Social models aim to create worlds to which all may belong; medical models aim to improve individuals so that they may become more acceptable to the world. A contemporary aim of inclusive education is to examine, promote, and practice building design, curriculum design, and teaching techniques that reflect and forward a vision of integrated societies. For many societies around the globe, moving toward inclusivity in schools and communities has required shifts in cultural, political, and economic beliefs and policies that have traditionally allowed the exclusion of children and people with disabilities.

One of the most striking contrasts between medical and social models of disability may be gleaned from comparing early 1900s policies that sought to advance eugenics with contemporary policies that forward civil rights and inclusivity. In the late 1800s, the study of human genetics and **biometrics** was burgeoning in North America and Western Europe (i.e., the "global north"). Heritable or genetic features were inferred from observable characteristics and intelligence tests were introduced. Quantifying and comparing human measurements led statistician Francis Galton to rank and order characteristics, thus leading to a quantifiable—apparently scientific—way to express desirable, "normal," and

	Medical Models	**Social Models**
Building Design and Materials	Provisions are made for individuals with disabilities according to the type and degree of impairment	Places, spaces, and materials that are likely to be adaptable to varied needs are initially designed and selected
Curriculum Design	Learners are offered an individualized curriculum and elective or extra-curricular opportunities correlate with anticipated post-school goals	Learners are offered access to the general curriculum and to similar opportunities that are offered to all students
Instructional Design and Support	Individuals are provided support, accommodations, and modifications, as determined by the type and degree of impairment	Flexible support is offered to any individual who is experiencing difficulty within any given instructional context

nondesirable human features. The concept of eugenics was born. **Eugenics** is the study and promotion of desirable human features through encouraging coupling between "well-born" people in order to further humanity. The flip side was discouraging or preventing those deemed "unfit" from having children. Thirty-three states in the USA created laws that allowed forced sterilization, with institutionalized, "feeble-minded" women the largest group of victims. At the same time, by 1918 all states in the USA instituted compulsory school attendance policies, which aimed to curb child labor, serve as an acculturating force for immigrants, as well as advance the progress of democratic engagement. The influence of eugenics—especially in the proliferation of intelligence testing—created a context in which disabled children could be justifiably excluded or removed from the education that was being made compulsory for others.

Attitudes toward disability would change in the USA and globally over the next decades. The high social status of returning war veterans disabled by battle greatly influenced the way disability was regarded. The unlawfulness of racial segregation marked by *Brown v. Board of Education of Topeka* (1954) would influence the fight for disability rights in education, leading to the 1975 establishment of the policy now known as the *Individuals with Disabilities Education Improvement Act* (2004), which guarantees a public education to children with disabilities. In 1990, UNESCO commenced the *World Declaration on Education for All* (EFA). The declaration forwards the importance of education to advance global interests and quality of life and names inclusion of groups who have been historically left out of education as integral to the its work. The table below offers an overview of key ideas and policies that characterize societal views and responses to disability at the publication of the example texts that are described in the next section.

	Dominant Global Views	U.S./Global North Context	Understanding of the Phenomenon
The Kallikak Family (1912)	Disability is a moral condition related to sin or moral lapse of the individual or kin. Disability is expression of divine will or a test of faith Responses to disability vary widely among region and cultures	Compulsory education Nativism, racism, and Protestantism USA Court rulings allow schools to expel children because they are disabled (*Watson v. City of Cambridge*, 1893; *Beattie v. Board of Education,* 1919)	Eugenics: • Involuntary sterilization laws are enacted in 33 states (1907–1930). Until 1950, 50,707 sterilizations had been performed
Salamanca Statement and Framework (1994)	1990: World Declaration on Education for All (UNESCO) 2000: Dakar Framework for Action 2007: United Nations' sweeping statement on human rights and disability, *Convention on the Rights of Persons with Disabilities*, is opened for signatures As of 2017, 160 nations are signatories on the convention (United Nations Treaty Collection, 2017)	1945: Forced sterilization and experimentation on disabled persons carried out during the Holocaust are globally decried as war crimes during the Nuremberg Trials 1975: First iteration of the *Individuals with Disabilities Education Act* asserts right to public education for students with disabilities 1990: *Americans with Disabilities Act* prohibits discrimination	Disability as a moral condition remains the most prevalent view worldwide As of 2017, human rights and antidiscrimination policies specific to disability are present in over 80 nations. More than 150 nations include disability rights or protections as part of their constitutions.

TOWARD INCLUSIVE SCHOOLS AND SOCIETIES: INTRODUCING EXAMPLE TEXTS

This section introduces changing societal beliefs about disability exemplified by the 1912 publication of Henry H. Goddard's 1912 study, *The Kallikak family,* and UNESCO's 1994 *Salamanca Statement and Framework for Action on Special Needs Education.* Goddard's study of "The Kallikak family" does not mark the beginning of disability in society, nor is it the advent of schools for children with disabilities. It emerged, however, in a cultural milieu that gave it influence on immigration policy, education, and public health in the USA and beyond.

Goddard was Director of Research at the Vineland Training School for Feeble-Minded Girls and Boys in the USA from 1906 to 1918. Institutions for the "feeble-minded" were places that people were sent for a range of reasons and offenses—from not being able to care for oneself or hold a job, to prostitution, having syphilis or epilepsy. Goddard's research into feeble-mindedness, education, and eugenics led to his writing on the Kallikak family. *Kallikak* is an extensive case study that documents the life and lineage of one of Vineland's residents, "Deborah Kallikak," in order to make an argument for the heritability of feeble-mindedness. He recommends identification and containment of a class of "morons" demonstrated to be genetically unfit for public life. The work is a most extreme example of a medical model of disability. Individuals are labeled as disabled using protocols deemed scientific and then removed from communities to receive specialized treatment and preserve personal and public safety. The methodology of the study was steadily discredited and by 1928 Goddard recanted his findings and stated his belief for the educability of "morons" and against their segregation into institutions. Despite his renouncement, however, the story of the Kallikak family persisted and "functioned as a primal myth of the eugenics movement for several decades" (Gould, 1996, p. 198).

Excerpt from *The Kallikak family* (1912)

https://archive.org/stream/TheKallikakFamily?ref=ol#page/n23/mode/2up

This is a typical illustration of the mentality of a high grade feeble-minded person, the moron, the delinquent, the kind of girl or woman that fills our reformatories. They are wayward, they get into all sorts of trouble and difficulties, sexually and otherwise, and yet we have been accustomed to account for their defects on the basis of viciousness, environment, or ignorance. It is also the history of the same type of girl in the public school. Rather good-looking, bright in appearance, with many attractive ways, the teacher clings to the hope, indeed insists, that such a girl will come out all right. Our work with Deborah convinces us that such hopes are delusions . . . She has been persistently trained since she was eight years old, and yet nothing has been accomplished in the direction of higher intelligence or general education. Today if this young woman were to leave the Institution, she would at once become a prey to the designs of evil men or evil women and would lead a life that would be vicious, immoral, and criminal . . . she has no power of control, and all her instincts and appetites are in the direction that would lead to vice.

Eight-two years after Goddard's study and shortly after the 1990 Education for All declaration, the World Conference on Special Needs Education adopted the *Salamanca Statement and Framework for Action on Special Needs Education* in 1994. The intent of the document was to reaffirm the commitment of the ninety-two governments in attendance to the EFA and layout provisions and recommendations to guide the global development and reform of education for students with disabilities. It is "Arguably the most significant international document that has ever appeared in the special needs field" (Ainscow & Sandill, 2010, p. 401).

Many nations, by 1994, had implemented policies to enable children with disabilities access to "special education," as in the United States, or "Special Educational Needs" (SEN)

> Excerpt from *The Salamanca Statement* (1994):
>
> http://www.unesco.org/education/pdf/SALAMA_E.PDF
>
> . . . regular schools with this inclusive orientation are the most effective means of combating discriminatory attitudes, creating welcoming communities, building an inclusive society and achieving education for all; moreover, they provide an effective education to the majority of children and improve the efficiency and ultimately the cost-effectiveness of the entire education system.
>
> A change in social perspective is imperative. For far too long, the problems of people with disabilities have been compounded by a disabling society that has focused upon their impairments rather than their potential.
>
> Special needs education incorporates the proven principles of sound pedagogy from which all children may benefit. It assumes that human differences are normal and that learning must accordingly be adapted to the needs of the child rather than the child fitted to preordained assumptions regarding the pace and nature of the learning process.

provisions, as in the UK. The particular emphasis of Salamanca on *inclusive* education as a means to create antidiscriminatory communities that are welcoming to people with disabilities, however, makes it a clear example of views associated with social models of disability. Aims of the *Salamanca Statement* extend beyond merely improving the quality of or access to education for children with disabilities and also understand systems of education and schools as places through which societal attitudes and contexts are shaped. *Salamanca*'s ambitious goals for social and cultural change in disability strive toward an ideal of inclusivity that is not stated in U.S. educational policy.

The authors of this chapter, who hold differing identities, experiences, and orientations to education, gathered to engage in discussion on the ideas presented in *The Kallikak family* and *The Salamanca Statement*. Our two-hour discussion produced 17,000 transcribed words from which emerged varied perspectives drawn from our experiences as teachers, parents, school specialists, researchers, and students and professors of teacher education. We present a thematic organization of key points of dialogue to highlight our impressions of reading *Kallikak* and contemplation of *Salamanca*'s vision of inclusive education.

HOW CAN WE READ *THE KALLIKAK FAMILY* THROUGH A CONTEMPORARY LENS?

Terms such as "idiot" and "moron" that are now used as taunts and epithets to denigrate people's intellect were once scientific categories used to describe people with intellectual disabilities. Although terms for how we describe disability have changed, we raise questions as to whether practices and beliefs have changed despite different contemporary vocabularies to describe disability.

Susan: The modern era of public education in the United States developed in a sociocultural context that excluded children with disabilities and justified those decisions through **scientism**, as are exemplified in the *Kallikak* writing.

Ellen: Goddard described the earliest identification of disabled children based on heredity and recommended separation from society because they were a burden and expense, and argued that there was no way they could rise above it.

Laurie: While reading Goddard I kept underlining the language being used and all the other words he used for labeling feeble-minded people—moron, imbeciles, idiots. He brought in immorality and poverty, heredity and intellectual capacity and he tied it all together. Toward the end of the document he admitted that he couldn't *prove* that criminality was related to disability, but argued that it must be. Considering the work that I do evaluating students as a speech language pathologist and working with special education documents, it almost looked like a caricature of what is being done now—judging children and in some ways using very subjective judgments and trying to make them scientific. It was really like looking at a caricature of the work that I'm involved in with special education. It was insightful yet disturbing in a lot of ways. I still see the effects of eugenics. In current rhetoric of ridding the United States of immigrants, the argument is, "They are criminals, they are terrorists," yet statistically they are not. The idea of making someone "other" and proclaiming it is good for society is still present.

LaChan: While reading and working through the language Goddard used for disability, I found myself saying, "I hope he doesn't talk about race; I hope he doesn't talk about race," hoping it wouldn't talk about race because I just knew if he was saying this about other White people I could only imagine what they were thinking about brown people.

Susan: Contemporary readings of Goddard are challenging because of the dehumanizing character that words such as feeble-minded, moron, imbecile, and idiot eventually took on. It is important to read these ideas about disability in relation to other marginalized groups. Eugenics *is* a social practice. The characteristics and notion of intelligence deemed desirable were those associated with White men of Western European descent. As Gould (1996) extensively describes, biometrics, including the rise of intelligence testing, served the purpose of comparing Caucasian qualities to those of people from other regions in order to illustrate the inherent inferiority of those the Western European/North American world sought to exclude, enslave, exploit, or colonize. That White, protestant men were most successful in the Western world transformed from a situation reflective of White supremacy and privileged social class to a *scientifically* ordained destiny through biometrics. Goddard popularized the concept and term, "moron," largely through the Kallikak study. It was his intent to create a language and classification system to describe a new class of inferior "others" that rationalized poverty and social injustice. This is the legacy of the medical model of disability that was propelled by Goddard and other thinkers of his time. Is it only the terms that are repellent or the ideas about people at work in them?

David: I believe we are still doing what Goddard describes today, to students at the end of the disability spectrum. Maybe we do not do it to 95% of students, but for 5%, we still do it. We have regional schools that we dump kids into.

Laurie: I do not think we can look at this study and say we are beyond its ideas about people. I believe his work informs what our practices look like today. But I would say that changing the words that we use leads to changes in our thinking.

Susan: We still label the folks Goddard was writing about. Moron, imbecile, and idiot became—in education—"educable," "trainable," and "profoundly" mentally retarded, which then became "mild," "moderate," and "severe" intellectual disability.

LaChan: It seems like in changing terms we are sanitizing or medicalizing. We are just trying to appease whomever is uncomfortable with the words. Having a child with autism, I have lived through his name change. I'll keep autism—it's fine with me.

Daniel: In changing words I think we are changing from that tradition to what society would want us to do. I think changing the words is a good thing. The words themselves don't change it, you have to change the definitions of them.

Laurie: I think there is a huge difference in "**neurodiversity**" and "moron" and "feeble-minded." It does not mean that the person using the words has changed their thinking, but over time changing the language can change the framework of thinking for many people.

LaChan: The section on community in the *Salamanca Statement* relates to the importance of personal narrative and the importance of choosing an identity that reflects how you identify and not letting others choose that for you. Considering how people identify themselves and being respectful of that is an important part of community engagement in inclusive education.

Two questions raised in the discussion are: (1) Do beliefs about people change as words used to describe them change? (2) Do the ideas about intelligence as innate and scientifically measureable advanced in eugenics still influence our educational practices? Some see changes in terminology as reflecting contemporary beliefs about disability and promising to lead change in how we think about disability and attend to individuals' understanding of self. Others perceive the use of different words as a continuation of medicalization, in which new vocabularies do not change the beliefs and practices that justify the marginality of people with disabilities through labeling.

WHAT ARE CHALLENGES TO CREATING INCLUSIVE EDUCATION?

The Salamanca Statement of 1994 portrays inclusive education as the right of all children to seek personal betterment and academic achievement in schools. The argument that children with and without disabilities are best served by integrated education in "regular" schools calls societies to critically examine the ways that cultural attitudes toward disability have allowed for discrimination or marginalization of children with disabilities in education. Societal change toward inclusive education seeks to reform educational practices that have led to poor outcomes for children with disabilities. Special education—as practiced in the United States—is plagued by persisting achievement gaps between students with and without disabilities, with little evidence that education received in specialized settings accelerates or equalizes academic progress on a national scale (Artiles, Kozleski, Trent, Osher, & Ortiz, 2010). Inclusive reform strives to re-think practices that do not appear to improve the national portrait of educational progress, while also promoting broader community inclusion as new generations of young people experience integration, rather than segregation, as the norm. Our experiences of inclusive practices in the United States exemplify the massive effort required to move toward inclusive school reform in a system that has long practiced special education as a system separate from regular education.

Laurie: Although the *Salamanca Statement* included a lot of good ideas about the development of inclusive schools, the question is always, "how?"

Daniel: I find that the American system has special education classrooms different from regular education. Some of the students, when placed in the inclusion classes they have in my school, do not benefit. If you have a separate classroom for students with disabilities and a trained teacher for them, *then* you give education equality. That is my experience. I think the American system is trying to do what the Statement recommends, but it is not always beneficial.

Laurie: Teachers who I work with who do not want students with disabilities in their classrooms say they do not have support for their educational needs. They have an intensely rigid curriculum and standardized testing to deal with. They feel like having students with disabilities is one more thing put on them.

Ellen: Teachers feel very defeated by policy.

Daniel: I feel sometimes that my kids are not learning anything in the classroom. I teach mathematics and we have unit assessments, so you have the curriculum to cover for the unit assessment. Usually we have five assessments, but they reduced it to four in my inclusion class. So I teach to the level of my students, but the unit assessment wants me to "cover" everything, too, so I realized that they are not learning anything. Then they are going to use the students' score on the test to assess my teaching.

Susan: I wonder if developing schooling systems with inclusive values from the start is easier than trying to reform a system that is already in place?

LaChan: In the USA's separate system of regular education and special education, we are not preparing teachers to teach all students in the ways we could. We are saying these students' needs are outside your wheelhouse—you need a specialist for this. We are not preparing general education teachers to work with *all* kids. Although we are saying we are creating inclusive environments, teachers are ill prepared. We are giving the teachers half of what they need. There is tension between the roles of the regular education teacher and special education teacher, which leads to a crisis between what each is supposed to do because we have separated their roles.

Erika: In my work in postsecondary education, students do not get support unless they come with documentation of disability. Some professors wonder why they were not in special education in earlier education. They do not realize that parents with less **social or cultural capital** may not know the rights of their children to be evaluated for special education.

Susan: In this example, access to support for learning is restricted by the requirement of having a disability label. We can refer back to the influence of Goddard's ideas and a medical model here. Do you think that some children—by virtue of disability—are more deserving of support for learning? If we imagine child-centered pedagogy as emanating from the individual strengths and needs of each child, as Salamanca suggests, why wouldn't learning support be available for all children? Why do we see disability as such a different category of need than other ways that children are different from one another?

Ellen: People have expressed ideas for so long about community-oriented education and child-centered curriculum and argue that this is what we should be doing for *all* children, but nobody does it. It doesn't change. I find in education that we have an idea and then it is sort of done and sort of not done. There's always a way around doing it the way it was meant to be done.

LaChan: What is the purpose of schooling? Is it for democracy? Is it for social mobility? I think that has everything to do with asking, "who benefits from school change?" What company benefits? What new innovative technology tycoon benefits? The reasons we have for education will dictate how we are creating schools, how we finance them, and who benefits from them.

Daniel: Capitalism has eaten too much of American society. We lose sight of justice; we just chase the money. It is benefitting an individual but not the society.

Laurie: I don't think there is anything wrong with parents or students inherently wanting schooling to improve their lives, but I think there's a problem with opportunity for all.

Ellen: What if, in capitalist competition, the only way for my child to win means that your child loses?

We raise a wide range of observations about challenges to realizing inclusive practice in the United States. Accepting that difference among children is not a rationale for separation in schools must lead to critical analysis of the many facets of school practices that have been built on the presumption of segregation. Teachers are not all prepared to consider the needs of students with disabilities. Standardization of curriculum and testing instantiates an expected norm for student performance and teachers' performances are evaluated by the number of students meeting these norms. The privilege of the "normal" student in schools is reinforced by a capitalist system that equates school success with later economic potential, thus pitting students against one another in competition. Moving toward inclusive education requires significant reform efforts in how societies conceive of human difference and the role of education for individuals and communities. Medical models of disability that understand people with disabilities to be individually deficient allow "regular" society to ignore their systematic marginality; it is presumed that their life conditions are related to their personal defects. Social models of disability ask communities to examine how educational, political, and economic systems create or even insist upon exclusion. If teacher preparation, teacher evaluation, and student achievement are narrowly conceived to continue to emphasize single and standardized measures of success, the system of education continues to incentivize exclusion, rather than enforce a value for inclusion.

THINKING INCLUSIVELY: RECOMMENDATIONS FOR TEACHERS

Moving toward inclusive education requires societal reform in how we understand the roles of schools in society, the ways we prepare teachers, and the ways we gauge student success. What, then, are the roles of individual teachers in this work toward building inclusive schools and communities?

Laurie: We have a tangled ball of wants and hopes for education. A lot of our values are subconscious and implicit. Critical consciousness is necessary to make our values explicit. There is not a lot of stepping back and thinking. Instead, we respond to new initiatives asking, "what do we have to do?" We comply; we conform. There is not a lot of stepping back from the system to critique the system and ask, "Is this a reflection of our values related to the purposes of school or disability?"

LaChan: Reflection requires a safe space to step back. Educational leaders must be intentional about their own reflection, as well as create spaces for teachers to reflect. Teacher education programs also have to be intentional about how they encourage reflection for students while they are in programs, but also communicate ways that teachers can be intentional about their reflection when they are in their jobs.

Erika: A positive thing in incorporating the community, as recommended in the *Salamanca Statement*, is being able to help parents—especially those with less cultural capital—know how special education works. Getting to know students as individuals enables teachers to focus on their strengths and not just weaknesses.

LaChan: Teachers should also get to know students' parents. Even just one interview can help.

Laurie: I wish we could give these documents to teachers and administrators and use them as critical thinking tools for their practice.

Steps that teachers can take include seeking their own critical awareness and engaging in reflective practice that attends to disability. We provide extension questions that invite readers to begin reflection on disability. As we, as teachers, see working with students with disabilities as an expected part of our work, we can seek personal and professional development related to disability. We can build strong relationships with parents and families to gain understanding of students' hopes and needs with fuller awareness of how education can differently impact individuals. In short, a first step is seeing ourselves as teachers of all *students and understanding that learning to teach is an ongoing journey of professional growth informed by our efforts to understand each student in their complexity.*

CONCLUSION

Our dialogue raises questions about disability and schooling emerging from our reading of *The Kallikak family* and *Salamanca Statement*. Intersections among disability, race, and class, the impact of economic systems and educational policy, and aims for teacher education and professional development are all factors that shape national and global values that impact our will and ability to construct inclusive schools and societies. Inclusive education is here proposed as a value system that teachers can strive to realize through intentional reflection on past and present perspectives on disability and difference toward the development of affirming responses to all children, families, and communities. Works, such as *Disability and the Politics of Education* (Gabel & Danforth, 2008) and *Inclusive Education: Twenty Years After Salamanca* (Kiuppis & Hausstatter, 2015), offer portraits of nations around the globe that are seeking inclusive education. Work toward inclusive education is a worldwide effort that is increasingly coherent in its aims since the *Salamanca Statement*.

EXTENSION QUESTIONS

1. How do social and medical models of disability seem evident in your personal experiences or educational studies?

2. What personal beliefs and values about education and disability impact your understanding and practice of inclusive education?

3. The book *Disability and the Politics of Education* (Gabel & Danforth, 2008) offers an overview of global contexts that illustrate varied ways that nations strive toward inclusivity. *Inclusive Education in Italy* (2012) by D'Alessio is an analysis of the title nation's frequently touted model. Explore the ideas in these works for ideas about how to seek inclusivity in school policy and practice.

REFERENCES

Ainscow, M., & Sandill, A. (2010). Developing inclusive education systems: the role of organisational cultures and leadership. *International Journal of Inclusive Education, 14(4),* 401–416. http://dx.doi.org/10.1080/13603110802504903

Artiles, A. J., Kozleski, E. B., Trent, S. C., Osher, D. & Ortiz, A. (2010). Justifying and explaining disproportionality 1968–2008: A critique of underlying views of culture. *Exceptional children,* 76(3), 279–299. https://doi.org/10.1177/001440291007600303

D'Alession, S. (2012). *Inclusive education in Italy: A critical analysis of the policy of Integrazione Scolastica.* Rotterdam: Sense.

Gabel, S.L. & Danforth, S. (Eds.). (2008). *Disability and the politics of education: An international reader.* New York: Peter Lang.

Goddard, H. H. (1912). *The Kallikak family: A study in the heredity of feeble-mindedness.* Macmillan Company.

Gould, S. J. (1996). *The mismeasure of man* (Revised). New York: W.W. Norton & Co.

Individuals with Disabilities Education Improvement Act, H.R. 1350, 108th Congress (2004).

Kiuppis, F. & Hausstatter, R.S. (Eds.) (2015). *Inclusive education: Twenty years after Salamanca.* New York: Peter Lang.

UNESCO. (1990). *World declaration on education for all and framework for action to meet basic learning needs.* Adopted by the World Conference on Education for All, Jomtien, Thailand, March 5–9. Retrieved from http://unesdoc.unesco.org/images/0012/001275/127583e.pdf

UNESCO. (1994). *The Salamanca statement and framework for action on special needs education.* Adopted by the World Conference On Special Needs Education, Salamanca, Spain, June 7–10. UNESCO. Retrieved from http://www.unesco.org/education/pdf/SALAMA_E.PDF

United Nations. (2017, August 10). *United Nations Treaty Collection.* Retrieved from https://treaties.un.org/pages/ViewDetails.aspx?src=IND&mtdsg_no=IV-15&chapter=4&clang=_en

World Health Organization. (2011). *World report on disability.* Geneva: WHO. Retrieved from http://www.who.int/disabilities/world_report/2011/report.pdf

GLOSSARY OF TERMS

Accessible/accessibility—refers to the design of physical and attitudinal environments, products, and services that ensures or increases usability for people with disabilities.

Biometrics—the measurement and statistical analysis of physical, behavioral, or cognitive characteristics.

Cultural capital—a sociological concept that describes nontangible social assets of a person that promote social mobility in a stratified society. Assets that act as capital may relate to knowledge, education, or style of speech, for example.

Disability studies—an interdisciplinary academic discipline that examines disability and experiences of disabled people in social and cultural dimensions.

Eugenics—a term coined by Francis Galton derived from the Greek term for "well born." Beliefs and practices that seek to shape the genetic quality of the human population by controlling reproduction. Eugenics is often associated with concepts such as biological determinism and social Darwinism.

Medical model of disability—understandings of disability that emphasize pathology of impairment in order to cure or manage a disorder through clinical treatment of the individual.

Neurodiversity—conceptualization of the range of difference in learning and behavior associated with the brain as natural, "normal," and expected variations.

Scientism—excessive belief in the power of scientific knowledge and techniques.

Social capital—value that comes from social networks, or groupings of people, which allow individuals to achieve things they could not on their own. It relates to actual and potential access to social networks established by acquaintance (i.e., people you know) or recognition of membership (i.e., people who think you are like them).

Social models of disability—various approaches to understanding disability as experiences and identities that are characterized by social, cultural, and environmental factors that restrict or enable people with extraordinary bodies to participate in community life.

12

WHAT TO MEASURE AND HOW TO MEASURE STUDENT LEARNING: UNDERSTANDING THE CONTEXT OF CLASSROOM DATA AND ASSESSMENT

CHARITY DACEY
TAMMY MILLS

INTRODUCTION

In this chapter, we explore how educational research has shaped teachers' classroom assessment practices via a dialogic exploration using two primary documents. The two documents, Cronbach's 1957 presidential address to the American Psychological Association (APA) and Black and Wiliam's 1998 literature review of classroom assessment practices, are set about 40 years apart and denote pivotal moments in the history and philosophy of testing and accountability within the context of larger social movements taking place in the country. Over the span of 40 years, these two major documents influenced how teachers thought and planned for classroom assessments. Cronbach's (1957) groundbreaking presidential address to the APA was the first to connect the theories and research on learning and the assessment of individual differences in cognitive abilities. He set out to bring testing from lab contexts of experimental psychologists to natural settings such as classrooms using correlational means. However, while he promoted testing in natural setting using correlational methods, Cronbach's focus of assessment still privileged a scientific view of the measurement of learning. That is, he promoted the idea that learning was cognitive act that could be quantified and measured through testing as long as the test was valid, reliable, and created by psychologists and researchers, not teachers. The questions remain, what progress was made in the 40 years since Cronbach's address related to classroom assessment practices? What were the influences of the larger social movements on that progress? A look at Black and Wiliam's (1998) literature review of classroom assessment practices within a historical context provides us with some answers. There are a number of important aspects to examine more closely in these pivotal works, yet prior to exploring them, first consider the following questions:

1. How as a classroom teacher might you determine your tests will measure what you intend them to measure (the construct validity of an assessment)? How will you know?

2. What are your strengths and weaknesses as a learner and how have you identified and utilized strategies during your education to capitalize on the strengths and manage and improve on your development areas?

3. As a future teacher, what are the advantages of utilizing self-assessments with your students and how can you envision making self-assessment an important classroom routine in the teaching and learning process?

4. Since the feedback you provide to students about how to improve is essential, what are some effective aspects of giving good feedback that you have experienced or witnessed in your own educational program?

5. Why is it important to avoid comparisons between students when providing feedback about performance or areas for improvement that involve particular qualities?

THE SHIFTING HISTORICAL CONTEXT OF CLASSROOM ASSESSMENT

Black and Wiliam (1998) conceptualized assessment as a *process* engaged in by teachers and students that includes goal setting, questioning, and a great deal of feedback. They did not view assessment as evaluating individual capabilities by outside researchers as proposed by Cronbach (1957). To help contextualize this shift, classroom data and assessment must be examined in relation to the broader social, political, and international events for the 40-year time span from 1957 to 1998. Below, a few pivotal events are highlighted that had either major theoretical or practice implications for teachers and students in K-12 classrooms. The following brief review of the evolution of testing also provides the historical groundwork, contextualizes the importance of classroom data and assessment, and clarifies the contributions of, and tensions between, what Cronbach (1957) proposed and the practices espoused by Black and Wiliam (1998).

	Global	National	Educational Policies	Understanding of Phenomena
Cronbach (1957) Primary focus is intelligence and aptitude	• World War II ends (soldiers return) • Sputnik (1957) • Expansion of universities Cold War: concerns of spreading of communism Formation of the United Nations • Bruner (1960) published *The Process of Education*	Alfred Binet (1908) developed a screening tool for the army First SAT developed (1926) Post-war competition for jobs; returning soldiers reclaimed leadership positions from women Sorting economic class/social stratification Means to restore American dominance and preeminence	A *Nation at Risk* called for an increase in academic rigor (1983) from the National Commission on Excellence in Education Common Core focus Americans with Disability Act (ADA) Mandatory, Basic Skills testing, SAT, ACT • Race to the top	• United the disciplines of scientific psychology and experimental psychology. • Proposed linking theories and research on learning and instruction with the tradition of assessing individual differences in cognitive abilities. • American Psychological Association (APA) interest in studying learning differences in context
Black & Wiliam (1998) So-called *21st-century skills* emphasizing higher-order thinking and deeper learning	Sorting for a knowledge economy instead of mechanical production Multimedia and technology boom Global interconnectivity	Dewey becomes the face of progressive education (1928) Expectations of college attendance expansion Increase focus on secondary education access Civil rights movement/shifting definitions of equality	Title IX provided tangible consequences for discrimination in sports Education for all Handicapped Children Act/ Least Restrictive Environment *No Child Left Behind Act* (2001) represents public demand for wide-scale assessment	Formative assessment is characterized not as a test, but rather a process engaged in by teachers and students (goal setting, questioning, feedback) Expansion of definition of assessment beyond traditional tests to focus on the student and student learning

EMERGING TENSIONS BETWEEN TRADITIONAL TESTING AND THE PROGRESSIVE APPROACH

In 1908, Alfred Binet developed a way to screen recruits for the army that was further refined and developed into a multiple-choice test primarily used to determine intelligence quotient (IQ) for the purpose of screening and categorizing individuals (Peterson, 1925). The National Intelligence Test was revised and adapted for many venues in subsequent years and applied in school settings and work environments (Freeman, 1926). Then, roughly twenty years later in 1926, the first SAT test was developed. Colleges and universities began to use the SAT for admissions criteria in addition to making predictions about students' abilities to succeed, a decision that was controversial from the start. The creation and use of the SAT created an assessment context characterized by the use of *norm referenced*, standardized tests used to measure students' intelligence for educational and various sorting purposes.

Conversely, a competing progressive education movement picked up momentum. Based on the pragmatist theories of William James, progressives, such as John Dewey, believed that educators should focus on problem solving, thinking over memorization, and experimental, purpose-driven education. These ideas pushed against the more authoritarian, preordained teaching of traditional education that was concerned with *delivering knowledge*, rather than *understanding students' real experiences* (Ravitch, 1983). Rather than focus on using measures in education such as the IQ test or the SAT, William James' pragmatist theories emphasized instead the mind as an instrument for realizing purposes, a radically different focus for educational assessment. The reason for assessment was to evaluate whether students were realizing their potential, becoming a fully developed human being (Rocheleau, 2004).

POST-WORLD WAR II: SHIFTING MOBILITY AND ACCESS TO EDUCATION

Generalizing about postwar schools in America is complicated by their size, complexity, and diversity. However, the postwar tensions that framed the national and the international milieu of the 1950s influenced education widely. While there were more opportunities for women to take advanced courses in high schools and colleges when soldiers were serving in the military, as soldiers returned, many women were forced to relinquish positions of leadership in education, at the classroom, school and district level as superintendents (Blount, 1998). The baby boom and postwar expansion of the middle class prompted the notion that most children *should* and *will* go to college, a socially constructed shift in attitude and belief about higher education, away from earlier notions that only the powerful and privileged had access to elite educational opportunities. This notion, that more students should have access to higher education, increased the pressure, and focus on the reliance of standardized testing as system of sorting and categorizing students into particular colleges and universities and as a method of predicting their future success.

In 1957, at the height of the Cold War, the Soviets launched Sputnik, spreading fear throughout the United States regarding the loss the "space race" and placing blame at the feet of the educational system. Postwar competition produced the STEM movement, a focus on reforming the curriculum of science, technology, engineering, and math and a move to privileging curriculum and testing, positioning the teacher as deliverer rather than decision maker in the classroom. Concurrently, the historic case of *Brown v. Topeka Board of Education* (1954) caused a seismic a shift in schools across the country as people questioned the definitions of racial equality. Dismantling segregated public schools was resisted by much of the United States located in the south, despite the moral authority leaders' call to disrupt the racial, economic class, and social stratification by seemingly objective criteria.

Amidst this global backdrop of post-WWII tensions and a national landscape of social stratification and shifting definitions of equality, Cronbach (1957) delivered his speech to the APA. Cronbach (1957) made a compelling case for establishing and following guidelines to ensure critical questioning, rigorous methods, and reliability whenever developing or using psychological tests. At the heart of Cronbach's work (1957) and work with his colleague Meehl (1955) was the question of whether students performed consistently and reliably on psychological and educational assessments. Cronbach (1957) created an opening for psychologists, test developers, and researchers to develop other types of assessments to be used for an array of purposes beyond simply sorting people into categories based on perceived intelligence or ability, but he did not believe teachers had the expertise to be involved in the field of scientific measurement and that schools should be assessing students' learning scientifically. In this way, Cronbach's speech represented the mindset of the time that placed emphasis and importance on researchers and psychologists, rather than teachers, as experts in education and in the field of assessment. Just a few years later Bruner's (1960) influential book *The Process of Education,* punctuated Cronbach's sentiment in which he essentially advocated bypassing the teacher, placing emphasis on the importance of the researcher as the educational expert.

INCREASED CONNECTIVITY AND GOVERNMENT INVOLVEMENT IN EDUCATION

At the same point in history, the governmental role in education expanded. This top-down, versus bottom-up approach, to reform in education was evident when President Johnson passed The Elementary and Secondary Education Act (ESEA) in 1965. The same year President Johnson instituted the Higher Education Act to provide scholarships and students loans, allowing increased access to college education for students from working-class backgrounds. The National Teacher Corps was established (a precursor to Teach for America) and desegregation of schools was made a priority. As the 1970s began under the Nixon administration, Title IX provided tangible consequences for gender discrimination in sports and the Education for All Handicapped Children Act ensured Least Restrictive Environments for students with disabilities. These events signaled a shift, whereby learning experiences for students in local classrooms were influenced as much by broad national policies as much as by decision made by their teachers who directly influenced their learning. As educational access and opportunities were more available to a wide a variety of students from myriad backgrounds, accountability pressures increased to show how schools measured up to one another in the race to meet the demands of offering high-quality education. There were implications for states and national testing for public schools as the assessment landscape shifted in response.

A consequence can be seen as a different type of testing gained a foothold in the 1970s in response to the progressive, educational policies instituted by Johnson and Nixon administrations. In the past, educators relied on *norm-referenced* testing. However, John Dewey and the progressive movement had long advocated for a standards-based model of education in which student learning is aimed at achieving specific outcomes, and academic success is determined by comparing students to a predetermined outcome, not to each other. This type of assessment is referred to as *criterion-referenced testing*. Educational leaders began to experiment, advocating for the establishment of specific standards to be met by students in the learning process. Gaining momentum, in theory, during this era was the notion that (1) teachers should use rigorous academic standards when planning classroom instruction and assessments, and (2) if students failed to reach these standards, teachers should pursue alternative strategies to ensure students meet learning objectives.

As we have seen, from the 1950s through the 1980s, the civil rights movement led to more integrated classrooms; open classrooms were beginning to form in particular places; school choice gained in popularity; and special education gained in significance. However, in spite of this evidence of progressive reform, the foundational aspects of schools and schooling remained unchanged. The progressive reform in terms of assessment remained at the surface level. While some schools were experimenting with student-centered assessment practices, most students and teachers still focused on covering content of textbooks, workbooks, and supplementary reading materials, and standardized tests were still used to group students by ability and to measure student achievement. In fact, schools resembled the structure and practice of many decades prior to the 1950s. Hope of progressive reforms taking hold and influencing true change was dashed with upcoming decades of 1980s and beyond.

An influential report on declining SAT scores was circulated in important circles in 1977, creating anxiety among leaders and policy makers. The publication of *A Nation At Risk* further punctuated this panic five years later in 1983. The overarching message was the United States was falling behind on the world stage. More accountability and tougher standards were the proposed solutions for the concerns shared by many and expressed by government officials and the public that the U.S. educational system was not keeping pace with competitors internationally (Gardner, 1983). As a response, government leaders formed task forces to strategize about how to improve global standings and explain how to correct the perceived sharp decline in student achievement (Schwartz & Robinson, 2000). A back-to-basics approach was the preferred solution, swinging the pendulum sharply away from progressive education. This new back-to-basics approach included an increased focus on testing and a common curriculum for all students and a way that their learning could be scientifically measured, by psychologists, not teachers. In 1993, the Massachusetts Education

Reform Act decreed the first statewide common curriculum and statewide, standardized tests. The emphasis on a common curriculum and subsequent testing allowed textbook publishers to take charge of designing scripted curricula, creating partner texts, and developing aligned, standardized tests.

Additionally, global interconnectivity increasingly became a reality in the 1990s. The emphasis on mechanical production shifted to sorting for a knowledge economy, and the multimedia and technology boom changed the nature of communication and education. Nationally, political leaders called for 21st-century skills, emphasizing higher-order thinking and deeper learning as a means to restoring American dominance and preeminence, leading to increased expectations for college attendance expansion and an increased focus on secondary education access. Notably, *A Nation At Risk* also set in motion a plethora of federal and state inquiries and attempts to assess teacher quality as a means to improve education overall, sparking the emergence of accountability-focused assessments for students, teachers, and schools. *Accountability-focused assessments* are designed to evaluate teacher, school, or program effectiveness, and can be used to determine student readiness for entrance, promotion, or graduation at any educational level (Conway, Goodell, and Carl, 2001). In 2001, No Child Left Behind was passed, reauthorizing the ESES Act of 1965, holding schools accountable for the achievement of their students. Schools were penalized if students did not meet adequate yearly progress, standards set by the federal Department of Education. It is in this context that the framework emerged for initiatives such as the Common Core State Standards Initiative (2010).

As the use of accountability-focused measures continued to build momentum, some assessment researchers associated with the APA also incrementally addressed educational reform and advocated for a shift in focus *away* from teaching, and *to* learning, the needs of learners, learning differences, the learning process, and how learners make sense of the world around them (e.g. Bartolome, 1994; Noddings, 1995; McCombs, 2003). Students were exposed to multiple means of assessment and some teachers employed a *constructivist learning approach to instruction that honors and respects students' perspectives.* Based on the notion that knowledge is socially constructed among students, this approach encourages teachers to provide students with opportunities to learn within classroom environments that support social interactions. Thus, while school administrators still relied on norm-referenced tests to determine student progress and the progress of their school as a whole, teachers were more likely to consider incorporating the use of criterion-referenced tests, portfolios, and rubrics to measure students' progress toward determined criteria. In some cases, teachers also began to assess nonacademic areas of development such as social and emotional development in classrooms and other learning environments that would not be considered in school settings prior.

CRONBACH'S CHARGE: ASSESSMENT HAS A ROLE IN EDUCATION

In his presidential address to the APA in 1957, Cronbach noted a schism had occurred between personality, social, and child, psychologists who worked in naturally occurring contexts and psychologists who studied perception and learning, conducting research in controlled laboratory settings. Thus, related to assessment specifically, there existed a divide between correlational psychologists and experimental psychologists. Correlational psychologists thought it their task to observe and gather data about individual differences with the potential to be influenced by multiple variables in natural settings. In contrast, experimental psychologists tested for outcomes in settings where variables were tightly controlled. Cronbach did not advocate for one discipline over the other, but argued each discipline, correlational and experimental, had the potential to inform a fuller understanding of testing. He emphasized the notions of construct validity and aptitude-treatment as evidence for how the combined efforts of each discipline can be applied to testing in natural contexts such as classrooms.

Construct validity refers to how well a test accurately measures the construct it was designed to measure. A construct is a variable that can be theoretically defined, but not directly observed, for example, motivation or attitude. For example, it is important to know that a test or assessment of an individual's motivation actually measures the construct of motivation. This means, the test score aligns with theoretical definition related to the construct of motivation and that test score and theoretical definition can be used to create predictions. *Aptitude treatment* refers to measuring an individual's readiness for different types of teaching (aptitude) and designing teaching methods to fit that individual's readiness level (treatment). For example, by assessing a student's knowledge of print, a teacher can make decisions about where to begin with that student's reading instruction. Thus, by considering the work of both correlational and experimental psychologists, Cronbach provided the foundation for classroom teachers to clearly define constructs, assess learner's readiness to learn, create student-centered learning opportunities focused on those constructs, and design assessments to evaluate student learning about constructs (construct validity). Forty years later, Black and Wiliam (1998) reviewed the literature and provided us with an evaluation of the state of Cronbach's vision.

BLACK AND WILIAM: ADJUSTING TEACHING AND LEARNING ACTIVITIES

Black and Wiliam (1998) suggested that assessment includes activities undertaken by teachers, and by their students in assessing themselves, which provides information such as feedback to adjust teaching and learning activities (p. 2). Rather than tests being developed by psychologists to be administered on students, Black and Wiliam (1998) posited that the way to improve educational standards is if teachers and students work closely together to engage in the formative assessment process consistently, over time. That is, student learning must be continuously informed by evidence collected in classrooms by teachers and students. Thus, based on Cronbach's original premise, the classroom is the most natural setting to collect data and use it to inform and exchange feedback between teachers and students for the purposes of improving student achievement. However, Cronbach did not believe teachers should do the work of assessment and would consider the process of formative assessment to be somewhat "unscientific" as it is not quantifiable data. Forty years after Cronbach, footprints of the progressive movement and of the shifts in historical context are evident in Black and Wiliam's (1998) review as they indicated that to see education improve over-all, teachers should be at the forefront of assessment. Teachers should enhance how they deliver feedback, engage students in the process, and plan for the potential impact of assessments on students' self-esteem and motivation. Whereas the majority of the studies Black and Wiliam (1998) reviewed focused on assessing individual capabilities as the backbone of assessment, they posited that it is critical that teachers use classroom assessment data for multiple purposes.

It is easy to understand why preservice and novice teachers can become overwhelmed by their assessment responsibilities. Teachers today are routinely expected to be (1) gathering and interpreting student learning data; (2) creating effective formative and summative classroom assessments; (3) providing feedback to students and families; (4) use feedback to modify teaching; and, (5) positively contributing to school and district-wide accountability measures. Complicating matters, specific expectations for classroom data collection varies from school to school, often depending on the values and beliefs of a particular community and the human and financial resources schools have available to put toward curriculum and assessment initiatives (Stiggins, 2002).

WHAT IS CLASSROOM ASSESSMENT AND CLASSROOM ASSESSMENT DATA?

Assessments at the classroom level are tools that teachers utilize to gather information and evidence about their student's' knowledge, skills, and learning (Barnes & Dacey, 2016). Classroom-level assessments can include traditional assessments, such as graded homework, quizzes, and chapter tests, or more authentic *performance assessments* with varying intentions and purposes. One result of the focus on accountability over the last thirty years has been a significant increase in the use of *performance assessments*. *Performance assessments* are often viewed as less traditional and assess how well students can demonstrate the execution of tasks that echo real-life situations (e.g., students planning for and implementing structured debates). Teachers often use portfolios or projects that demonstrate evidence of student mastery of multiple learning goals or that incorporate interdisciplinary themes, such as addressing goals in health, math, social studies, and communication by planning an instructional unit about running a cafeteria or café that includes the development of menus, budgets, and presentations to funders. Teachers also create and implement *formative assessments* at key points in their instructional units to gauge if instruction requires modification, maximizing opportunity for student learning, as opposed to *summative assessments*, which are administered at the end of instructional units (Dacey & Barnes, 2016).

Regardless of type of assessment, when teachers are trying to gauge the success of their instructional planning and implementation, they gather *assessment data*, any form of evidence of learning, formative or summative, that reveals how well students understand concepts or the level of students' ability with particular skills. A common misconception of assessment data stems from the assumption that data must be a number, bar graph, table, or other forms of quantitative information. Ultimately, it is critical to understand the purpose behind each assessment or evaluation in the interpretation of classroom data.

A TEXTUAL CONVERSATION BETWEEN CRONBACH AND BLACK AND WILIAM

Since most new teachers use performance assessments (and accompanying rubrics) for assessing student learning, examining the below performance assessment used in a science classroom helps bring to life the principles that both Cronbach (1957) espoused and the ideas reviewed by Black and Wiliam (1998). This assessment also exposes the tension between these ideas and why assessment can be a difficult landscape for teachers to navigate. What might two middle teachers, Mr. O'Meara and Ms. Fox, discuss when deciding if this assessment is appropriate to evaluate a students' ability to engage with scientific reasoning? First, examine the task being addressed:

Use data from your investigation to write a scientific explanation below to answer the question *What effect does increasing atmospheric CO$_2$ have on ocean pH?* Make sure to include evidence and reasoning to support your claims.

The following answer is just one example of a possible answer. Students may come up with additional/different evidence and/or reasoning.

Claim (answers the question): Adding carbon dioxide to salt water causes the pH of salt water to decrease.

Evidence (from your investigation):	**Reasoning** (scientific ideas that connect your evidence to your claim, explains why the evidence is important):
• The pH of salt water with no carbon dioxide introduced is 7.3. • The pH of salt water after blowing into it is 6.7.	• When we exhale, we release CO$_2$. By blowing into the beaker with the straw, I introduced CO$_2$ into the water. • The pH scale goes from 0 to 14 and indicates how acidic or basic a substance is. • If the pH is lower than 7, the substance is considered acidic. • If the pH is 7, the substance is considered neutral. • If the pH is above 7, the substance is considered basic. • The introduction of carbon dioxide results in a decrease of pH. • Carbon dioxide can make oceans less basic and more acidic.

Claim-Evidence-Reasoning Rubric

C-E-R Element	Zero (0)	Early (1pt)	Emerging (2pts)	Sophisticated (3pts)
1. Claim	Does not make a claim that responds to the question.	The claim responds to the question, but is an inaccurate claim.	Makes an accurate but incomplete claim in response to the question.	Makes an accurate and complete claim in response to the question.
2a. Evidence Use of data	No evidence is provided.	The evidence contains some of appropriate data from an observation.	The evidence contains most of appropriate data from an observation.	The evidence contains all appropriate data from an observation.
2b. Evidence Interpretation of data	Does not interpret any evidence.	Interprets only some data accurately.	Interprets most of the data accurately.	Interprets all of the data accurately.
3a. Reasoning General statement	Does not provide any reasoning.	Answers why or how the evidence supports claim with no relevant scientific principles (disciplinary core ideas).	Answers why or how the evidence supports claim with insufficient relevant scientific principles (disciplinary core ideas).	Answers why or how the evidence supports claim with sufficient relevant scientific principles (disciplinary core ideas).
3b. Reasoning Use of pieces of evidence	Uses no evidence or relevant big ideas accurately to explain the relationship between claim and evidence.	Uses some piece(s) of evidence and relevant disciplinary core ideas accurately to explain the relationship between claim and evidence.	Uses most pieces of evidence and relevant disciplinary core idea accurately to explain the relationship between claim and evidence.	Uses all pieces of evidence and relevant disciplinary core ideas to accurately to explain the relationship between claim and evidence.
4a. Persuasion Complete sentences	No sentences are complete.	Only few sentences are complete.	Most sentences are complete.	All sentences are complete.
4b. Persuasion Grammatical Choices	Most of CER contains many grammatical errors.	CER contains some grammatical errors.	CER contains few grammatical errors.	CER contains minimal grammatical errors.

Rubric developed and adapted from material at http://slider.gatech.edu/student-edition.

Cronbach's (1957) work facilitates our understanding of assessment in natural contexts, rather than in laboratory settings, and helps us specifically understand classroom assessment practices addressing construct validity, questioning how the assessment field could really know whether a test or assessment measures what it claims it is trying to measure. Black and Wiliam, however, questioned the concept of "scientific measurement" in classrooms and instead advocated for performance assessments within authentic contexts that allows for differentiated methods of completion, different levels of student understanding, and multiple attempts in meeting learning goals. Use of performance assessments supports the stance that learning as a relational, complex, dynamic, continuous process rather than the notion that students' knowledge is fixed and static.

The assessment shown above is asking students to craft a scientific explanation about the effect of increasing atmospheric CO_2 have on ocean pH. The teacher-created assessment *may or may not* demonstrate construct validity for measuring students' ability to engage in scientific reasoning. There could be an argument made that this assessment also measures their scientific content knowledge, their scientific literacy; even students' ability to read and to write. The rubric used to evaluate students' learning illustrates what Black and Wiliam (1998) conceptualized about assessment as a *process* engaged in by teachers and students working in classrooms (natural settings) that includes goal setting, questioning, and a great deal of feedback. They posit that students can and should be assessing themselves during instruction, and teachers must make changes to their planned activities based on classroom data during the teaching and learning process. By providing students with a rubric prior to completing an assignment, teachers can be more explicit about their expectations for student performance and create opportunities for students to ask questions and obtain clarification about the purpose of the task at hand.

In the assessment pictured above, the students are involved in a formative assessment, a performance task in an authentic context that requires them to make decisions about how to go about completing the task based on their prior and developing knowledge. Similarly, in the rubric pictured above, teachers use this framework to evaluate student work using the criteria they set out to measure. This theory of learning pervaded the studies reviewed by Black and Wiliam. The notion that abilities are a product of learning and learning is a result of previously acquired abilities undergirds much of the classroom assessment literature (e.g. Ames, 1992; Ames & Archer, 1988) at such a deep level it nearly goes without saying. Black and Wiliam noted that researchers seemed to be working from this theory as an assumption. As evidenced in the performance-based assessment above, the teacher understands her students as bringing a variety of different understandings and depths of prior knowledge to the task. Some students may have previous experience with ocean acidification and pH levels, while others might have no previous knowledge and are using only what they have learned in class and what they are learning while in the process of engaging with the assessment. The use of the rubric allows the teacher and the students (1) to determine current levels of knowledge and skills, and (2) to adjust current learning activities and pacing, and (3) to adjust or set new goals for future learning. The use of the rubric in the above assessment allows for continued growth and multiple attempts. Students can engage with this task, or similar tasks regarding the same concept of decision-making and the topic of carbon monoxide, and continue to make connections, develop knowledge, and work toward meeting learning goals.

This particular assessment speaks to Cronbach's notion of designing teaching and assessment methods that fit different types of readiness. For example, the teacher allows students to connect their scientific ideas and reasoning to their claims and evidence. The teacher can then assess their readiness to move on and deal with more complex scientific reasoning tasks. This assessment allows the teacher and the students to assess students' scientific thinking and knowledge and differentiate further instruction accordingly.

DIALOGUE BETWEEN AUTHORS

Provided below is a conversation between the two authors that embodies the tension that exists within today's assessment landscape, balancing Cronbach's scientific approach of assessment in a natural setting that has led to the concept of data-driven instruction with an emphasis on testing and Black and Wiliam's process-focused conception of ongoing formative assessment methods that are tightly linked to instruction.

Charity: *From my perspective, one of the issues at the heart of assessment is determining how teachers evaluate what students really know. For new teachers it can be tempting to rely on more standardized assessments, textbook-supplied exams, rather than accepting the challenge of designing their own assessments.*

Tammy: I agree. Similarly, teachers can fall into the trap of preparing students for summative assessments by giving them a few problems to solve, some solutions to choose from in a multiple-choice format, some true-false questions, and a couple of constructed response questions that are not as authentic or complex as the example provided earlier in the chapter.

Charity: *I found the assessment task provided earlier in the chapter effective; however, I believe some would question the assessment's content validity.*

Tammy: Overall, I think this assessment task demonstrates how scientists think. It is a real-world scenario. It is a great example of the type of assessment that pushes student thinking and learning. *Looking at what is being measured is important, is it the students' understanding of the effects of increasing atmospheric CO_2 on ocean pH, rather than the students' writing skills?* Some students may be strong in their content knowledge but are activity engaged in developing their writing skills. It is critical that teachers' assessments measure what they intend to measure. Content validity is that simple in theory, it is just not always easy to execute in practice.

Charity: *One of the most pressing challenges for teachers to creating and implementing effective assessments is juggling the host of demands on their time and attention. While we know that effective assessment is a process engaged in by teachers and students, a great deal of* *planning and time is necessary in order to engage in goal-setting together, questioning, and delivering specific individualized feedback to students.*

Tammy: Yes, teachers' responsibilities seem to be increasing all the time. It is critical that teachers' find the time to prioritize and analyze results from both formative and summative assessments. This step will ensure they can make instructional changes that will improve the learning process and possibly even increase differentiation of instruction for students.

Charity: *Agreed. Another challenge teachers' experience is the increase in accountability in recent years. Now more than in the past, schools and districts are evaluated and ranked based on students' performance on standardized tests. At the classroom level, teachers struggle with instructional time being spent more than ever before on students' test preparation and administration. Giving students periodic practice in answering the types of questions found on standardized tests is probably beneficial since taking standardized tests is a skill unto itself.*

Tammy: Yet, we have an idea that most teachers prefer formative assessments and would avoid using assessments primarily for producing grades, categorize students, or evaluating individual capabilities if given the choice. With this in mind, it would be valuable to expand our view to explore and learn about what other nations are prioritizing with regard to assessment. Our global context can inform our knowledge of assessment best practices, help us reevaluate priorities, and perhaps influence policy changes in the future. As teachers invested in our students' futures, we are obliged to share our assessment experiences, to inform and shape the larger discussions about assessment at the local, state, and national levels.

PRIMARY IMPLICATIONS FOR TEACHERS

Advances in assessment research in the areas of content validity, goal-setting, providing specific feedback, and differentiation of instruction have implications for teachers. It is essential that teachers create and utilize assessments that accurately and fairly measure what students are learning in the classroom; tests must be valid and assess what they are designed to measure. Similarly, results of assessments must be utilized to improve the learning process, rather than primarily being used to produce grades, reports, or categorize students for further teachers. However, the increasing focus on achieving accountability in a global context means it is more challenging for teachers today to generate their own assessments and make their own instructional choices. As Klenowski (2009) posited, teacher empowerment in this era is increasingly about respecting local and cultural contexts for assessment practice. Teachers must attend directly to cultivating culturally responsive assessment practices "for and with students" (Klenowski, 2009, p. 78). The future entails teachers, students, educational leaders, and policy makers approaching assessment as deeply social and personal work if we are going to improve educational quality. All stakeholders have a role in continuously improving classroom assessment. (1) Teachers should provide a plethora of detailed feedback about students' performance in a variety of forms. (2) Students must be more meaningfully engaged in the assessment process, such as becoming adept in self-assessment. (3) Administrators and family members must play a more active and supportive role in the teaching and learning process, collaborating with teachers and students as they engage in assessment activities. (4) Finally, the future also must include more focused research and detailed illustrations and examples of innovative, successful, and culturally responsive assessment practices.

CONCLUSION

These two documents are related in two important ways. First, it is evident that the linking of the two disciplines have led to the undergirding belief that individuals can be assessed for their capabilities. Second, teachers can provide instruction for students in ways that can improve and enhance those capabilities, and assessments can be developed to accurately determine instructional outcomes. With regard to assessment, what began as a focus on the individual has evolved into a focus on the relationship among the student, the teacher, and the assessment data. Now more than ever, it is important that teachers understand *what* to measure, and *how* to effectively assess student learning, and then to make any necessary adjustments to instruction. Despite the fact that the context of using classroom data and assessment is complex, teachers must ensure students' learning needs are planned for, implemented, and assessed accurately. Learning in the twenty-first century has become increasingly personalized. Instruction and assessment occurs using more flexible formats than ever before in history, often in online and hybrid spaces enacted with computer technology. With proficiency-based learning on the rise, student's now more than ever can test in and out of subjects; learn anywhere, with any device, at any time. These are some indications that suggest we may be on the cusp of another major paradigm shift in thinking about assessment. Take a test, meet the standard, and pass the course from the comfort of a computer screen at home or at school. Now more than ever, teachers must engage in reframing what is the essence of effective assessment. Being principled about the ethics of assessment is also necessary. For instance, teachers cannot falsify grades, and they must be mindful of the cultural bias often found in assessments and work to minimize their impact. Finally, teachers often operate with the assumption that learning is fundamentally an act of creation rather than simply delivery and regurgitation of information. As a result, it is tantamount that teachers approach assessment in this same manner.

GLOSSARY OF TERMS

Accountability-focused assessments—assessments designed to evaluate teacher, school, or program effectiveness, or used to determine student readiness for entrance, promotion, or graduation at any educational level became customary.

Aptitude-treatment—refers to measuring an individual's readiness for different types of teaching (aptitude) and designing teaching methods to fit that individual's readiness level (treatment).

Assessments—tools or methods that teachers utilize to gather information and evidence about students' knowledge, skills, and learning at any stage of an instructional unit.

Assessment data—any form of evidence of learning *which does not have* to be a number, bar graph, table, or other form of quantitative measure.

Construct validity—whether a test measures what it claims it is trying to measure.

Constructivist learning theory—belief that people make meaning or knowledge built on their experiences and therefore learning experiences should be through *doing*.

Content standards—defined areas of knowledge within each grade level and subject area that students are expected to learn and demonstrate growth and achievement.

Criterion-referenced tests—assessments that indicate how well test takers performed based almost solely on the mastery of specific criteria covered in the test questions/material.

Formative assessments—method or tool that teachers use to monitor student learning during the instructional unit and provide feedback to students to make adjustments and improve their performance.

Norm-referenced tests—assessments that indicate whether test takers performed better or worse than other test takers and are often used in rankings of students.

Performance assessments—tasks that assess students' knowledge and skills in which students are required to demonstrate their learning.

REFERENCES

Ames, C. (1992) Classrooms: goals, structures, and student motivation. *Journal of Educational Psychology*, *84*(3), 261–271. doi:10.1037/0022-0663.84.3.261

Ames, C., & Archer, J. (1988). Achievement goals in the classroom: student's' learning strategies and motivation process. *Journal of Educational Psychology, 80*(3), 260–267. doi: 10.1037/0022-0663.80.3.260

Barnes, N., & Dacey, C. (2016). Using traditional assessments to effectively inform your teaching. In D. Schwarzer & J. Grinberg (Eds.) *Successful teaching: What every novice teacher needs to know* (pp. 169–182). Lanham: Rowman & Littlefield.

Bartolome, L. I. (1994). Beyond the methods fetish: Toward a humanizing pedagogy. *Harvard Educational Review, 64*(2), 173–194.

Black, P., & Wiliam, D. (1998). Assessment and classroom learning. *Assessment in Education,* *5*(1), 7–74. doi: 10.1080/0969595980050102

Black, P., & Wiliam, D. (1998). Inside the black box: Raising standards through classroom assessment. *Phi Delta Kappan, 80*(2), 139–148.

Blount, J. (1998). *Destined to rule the schools: Women and the superintendency, 1873–1995.* Albany, NY: SUNY Press.

Bruner, J. S. (1960). *The process of education*. Cambridge, MA: Harvard University Press.

Common Core State Standards Initiative. (2010). *Common Core State Standards for English Language Arts and Literacy in History/Social Studies, Science, Science, and Technical Subjects*. Retrieved from http://www.corestandards.org/ELA-Literacy/

Conway, P. F., Goodell, J. E., & Carl, J. (2001). Educational reform in the USA: Politics, process, and purpose. In R. Griffin (Ed.), *Education in transition: International perspectives on the politics and processes of change* (83–108). United Kingdom: Symposium Books.

Cronbach, L. (1957). The two disciplines of scientific psychology. *American Psychologist, 12*, 671–684. doi: dx.doi.org/10.1037/h0043943

Cronbach, L. J., & Meehl, P. E. (1955). Construct validity in psychological tests. *Psychological bulletin, 52*(4), 281–302. doi: http://dx.doi.org/10.1037/h0040957

Dacey, C., & Barnes, N. (2016). Authentic performance assessments. In D. Schwarzer & J. Grinberg (Eds.) *Successful teaching: What every novice teacher needs to know* (pp. 183–194). Lanham: Rowman & Littlefield.

Freeman, F. N. (1926). *Mental tests: Their history, principles, and applications*. Boston: Houghton Mifflin.

Gardner, D. P. (1983). *A nation at risk: The imperative for educational reform*. Washington, DC: National Commission on Excellence in Education.

Klenowski, V. (2009). Respecting local, cultural contexts for assessment practice in an era of globalization. In E. Grigorenko (Ed.), *Multicultural psychoeducational assessment* (pp. 77–94). New York: Springer Publishing Company.

McCombs, B. L. (2003). Defining tools for teacher reflection: The assessment of learner-centered practices (ALCP). *Paper presented at the Annual Meeting of the American Educational Research Association* (Chicago, IL, April, 2003).

Noddings, N. (1995). Teaching themes of care. *Phi Delta Kappan, 76*(9), 675–679.

Peterson, J. (1925). *Early conceptions and tests of intelligence*. Yonkers-on-Hudson, NY: World Book.

Ravitch, D. (1983). *The troubled crusade: American Education, 1945–1980*. Basic Books, New York.

Rocheleau, J. (2004). Theoretical roots of service-learning: Progressive education and the development of citizenship. In B. W. Speck & S. L. Hoppe (Eds.), *Service-learning: History, theory, and issues* (pp. 3–21). Westport, CT: Praeger.

Schwartz, R. B., & Robinson, M. A. (2000). Goals 2000 and the standards movement. In D. Ravitch (Ed.), *Brookings papers on education policy: 2000. Washington, DC: Brookings Institution.*

Stiggins, R. S. (2002). Assessment crisis: The absence of assessment for learning. *Phi Delta Kappan, 83*(10), 758–765.

13

UNDERSTANDING THE CONTEXT OF PARENTAL INVOLVEMENT THROUGH THE NATIONAL STANDARDS FOR FAMILY–SCHOOL PARTNERSHIP

Veronica R. Barrios
Clarissa Barrios

W hat role do parents play in the education of their child? What are the expectations for parental involvement as it relates to academic achievement? Are parents responsible for their child's education or are teachers? These are some of the questions that come to mind when discussing parental involvement. This chapter will offer a definition of parental involvement as well as some examples of what a school might expect regarding parental involvement. The chapter will then discuss the history of the National Parent Teacher Association, their first-released standards for parental involvement and their revised standards as well. A discussion of influences on parental involvement will be presented.

PARENTAL INVOLVEMENT DEFINED

Parental involvement has been defined in a multitude of ways. Broadly speaking, parental involvement refers to some level of contact between parents and teachers regarding academic matters (Fan & Chen, 2001). Others define parental involvement as attendance by the parent to at least one school event or meeting (Child Trends). It is also important to note that the definitional inconsistency surrounding parental involvement also poses a problem for how we define parental involvement. Nonetheless, parental involvement does seem to have benefits for the child. As practitioners however it is important to be clear on what is meant by parental involvement in one's institution and classroom.

DIFFERENT FAMILY STRUCTURES

There has been movement to create more inclusive attitudes regarding family structures within the education community (Edwards, n.d.). **Kin** are not the only ones involved in a child's education. Edwards (n.d.) outlines 14 different family structures ranging from nuclear families to transnational families. Often, **nuclear families** are the family structure from which all other structures are "judged." This could be a problem for educators since children come from single-parent families (i.e., mother-only, father-only), foster families (i.e., foster parents), queer families (i.e., same-sex parents), extended families (i.e., grandparents are caretakers), **blended families** (i.e., step-parents/siblings), adoptive families (i.e., adoptive parents), and **transnational families** (i.e., one parent lives in a different country) to name a few (Edwards, n.d.). Similarly, there are **parentified children** (Boszormenyi-Nagy & Spark, 1973) caring for their sibling's educational attainment by consistently advocating and assisting with school activities. In any of these family structure, it is not only a biological parent may assume the role of parent to a child. Educators working from a place of acceptance and understanding of these different familial structures may have more success gaining parental involvement.

IMPORTANCE OF PARENTAL INVOLVEMENT

A large **meta-analysis** identified parental involvement and its influence on student achievement (Fan & Chen, 2001). Findings demonstrated that parental involvement had a strong positive influence on students' overall GPA. Child Trends, a national **think tank**, also released similar findings regarding the positive impact of parental involvement on children's academic achievement. Practitioners value and depend on parental involvement to reinforce the academic and social skills that are being taught in the classroom on a daily basis. Parental involvement in the form of having high aspirations for the child had a more positive effect on academic achievement than did parental home supervision (Fan & Chen, 2001). Because their parents value the dedication required to achieve success by providing positive reinforcement at home, these children adopt similar values that transfer into the classroom. It also is a clear indicator to the student that their teacher and parents are working together and can easily/quickly communicate their daily progress. Academic research has supported the link between parental involvement with teachers and in turn the enhancement of social functioning and reduction in problem behaviors within children (Nokali, Bachman, & Votruba-Drzal, 2010). Parental involvement decreases at-school behavioral problems, increases within-school academic performance, and increases the chances of completing high school (Child Trends, 2013). It is important to note that much of the research done on parental involvement does not include older children (Nokali et al., 2010).

Parental involvement is an essential part in the success of individual children and the classroom as whole. Most schools have a "back to school night" built into the beginning of the school year specifically to allow for the introduction of parents and school community to occur. During this time, some educators may include a presentation with general information and provide parents with the opportunity to visit the classroom, explore student materials and work, and meet with the teacher. A stance often undertaken by educators is that education begins at home with the parents, is enhanced in school, and should be reinforced at home afterward.

There are a variety of dynamics that can prevent parents from being able to meet the expectations set by administration and/or classroom teachers. Work, language barriers, and the inaccessibility to technology are just some of the roadblocks that can negatively affect the bond between school and parents. It is advantageous to include parents in the creation of school policies and documents regarding parental involvement. Not acknowledging macro- and micro-level barriers to parental involvement only exacerbates lack of involvement and miscommunication.

THE HISTORICAL BASIS FOR PARENTAL INVOLVEMENT

The National Parent Teacher Association was founded in 1897, as the National Congress of Mothers by Alice McLellan Birney and Phoebe Apperson Hearst (www.pta.org). In 1908, they changed their name to the National Congress of Mothers and Parent-Teacher Associations in response to the national growing importance of the partnership between parents and teachers. The organization changed its name again in 1924 to the National Congress of Parents and Teachers, and began to collaborate with other PTAs in the Southern and segregated states. The National Congress of Colored Parents and Teachers, who closely followed the National PTA's objectives in Washington, DC and other segregated states, was founded in 1926, by Mrs. Selena Sloan Butler, who served as president. The two organizations remained separate but inextricably linked for many decades. Special committees existed between the two organizations encouraging collaboration and understanding between them. Later, in 1970, after the civil rights movement, the National Congress of Parents and Teachers merged with the National Congress of Colored Parents and Teachers and became the National Parent Teacher Association (National PTA), as we know it today. It would take another 27 years for the National PTA to develop its first set of national standards for parental involvement released in 1997.

NATIONAL STANDARDS ABOUT PARENTAL INVOLVEMENT

A short history lesson is necessary in order to understand how a parental involvement national standard was created in the United States. While the concept of parental involvement has existed in the U.S. education system since 1642, it has been a topic of focus for researchers here in the United States only over the last thirty years (Hiatt-Michael, 1994). The 1980s introduced attention toward national standards in education. In particular, educational policy influences seem to drive the creation of the National Education Goals (NEG) Panel in 1989. The NEG generated six standards to address our nation's continuous drop in educational ranking, and added two more in 1994, one of which was on parental involvement. The goals were set to be met by 2000. As was mentioned earlier in the chapter, parental involvement was also beginning to gain support by academic researchers studying its impact on academic achievement. Interestingly enough, the first National Education Goals (NEGs) were developed in 1989 under President George H. W. Bush, and by 2001, his son, George W. Bush, passed the No Child Left Behind Act, continuing his father's efforts, and continuing the attempt to increase our ranking.

The eighth goal of the NEG, "Schools will promote parental involvement and participation," prompted the National PTA to create their six standards on parental involvement. This goal was added to the original NEGs in 1994. By 1995, Spain passed a law (LOPEG-Ley Orgánica de la Participación, la Evaluación y el Gobierno de los centros docentes) that reinforced parental involvement in the running of individual schools (Eurydice, 1997). Ireland, Iceland, Sweden, Austria, and Scotland each passed variations of LOPEG in their respective countries (Eurydice, 1997). Parental involvement was gaining attention around the world as can be seen. This chapter will discuss the original standards from 1997, National Standards for Parent/Family Involvement Programs, and the updated version released in 2007, National Standards for Family–School Partnership. In 2007, the National Standards were updated in the midst of the No Child Left Behind policy. Globally, initiatives, such as Children's Plan in the UK and the Schooling Strategy in New Zealand, were also targeting the link between parental involvement and educational improvement (Savelsberg & O'Hehir, 2014).

The standards were selected for inclusion in this chapter, instead of other historical documents, because they were the first attempt by a national organization, supported by the U.S. government, to provide a unified approach to parental involvement for all public educational institutions. Given that parental involvement is not a legal obligation, creating national standards seemed to allow administrators/educators to **operationalize** parental involvement for the communities they served. Table 13.1 is included to help readers understand both global and national movements, which were, and are, affecting parental involvement.

It should be noted that there were other movements occurring within the education system in the United States at this time as well. Two such movements demonstrated the parents' power in choosing the best options for their children, with little government intervention. The voucher system allowed families to receive tax credits and deductions from their local government if their child attended a privately funded school. School choice allowed families to choose which public school they wanted their child to attend, even if it was not in their designated school zone. However, the criticisms around these choices focus on public school funds being allocated to schools other than their own. The National PTA was, and still is, firmly against these movements (www.pta.org). The PTA preferred to support local schools and parental involvement in their own public schools in order to improve them.

A review of the standards will ensue addressing how these standards are currently being implemented and how families may be affected by their adoption. The *National Standards for Parental Involvement* are available online if you follow these links: http://files.eric.ed.gov/fulltext/ED405405.pdf (1998) and http://www.pta.org/nationalstandards (2007). Take note that some of the standards have remained, some have merged, a new standard

Table 13.1 Global and national influences on parental involvement

	Global	National	Policies	Understanding Parental Involvement
1997–National Standards for Parent/Family Involvement Programs *(original)*	Between 1995 and 1996, Spain passes a law called LOPEG, which reinforced parental involvement in the running of individual schools. Ireland, Iceland, Sweden, Austria, and Scotland each passed variations of LOPEG in their respective countries.	In 1989, the National Education Goals (NEGs) was created in response to dropping academic standards in the United States. Academic research beginning to link parental involvement with higher academic achievement in the 1990s.	There were 6 goals set by the NEG panel in 1989. In 1994, two more goals were added, one of which is the 8th goal addressing parental involvement.	Parental involvement includes communication, promoting parenting skills, assisting student learning, volunteering, decision-making and advocacy, community collaboration.
2007–National Standards for Family–School Partnership *(current)*	International initiatives, such as Children's Plan in the UK and the Schooling Strategy in New Zealand, are targeting the link between parental involvement and educational improvement.	From 2001 until 2015, No Child Left Behind is implemented stating all children will meet specific educational standards in order to improve academic standards in the United States, and parental involvement is implicated.	Changes were released to the national standards on parental involvement in 2007.	Parental involvement includes welcoming families, communicating, supporting student success, speaking up for every child, sharing power, and community collaboration.

was introduced, and other standards were removed altogether. There were also language changes between the two releases.

We will now go through each standard and help the reader think critically about the standards by considering the perspective of a teacher (Clarissa) as well as that of a family (Veronica).

WELCOMING ALL FAMILIES INTO THE SCHOOL COMMUNITY

In order to achieve parental involvement, an investment of time from the child and their kin seems necessary. Yet, the extent of that involvement is influenced by the sense of community that may exist between the families and their school communities.

Veronica: *Currently, the first standard is welcoming all families into the school community. It acknowledges that families must first be welcomed into the academic community before discussing what is needed from families to support student success. This would seem necessary in order to understand who represents each child's family and who is responsible for that particular child's education. This establishes a relationship with the family and increases an understanding of the family structure and familial roles.*

Clarrisa: Administrators and teachers have a wide range of opportunity to welcome families into a school community in order to create an atmosphere of respect and cooperation. To assist, schools may hire staff to reach out to parents and families, plan/organize/implement workshops, and help advocate for students. Teachers find it helpful to immediately open the lines of communication with parents by exchanging contact information and providing parents with a schedule of availability for conferences. Important documents containing policies, expectations, and the school year calendar are amongst the most common documents distributed during an initial meet at the commencement of the school year.

Veronica: *Education for practitioners and administrators around family roles and rule surrounding education could prove useful for engaging families. For example, all families have roles for its individual members. Similarly, all families have rules of functioning, which dictate the conversation patterns and topics discussed. Given this information, how might administrators and teachers create an atmosphere that is respectful of the families whom they hope to engage?*

Inviting the family into the school community is not as a simple as an invitation. There is a need to consider factors that promote or inhibit the welcoming process.

COMMUNICATING EFFECTIVELY

In 1997, one of the standards described how supporting diverse parenting styles/skills could affect student performance. This standard seems to be fused throughout the current standards. Rather than focusing on just parenting styles and skills, the parents are now viewed as advocates working with the academic community to foster their child's development. In order to advocate, communication patterns will need to be established.

Clarissa: This standard emphasizes communication between parents and school staff, and was also present in the 1997 version of the national standards. In order to communicate effectively with parents, educators may find it helpful to use a variety of ways to maintain contact with families. For example, providing parents with the contact information of a teacher and administrator keeps lines of communication open. Also, being able to access progress monitoring records in real time through the use of software, not only keeps parents informed, it provides a log of proof that parents have been consistently contacted. The district, school, and classroom websites are more ways to regularly communicate with families. Administrators also make themselves available to families during school hours, including drop-offs and dismissals. When an administrator is consistently seen and available, it promotes a healthy, growing relationship with families that positively affects the performance of children in school.

Veronica: *The word effectively was added to the new standard, addressing the reality that communication requires at minimum two parties. It is not enough for the school to provide information, it is equally important for the families to engage the teacher. A common difficulty in doing so however is language barriers. As an institution whose funding is generated in part by the residents of town, translation services should be a welcomed aspect of the school community. Dissemination in representative languages, as well as interpreters, during school meetings should be considered. Keep in mind, older siblings, cousins, or other kin, may serve as gatekeepers for families. Additionally, it is important to consider cultural beliefs, specifically around rules for communication. For example, can the mother be present without a male or can a parentified child be present without an adult?*

Successful communication is certainly possible but it will require the school community's efforts in understanding the community they serve. It may also require consideration by both the school community and the parents regarding what needs to be in place in order to achieve positive and effective communication patterns.

SUPPORTING STUDENT SUCCESS

Ideally, both the parents and the school community have the child's success as the primary focus of their relationship. Yet, supporting student success seems dependent on supporting the varying actors present for the child.

Clarissa: This standard describes how parental involvement can support student success, an idea that was also present in the 1997 standards. Most school districts help support student success by offering a variety of before-school and after-school programs. These kinds of programs provide students with strategic interventions in order to help them achieve success. Some districts may choose to invite students to these programs based on their standardized testing scores and/or low quarterly grades. These students may be selected to attend extra academic programs in order for them to receive interventions that may be instrumental to their success.

Veronica: *Parents need to be engaged to successfully intervene with children. Creating opportunities for parental learning can help parents better assist their children. At times, I think it is expected that parents know how to support their children. Defining what parental support looks like for the child could be critical to improving involvement. In line with defining support, it seems important to consider what is realistically expected from parents. In some families, parents are hardly home to monitor work due to their own employment. In other families, parents may have less education than their own children and certainly as was discussed, may not know the language enough to assist.*

Clarissa: Although these academic programs are created in order to support students based on their individual needs, schools must provide teachers with the tools to do so. Curriculum should be available to teachers with time to plan, and parents should be made aware of the program expectations. Showing parents examples of quality work and providing a rubric for assignments are concrete ways to help families stay on task at home. Reviewing student work can help to keep a running record of grades and assist when discussing student strengths and areas of improvement. Teachers may also send home projects that reflect the learning happening in school and provide a fun, educational opportunity for families to work together. These projects can include options for different learners and provide little to no economic strain.

Veronica: *Understanding family structures and familial expectations can also help alleviate how parental involvement should unfold from one child to the next. It seems counterproductive to have the same expectations of all families when each family unit may look different. Similarly, most families are not equipped with information about developmental milestones, and may not be aware of what realistic expectations for their child may look like.*

Critical for supporting student success is supporting teachers and families. If the critical actors in the child's life are supported, then the child's experiences with supportive structures will be more successful as well.

SPEAKING UP FOR EVERY CHILD

Speaking up for Every Child replaced the original standard called volunteering. Focusing on parents volunteering may be a good way to gain parental involvement; however, its removal is likely indicative of its secondary importance to parental advocacy. As we know, all children need adults who can advocate for them. If, and how, adults advocate for a child is dependent on whether that adult knows their own rights as an advocate.

Clarissa: Advocating for the rights of every individual student is a part of being an effective educator. Parents, teachers, and administrators must be familiar with the district's policy for advocating for student rights. Schools may distribute a Handbook at the start of each school year that explains how to identify an issue, along with information on who to refer to in order for it to be resolved. Administrators and teachers should encourage parents to address issues early on so that a resolution can be reached efficiently.

Veronica: *Parental involvement also depends on their understanding of and advocating for their rights. Including information for parents regarding how to advocate for their child would boost involvement, particularly around meeting student goals. Another thing to consider is fear of retaliation on the part of the parents to advocate. In some cases, parents may not be legal residents or citizens and fear deportation if contact is not amicable between them and the school. Other families may also be new to children's rights and therefore expect that whatever the school personnel say about the child must be true, negating the child's right.*

An informed kin is very important for the success of the child. Similarly, teachers who are supported as advocates for the children they teach can provide better options for student success as well.

SHARING POWER

In 1997, the importance of the parental role in decision making regarding the child's academic success was highlighted. Yet, today, the language has shifted from a parent having a role in decision making to a parent having power in their child's academic success. This language showcases an equal partnership between parents and teachers/administrators, rather than stating parents are important to the process of decision making, but not necessarily equally important.

Clarissa: In practice, however, it seems that power is not equally distributed. Parents may be misinformed about their rights. They may also expect the teacher to do the bulk of the work in regards to what is best for the child academically. If there are language barriers, some parents may post blame on that regarding their inability to support their child's academic progress. If the teacher and parent do not agree, this conflict can negatively affect the child's academic and behavioral performance. Parents may assume that if they are not contacted about a school issue, there is no issue. Parents should be aware of the fact that their voices are more powerful than those of the teachers.

Veronica: *How do we balance and create a space for conversations between teachers and parents when both seem to be at odds regarding how to successfully move their child along? While both parties may be well meaning, parents often look to the teacher as the expert in educating their child. The teacher is often looking to the parent as the expert on the child. While the standard sounds ideal, there is also a lack of consideration for real-world application. Socioeconomic status affects the sharing of power. With more financial means, also comes tutoring and time for parental involvement, or at the least, financial resources to offset the lack of one-on-one parental involvement that leads to academic success, such as nannies or sitters who help with schoolwork. Similarly, more educated parents may be more aware of how to and the positive impact of their parental involvement.*

Clarissa: Accountability with follow up regarding student growth should be placed on both parents and teachers. Parental monitoring should regularly be a point of discussion.

Veronica: *It could be helpful for parents to know what is expected and when it is expected in order to capitalize on parental involvement. The reality is that parental involvement will look different for different families, and if educators are aware and involved in defining what it looks like for a particular family, it could facilitate it.*

Shared power seems to be in the best interest of the child. Parents who are knowledgeable about their power are positioned to better support their children.

COLLABORATING WITH COMMUNITY

The student's community does not necessarily have boundaries around the household and the school. Other resources may exist in the broader community that can enhance the student's success, as well as the kin's options in supporting their child's education.

Clarissa: Community collaboration is important in fostering student achievement. Collaboration is ideal but may be difficult to execute because although school districts normally have a good relationship with community service workers, there may not be strong connections with local businesses. Schools may invite service workers to visit classrooms, provide demonstrations, and hold workshops. School boards and local officials may collaborate to ensure the safety, and academic and social well-being of children in the community. Decisions may include building new playgrounds for recreational use, opening locations where community gatherings, added school security, and school closings. This collaboration can lead to open dialogue about new curriculum and services that would best support student achievement.

Veronica: *A family is already a unit in and of itself, however it is so heavily influenced by outside forces, in particular the school community. If the school community has a good relationship with the neighborhood then it can positively influence the family. Community programs that cater to schools can provide resources that families may lack or be unable to provide. For example, after school programs offered through religious centers, recreational clubs, or tutoring centers can help support student success. Similarly, schools that offer ESL and GED courses can help parents, in turn, helping the children. Children can also gain civic engagement and internship opportunities when community collaborations are fostered.*

The successful implementation of these standards requires involvement on the part of the kin, school community, and the broader community. Overall, parental involvement is possible with effort on the part of the kin, and understanding and support on the part of the school community.

CONSIDERATIONS FOR REVISED STANDARDS

More than ten more years have passed without revisions to the standards. Some things to consider going forward will be discussed. There may be a disconnect between what parents *think* is happening in school and what is actually happening. Creating a clear understanding of the academic and behavioral expectations placed on children through the Common Core and Every Student Succeeds Act is critical. Often national education acts, such as the Common Core, shift academic expectations and create new demands of teachers and students. These national acts change based on political climates, without much feedback or consideration of familial structures, teachers' workloads, and local political climates. Collaboration with developmentalists who provide training to teachers and families could curtail conflict between parents and teachers surrounding a child's academic and social tasks.

FUTURE STANDARDS

The content of the current standards are ideally what one would want and expect from families, even in the future. Yet, most teachers have likely not heard of these standards and not all parents are aware of their rights and need for parental involvement. Therefore, the successful implementation by both parents and instructors seems daunting. A recommendation for teachers in training is training in how to garner parental involvement as an agent of change and instruction in their own classrooms. However, it is important to also acknowledge that the teacher's personal agency is still nested within the larger educational system, which in the end exercises a considerable amount of power over teachers. A recommendation to reach future parents is to provide training at the high school level regarding parental rights and advocacy within the school district, perhaps in the form of lessons on the education system through civics courses. After all, the education system is one of the systems, which comprise our larger socio-political system. Empowering future parents about their rights and need as parents involved in their child's education seems critical.

PRACTICAL IMPLICATIONS

Parental involvement may look different depending on the population of the school community. Teachers may experience a shift in the level of parental involvement due to a variety of factors already discussed. Because of this, teachers and administrators are expected to be as accommodating as possible in order to meet the needs of the families. Most educators may find themselves working well before and past contractual hours in order to support the schedules of parents. Ensuring that each school have a PTA would help with limiting the amount of extra hours teachers use to communicate with families. A PTA would assist with **turn-keying** information from administration. It would also create a network of parents that can discuss current school-related events, and share ideas and concerns. Since not all schools have a PTA, parents can request from districts creating a policy that makes the PTA a requirement for all schools.

CONCLUSION

Fostering an honest dialogue between school personnel and families is likely the best way to gain and improve parental involvement and positive student outcomes. Working with families as opposed to telling families what to do gives families authority over their child's education and helps them become empowered agents within the school community. Educating staff on and implementing the aforementioned standards and creating PTAs at each school could facilitate parental involvement. Parents and teachers would benefit from collaborating, since student success would increase, and this is the ultimate goal of both parties.

EXTENSION QUESTIONS

1. What kind of courses help prepare teachers to work with diverse families?
2. What are the advantages and disadvantages of a school PTA?
3. As families are welcomed into the school community, what measures are taken to ensure that their participation is effective?
4. How can teachers/administrators provide parents with a concrete, updated image of today's educational expectations?

GLOSSARY OF TERMS

Blended families—refers to families in which one parent has remarried a partner who also has children and now the family includes stepparents and stepchildren.

Kin—referring to a family member.

Meta-analysis—a succinct analysis of major findings within all released publications over a specified timeframe.

Nuclear family—refers to a family with a mother, father, and their children.

Operationalize—to share a particular definition that will be common to all involved in that specific setting.

Parental involvement—contact between parents and teachers regarding academic matters.

Parentified child—when a child assumes the responsibilities of a parent.

Think tank—a group of experts in a specific subject area that provide guidance and findings to interested groups.

Turn-keying—a reference used amongst educators referring to the dissemination of new material from one educator to another/to a group; allows for the quick dissemination from one to many of new material.

Transnational families—refers to families residing in more than one country at a time but who still maintain regular contact with one another, often through technology and/or frequent visits.

REFERENCES

Boszormenyi-Nagy, I., & Spark, G. M. (1973). *Invisible loyalties: Reciprocity in intergenerational family therapy*. New York, NY: Brunner/Mazel.

Child Trends. (2013). Parental involvement in schools: Indicators of child and youth well-being. Retrieved from https://www.childtrends.org/?indicators=parental-involvement-in-schools

Edwards, J.O. (n.d.). The many kinds of family structures in our communities. Retrieved from http://www.scoe.org/files/ccpc-familystructures.pdf.

El Nokali, N. E., Bachman, H. J., & Votruba-Drzal, E. (2010). Parent involvement and children's academic and social development in elementary school. *Child Development*, *81*(3), 988–1005. http://doi.org/10.1111/j.1467-8624.2010.01447.x

Eurydice. (1997). The role of parents in the educational systems of the European Union. Brussels, Belgium: European Unit of Eurydice.

Fan, X., & Chen, M. (2001). Parental involvement and students' academic achievement: A meta-analysis. *Educational Psychology Review, 13*(1), 1–22.

Hiatt-Michael, D. B. (1994). Parent involvement in American public schools: A historical perspective 1642–1994. *The School Community Journal, 4*(2), 27–38.

National Education Goals Panel, (1990). History, 1989 to Present. Retrieved from http://govinfo.library.unt.edu/negp/page1-7.htm

National Parent Teacher Association. (1997). National standards for parent/family involvement programs. Chicago, IL: National PTA.

National Parent Teacher Association. (2007). National standards for family- school partnership. Retrieved from http://www.pta.org/nationalstandards

Savelsberg, H. & O'Hehir, J. (2014). Towards best practices in parental involvement in education: A literature review. Government of South Australia. Retrieved from https://www.decd.sa.gov.au/sites/g/files/net691/f/towards-best-practice-parent-involvement.pdf

14

BEYOND THE GENIUS AND THE MUSE: CREATIVITY IN LEARNING AND TEACHING

PABLO P. L. TINIO
SOFIA A. TINIO

INTRODUCTION

A kindergartener sits in front of the classroom reading aloud an alphabet book to her class: "M-mat, N-nap, O-ox." She suddenly looks up from the book and says, excitedly, "Look! Mat rhymes with hat, hat and cat, cat and bat!" Her classmates join in on the chant at which point the teacher interrupts the class and tells the reader to pay attention to the book and to continue with the pages. She then tells the class to be quiet and listen.

A fourth-grade class is working on analogies and a student comes up with an unusual, but appropriate, analogue pair of words. The teacher tells him that he can't use the pair because it is not on the list of possible answers.

The above scenarios play out on a daily basis in classrooms the world over. What seems like an insignificant insight to an adult could mean the world to a child at the moment of discovery. What situations like these have in common is that they deliver an unspoken message to ignore playful, imaginative, and inventive moments. They stifle creativity. This chapter looks at creativity in learning and teaching and will present the state-of-the-art of what we know about facilitating and nurturing creativity while also being responsive to the day-to-day demands of the school setting. The chapter will discuss the common ways in which creativity is defined, attempt to dispel myths about creativity, and present two key texts on creativity that serve as foundations for a dialogue about the important issues in creativity and how thinking about such issues have evolved since the 1950s. Finally, the chapter will address how the ideas discussed could impact learning and teaching and, importantly, will discuss practical implications for teachers and how they could establish learning and teaching environments that support creative behavior.

WHAT IS CREATIVITY?

A classic view of creativity states that for something to be considered creative, it must have two characteristics. The first of these is novelty—a product or idea must be new or unique. The second is that the product or idea must be considered useful within a given area. Thus, novelty *and* usefulness are necessary aspects of creativity. In following this view, a first-grade math curriculum that is new and exciting, but ineffective in teaching basic math concepts, is not creative; likewise, a lesson on life cycles of plants that is pedagogically effective, but has been part of the curriculum for a decade, is not creative. What would be considered creative would be a lesson that integrates math and the life cycle of plants in a manner that has never been done before, and in a way that promotes a deep understanding of facts and concepts related to the two subjects. Such a lesson is both novel and useful.

Creativity is typically thought of as a positive and desirable personality trait. Creativity, after all, is beneficial: Creative students are able to find novel solutions to problems, tasks, and projects that they must complete in the classroom; creative coaches are able to come up with new and effective approaches to training their athletes and to developing new tactics to help their teams succeed; and creative teachers are more likely to teach difficult and perhaps uninteresting subjects in new and engaging ways. Creativity is certainly beneficial, and there are, and have been, many attempts to teach people to be more creative (de Bono, 1992; Renzulli, 2005). However, most of these attempts have had limited or no results (Plucker, Beghetto, & Dow, 2004). With creativity clearly being beneficial in so many ways, why is creativity so elusive? The major reasons are the ways creativity is viewed in our society and people's beliefs about creativity.

BELIEFS ABOUT CREATIVITY AND CREATIVE EXPRESSION: THE GENIUS AND THE MUSE

Creative people have historically been held in high esteem, as part of a category of people with different levels of functioning and with special skills and talents, the typical idea of a genius—such as Albert Einstein, Pablo Picasso, Thomas Edison, Bill Gates, Stephen Hawking, and William Shakespeare. Highly creative people are often seen as having innately acquired skills: they are born creative. This view is also related to the belief that a person is either creative or not—the view that creativity is a fixed trait, as opposed to a skill or an ability that can be enhanced and nurtured, for example, by a caregiver or teacher. Creativity is also often associated with ambiguity and even mysticism—as involving mysterious processes, inspiration from a muse, or the work of a higher power.

When thought of in this way, it could be difficult to see creativity within the context of a living, buzzing, everyday, and at times boring and routine classroom. It becomes difficult to see that *all* schoolchildren (and not just an elite few) have the potential to be highly creative. And it becomes a challenge to teach students specific skills that could help them be creative and that could encourage them to assume a mindset in which they believe that they have control of their own creativity (Tinio & Barbot, 2016). A way to address this issue is to consider creativity not as mysterious and only within reach of a few people, but as a set of mental skills that every person is capable of having (albeit at various levels of quality and quantity) and as a concept that is influenced by specific factors. Every child is capable of being creative in his or her own way (Russ & Fiorelli, 2010). Because a significant amount of research has been conducted on creativity, we have a great deal of knowledge about the factors that impact creativity. Below, we will examine these through two key texts.

GUILFORD'S 1950 PRESIDENTIAL ADDRESS AND BEGHETTO AND KAUFMAN'S FOUR-C MODEL OF CREATIVITY

Guilford's 1950 Presidential Address to the American Psychological Association has influenced generations of creativity researchers and practitioners. It outlined the following four major points regarding creativity that are related to learning and teaching:

1. Everyone has the capacity to be creative, not just geniuses, and there are individual differences in levels of creativity.

    The general psychological conviction seems to be that all individuals possess to some degree all abilities, except for the occurrence of pathologies. The important consideration here is the concept of continuity. Whatever the nature of creative talent may be, those persons who are recognized as creative merely have more of what all of us have. It is this principle of continuity that makes possible the investigation of creativity in people who are not necessarily distinguished. (Guilford, 1950)

2. Expressions of creativity occur in all aspects of human life.

    The factorial conception of personality leads to a new way of thinking about creativity and creative productivity. According to this point of view, creativity represents patterns of primary abilities, patterns which can vary with different spheres of creative activity. (Guilford, 1950)

3. Creativity is influenced by specific personal, social, and environmental factors.

    What it takes to make the inventor, the writer, the artist, and the composer creative may have some factors in common, but there is much room for variation of pattern of abilities. (Guilford, 1950)

4. Creativity is not a fixed trait, but involves a set of mental skills that could be facilitated and nurtured.

> For I believe that much can be done to encourage its development. This development might be in the nature of actual strengthening of the functions involved or it might mean the better utilization of what resources the individual possesses, or both. (Guilford, 1950)

In his address, Guilford (1950) made an urgent call for more research on creativity, which was extremely limited at that time, especially empirical research. Guilford, purposefully or not, also laid the foundation for the work of creativity scholars who followed in his footsteps. The next text, by Kaufman and Beghetto (2009), represents the work of such scholars. In it they propose the *Four-C Model* of creativity. Their paper represents the state-of-the-art of creativity research during the beginning of the 21st century and reflects over half a century's worth of creativity research conducted since Guilford's address. In fact, Kaufman and Beghetto directly reference Guilford in their work saying "Guilford's call to arms resonated with psychologists around the world" (p. 1). The most important aspect of their paper is that they identify four types of creativity, a taxonomy, that has been revolutionary for the field: mini-c, little-c, Pro-c, and Big-C.

Mini-c creativity refers to creativity manifested at the individual, or personal, level. This is a type of creative expression that on the surface, might seem minor and could be easily overlooked or dismissed by others, but nonetheless is personally meaningful. An illustration of this is the above example of the kindergartener's sudden insight regarding the rhyming words as she read aloud the alphabet book, or the fourth grader's discovery of an unusual, but appropriate, analogue pair of words. Both creative expressions are personally meaningful, but not necessarily influential to others (Kaufman & Beghetto, 2009).

Little-c creativity refers to everyday creativity that is more easily recognizable and that could have greater impact for others than mini-c creativity. Imagine if the first-year teacher described above was given the opportunity to implement the new approach to teaching a math unit. If successful, the approach could have had a positive impact on the learning of all first-grade students in that school and would have been an example of little-c creativity (Kaufman & Beghetto, 2009).

Imagine then that the first-grade teacher's new approach would have taken off, so much so that the entire school district would have implemented the approach and shared it nationwide. The teacher might have given lectures throughout the country and have written books about the teaching method with formal guidelines on implementation. This type of creativity is not at the level of eminence or genius, but it goes beyond little-c, and Kaufman and Beghetto (2009) refer to it as *Pro-c* creativity.

Finally, *Big-C* is the type of creativity that we hear about when people talk about creative achievement. This is creativity at the highest level: historically eminent scientists like Einstein, artists such as Picasso, and writers such as Hemingway. Very few people reach this level of achievement, and it represents the most irrelevant type of creativity when we discuss learning and teaching. Kaufman and Beghetto (2009), through their categories of the Four C's, provide a fusion of the research completed since the 1950s and develop on the four major issues that Guilford (1950) had raised.

Much progress in our understanding of creativity has taken place during the six decades since Guilford's (1950) address. Positive developments have occurred at global and national levels as well as with educational policies (see table), developments that are reflected in Kaufman and Beghetto's (2009) *Four-C Model*, which has become one of the most important pieces of scholarship on creativity.

	Global Forces	National Forces	Educational Policies	Understanding of Phenomena
Text 1 *Guilford's 1950 Presidential Address to the American Psychological Association*	The time following the Second World War was relatively peaceful and prosperous especially in developed countries (Simonton, 2001).	Establishment of the National Science Foundation and the recognition that science and technology are fundamental to the growth and prosperity of the nation.	Creativity and innovation seen as central to educating an efficient, innovative, and productive workforce.	Creativity as a set of mental skills that could be studied, facilitated, and taught in schools.
Text 2 *Kaufman and Beghetto's (2009) Four-C Model of Creativity*	Globalization, the rapid dissemination of information through the Internet, and the rise of new technologies.	Americans' competitiveness in the global market requires 21st-century skills, which includes creativity.	Educational policy shifts its focus to accountability and empirical evidence of not only acquisition of knowledge in traditional subject areas (e.g., math, social studies), but also of "mental skills" such as critical thinking and creativity.	Understanding of the specific underlying cognitive, emotional, and social forces influencing the expression of creativity; new methods for measuring creative behaviors.

DIALOGICAL TEXT ANALYSIS

Below, we discuss (from both theoretical and practical perspectives) *motivation*, the *be creative effect*, and *creative metacognition* as examples of factors related to creativity that empirical research after Guilford (1950) has identified as key to the expression of creative behaviors.

MOTIVATION

PT: Everyone has the capacity to be creative, not just geniuses, and there are individual differences in levels of creativity. Such differences regarding creativity are rooted in specific personal, social, and environmental factors affecting people, which Guilford (1950) himself recognized, although did not develop upon because of the lack of empirical research on such factors. Motivation is one of these factors, and it affects the expression of all types of creativity (Kaufman and Beghetto, 2009). Motivation could be categorized as two types: intrinsic and extrinsic. Those who are intrinsically motivated perform a task because they find the task pleasurable or personally meaningful. In contrast, those who are extrinsically motivated do something for a reward, praise, or some other external factor.

ST: *The difference between intrinsic and extrinsic motivation could be seen in a scenario where one student who draws and paints at home because she simply loves art is intrinsically motivated while another student who does the same activities because his parents praise him each time he shows them an artwork that he made is extrinsically motivated. The former student will be more likely to be creative at art because she loves to draw and paint. People who are intrinsically motivated to perform a task are more likely to be creative (e.g., Amabile, 1985).*

THE BE CREATIVE! EFFECT

PT: Although conducive for creativity, intrinsic motivation is difficult to encourage. Thus, when intrinsic motivation is not present, teachers could encourage creativity through direct instruction, by explicitly telling a student to be creative and that he or she has the potential to be highly creative. On the surface, this approach seems overly simplistic. However, studies have shown the instruction to be creative could actually help increase a person's creativity. This classic "be creative effect" (Christensen, Guilford, & Wilson, 1957) has been replicated in numerous studies. Telling someone to be creative could have two possible outcomes: an increase in the number of solutions to a task or problem and an increase in the creativity of the solutions. Recent studies have shown that asking someone to be creative actually leads to fewer solutions, but an increase in the quality of the solutions (Nusbaum, Silvia, & Beaty, 2014).

ST: *Teachers may not want to instruct their students to be creative all the time for all tasks and activities. Instead, they could take advantage of the approach in a strategic way. Note that students who are intrinsically motivated to perform a task or engage in a particular subject is already at an advantage as far as creativity goes. In this situation, a teacher does not need to intervene. Intervention might even be detrimental to the creative process as the already motivated student possesses both the drive and the skills to perform in a creative way. The teacher might then focus on a task and an activity that the student is not intrinsically motivated to perform—but nonetheless could benefit from some level of creativity—and instruct the student to be creative in this area. In doing this, a balance in creative performance could be achieved amongst different subjects.*

CREATIVE METACOGNITION

PT: Explicitly telling students to be creative has its benefits, but as educators, what we would like is for our students to be able to control their own creativity. Therefore, it is important to help students become more aware about their creative strengths and weaknesses and when it is appropriate and advantageous to be creative (and when it is inappropriate and disadvantageous). Kaufman and Beghetto (2013) labeled this ability creative metacognition.

ST: *Because creativity is generally seen in a positive light, most people in most situations would like to be creative. There are, however, circumstances in which creativity might actually be inappropriate, or worse, disadvantageous. Creativity is beneficial to the student who is trying to come up with an idea for an artwork that will be submitted to an art contest and that will be judged for not only its technical execution, but also for its novelty and ability to express an underlying idea or concept. Creativity is also beneficial for the student who is writing a poem or fictional story for a creative writing class. The creations of dioramas, science projects, and collages would all benefit from some creative thinking. In general, executing a basic and prescribed science experiment in order to demonstrate a particular concept would not; neither would the application of a linear, sequential, and invariable mathematical formula. Memorizing spelling words and definitions, calculating averages, and knowing the sequence of events that led to an important point of history all benefit from following steps, routines, and repetition—rote learning—not improvisation or unrestrained invention.*

PT: Creative metacognition then allows sound judgment of the when and how of creativity (Kaufman & Beghetto, 2013). It also provides opportunities to help students become more aware of their own thoughts and beliefs about creativity, which at times could be the barriers to their creative expression and creative achievement. For example, children may have a fixed view of their creativity and believe that they are not as creative as other children, or in a more extreme case, they might think that they are not creative at all. Children who have such a fixed view of creativity could benefit from being taught specific metacognitive skills, such as identifying the subjects and activities that would allow them to be the most creative and then giving them opportunities to be creative in those areas. Metacognition would also entail helping the students identify instances of their own creative behavior as evidence that are contrary to their initial beliefs, they could indeed be creative. Metacognition could develop into a very useful habit of mind.

INTERACTION OF FACTORS

PT: Factors that underlie the expression of creativity, such as the three described above, could interact with each other. For example, some learning scenarios allow students to offer input on, and control over, their own learning or completion of a task, a prime example of the use of creative metacognition. Such scenarios would increase the likelihood that the students become more intrinsically motivated, which in turn, would have the benefit of promoting creativity.

ST: *Examples include giving students choices regarding a topic for a research paper or project, a story for a play, or a concept to be addressed in a science experiment. If a particular circumstance would not allow choices of topics, as when a particular topic is the focus of a learning unit, students could be given the opportunity to choose how they would like to work with that topic, for example, through an art, science, or other hands-on project, book report or other writing assignments, or a presentation or performing arts piece. When appropriate, students could also be given the chance to create their own collaborative groups instead of teachers assigning the groups.*

PT: When students have a sense of ownership of their learning and performance, intrinsic motivation and creativity are more likely to occur. In addition, interest in the subject or task would also increase, and studies have shown that increased interest also promotes creative behavior (Ruscio, Whitney, & Amabile, 1998). Finally, when appropriate teachers could provide explicit advice on when and in what activity students should try to be creative.

IMPLICATIONS FOR TEACHERS

External forces have seeped into the walls of the traditional classroom, forces that are presently shaping the teaching profession and how and what students are taught. Technology, and its influence on teaching and learning, is one such external force. Another are the educational policies at both state and national levels that have shifted educators' focus toward accountability, the need for evidence of educational outcomes, and development of 21st-century skills. Thus, what it means to be a teacher and what it is like to be a student have dramatically changed over the years.

This is why nurturing and promoting the creativity of our students is as important now as during Guilford's (1950) time. To be able to accomplish this, we must learn from the large body of knowledge about creativity that is now available to us. Creativity scholars have shown that creativity is expressed differently in different people at different intensities, and that creativity may be expressed in different spheres of life. Thus, developmentally appropriate pedagogy should also take into account individual expressions of creativity as well as the factors (e.g., motivation, interest) that influence such expressions.

As educators, our job, in the most basic sense, is to cause positive change in our students. As simple as this task may seem, its realization hinges on the fundamental belief that people have the *capacity* for change. As we believe that students could be taught to solve new math problems, to read complex texts, and to think critically about a pivotal historical event, we must also believe that they could be taught to not only be more creative, but also that they have control of their own creativity—a set of mental skills that could be strengthened and refined.

CONCLUSION

The age-old beliefs about creativity as involving the genius and a muse and as being a fixed personality trait are largely irrelevant when we consider learning and teaching. They are irrelevant when a student is trying to solve a math problem, come up with a unique idea for a project, or write a grammatically correct yet insightful sentence. What are relevant are motivation, desire to be creative, and being thoughtful about one's creativity. Important in these situations is not profound inspiration—possible yet highly unlikely—but those moments of small creative insights that permeate each day and progressively advance a student's work and life. These moments are within reach of all students. The critical work of the teacher is to facilitate and to be receptive to these moments.

GLOSSARY OF TERMS

Be creative effect—simply instructing someone to be creative could actually make them more creative

Creative metacognition—knowledge about one's creative strengths and weaknesses and when it is appropriate and advantageous to be creative.

Creativity—ability to produce something novel and useful.

Extrinsic motivation—doing something for an external reward such as praise or money

Four-c model of creativity—Kaufman and Beghetto's (2009) description of four types of creativity: mini-c, little-c, Pro-c, and Big-C creativity; also refers to the developmental progression of creativity.

Intrinsic motivation—doing something because it is pleasurable and personally meaningful.

EXTENSION QUESTIONS

1. What are some of your experiences with negativities regarding creativity when you were a student, and what would you do as a teacher to prevent similar experiences for your own students?
2. How creative are you generally? And how much of your beliefs about your own creativity come from messages from others that you received growing up?
3. Describe instances of mini-c creativity in your life or work.
4. How much were you aware of mini-c creativity prior to reading this chapter?
5. Consider the vignette of the student reading to the class. What would you do in that situation?
6. How has your definition of creativity changed after reading this chapter?

REFERENCES

Amabile, T. M. (1985). Motivation and creativity: Effects of motivational orientation in creative writers. *Journal of Personality and Social Psychology, 48*, 393–397.

Christensen, P. R., Guilford, J. P., & Wilson, R. C. (1957). Relations of creative responses to working time and instructions. *Journal of Experimental Psychology, 53*, 82–88.

De Bono, E. (1992). *Serious creativity: Using the power of lateral thinking to create new ideas.* New York: HarperCollins.

Guilford, J. P. (1950). Creativity. *American Psychologist, 5*, 444–454.

Kaufman, J. C., & Beghetto, R. A. (2009). Beyond big and little: The four c model of creativity. *Review of General Psychology, 13*, 1–12.

Kaufman, J. C., & Beghetto, R. A. (2013). In praise of Clark Kent: Creative metacognition and the importance of teaching kids when (not) to be creative. *Roeper Review, 35*, 155–165.

Nusbaum, E. C., Silvia, P. J., & Beaty, R. E. (2014). Ready, set, create: What instructing people to "be creative" reveals about the meaning and mechanisms of divergent thinking. *Psychology of Aesthetics, Creativity, and the Arts, 8*, 423–432.

Plucker, J. A., Beghetto, R. A., & Dow, G. T. (2004). Why isn't creativity more important to educational psychologists? Potentials, pitfalls, and future directions in creativity research. *Educational Psychologist, 39*, 83–96.

Renzulli, J. S. (2005). The three-ring conception of giftedness: A developmental model for promoting creative productivity. In R. J. Sternberg, & J. E. Davidson (Eds.), *Conceptions of giftedness* (pp. 217–245). Cambridge: Cambridge University Press.

Ruscio, J., Whitney, D. M., & Amabile, T. M. (1998). Looking inside the fishbowl of creativity: Verbal and behavioral predications of creative performance. *Creativity Research Journal, 11*, 243–263.

Russ, S., & Fiorelli, J. A. (2010). Developmental approaches to creativity. In J. C. Kaufman & R. J. Sternberg (Eds.), *Cambridge handbook of creativity* (pp. 233–249). New York, NY: Cambridge University Press.

Simonton, D. K. (2001). The psychology of creativity: A historical perspective. Retrieved from https://simonton.faculty.ucdavis.edu/wpcontent/uploads/sites/243/2015/08/HistoryCreativity.pdf

Tinio, P. P. L., & Barbot, B. (2016). Purposeful fulfillment of creative potential. In R. A. Beghetto, & B. Sriraman (Eds.), *Creative contradictions in education: Cross disciplinary paradoxes and perspectives* (pp. 115–128). New York: Springer.

CONCLUSIONS

DAVID SCHWARZER AND
JAIME GRINBERG

Congratulations! By concluding reading this book, you have just completed a first important step toward better understanding the current context of educational practices in the 21st century. The different chapters you read were crafted carefully to focus on the historical and sociocultural foundations of education. They also were intended to provide you with practical applications, specially designed for novice teachers like you. Furthermore, connections to global and local (glocal) insights were intentionally embedded in these chapters to better understand our current situations in the societal, schooling, and teaching arena.

Remember that the different tools provided throughout the book were designed to scaffold your journey into becoming a reflective and effective teacher. Connecting the current practices and policies to glocal and national understandings of the phenomenon at hand is a central goal of this book. In your academic future, remembering that each one of the "new" policies is always based on some past experiences and conversations in the United States and in the world should be helpful to contextualize and understand it. The most useful tool might be the descriptions provided on future trends—trying to predict what is coming next to future teachers in the United States is always complex and unpredictable and yet a valuable experience. The editors strongly believe that understanding education as a transdisciplinary phenomenon in which different content areas collaborate among them is very important. We hope that as a follow up, and a next step in your educational journey, you will become a more conscientious teacher who understands how society, school, and teachers are interconnected and influenced by global forces, national forces, and policies. Be active on your pursuit for a clearer and more critical understanding of the "new" ideas and "cutting-edge" developments that some school districts or workshop developers are sometimes trying to impose in your practice.

At this time, your personal reflection on a lifelong decision about entering the field of teaching and education should be much more informed than before reading this book as part of your introductory class. Engaging in a dialogical transdisciplinary conversation with other educators in your own educational context is an important practice because it fosters a sense of community among new teacher trying to better understand their trade. Moreover, it will be very beneficial for reflective practitioners interested in advocating for best practices for their students. Find a critical friend and use the insights gained from such conversations to convince administration or parents on your recommendations for new practices or policy changes. Make those connections user friendly with minimum "jargon" so everyone in the community can understand the major points you are trying to highlight and advocate for. You may even think about a few questions and/or activities for community members, parents, or colleagues that you are trying to influence in their understanding. Sharing tools to further self-reflection and/or group discussions to help everyone make informed decisions is fundamental.

SOCIETY, SCHOOL, AND TEACHERS: WHAT HAVE WE LEARNED?

This book was designed around three themes: Society, Schools, and Teachers. The deductive structure of this volume was intended to capture the more general concept first (society), moving through an intermediate concept (school) and to finish with the most specific one (teachers). Be reminded that in all cases, our most PRACTICAL daily practices or routines in the classroom (e.g., an "exit ticket") have socio-historical explanations and interpretations that are worthwhile to understand and reflect while deciding whether to adopt them or not as part of your practice. We hope that the interconnectedness between societal forces, schools' reactions to them, and teacher practices is now much clearer than before as a result of reading this book.

Do not stress if the connection between a particular chapter and the section of the book is not of your liking. Some of these placements were contested and decisions were made that may look idiosyncratic to you. It is much more important to reflect on the topics and their importance to you and your colleagues than their relative placement in the overall structure of the book. Much more important is to think about the following questions: Are there some topics that the book overlooked? Are there some topics that are crucial in your community that you would like to investigate? We hope that the basic structure of this book can become a pedagogical tool for you and your future colleagues to engage in an ongoing reflection and investigation that will impact your future teaching practices. Follow the same structure as a strategy for your ongoing discussions.

WHAT DO WE KNOW ABOUT THE SOCIETAL FORCES?

So, what do we know about societal forces and their historical impact on our practice? We do know that immigration has been a defining and continuous aspect of schooling and teaching since the inception of public education in the United States and how it has changed and yet it has remained the same——an ambivalent topic with strong political implications for all the parties involved (Gonzalez & Inoa, this volume). We also established that the intersections of class, capital, and student achievement were and still are part of the most powerful and predictable societal forces that remain almost unchanged during the last decades. This is true for all students but particularly important for urban minority youth (Rivera Rodas & Auffant, this volume). Language education policies in the United States were, are and will be an issue that is going to continue to be debated in public schooling. The importance of English as the main language of instruction and communication in the United States is not contested, but the importance of bilingualism/multilingualism or translingualism as a possible goal for the United States is clearly articulated in this book (see Schwarzer & Kopczynski, this volume). We also established that one of the glocal goals of public education as an arena where democratic muscles are developed and enacted. Public schooling is becoming the first place where democratic citizenship is developed and enacted. Finally, we know that societal forces are moving the teaching profession to engage more and more with glocal forces worldwide. In light of the knowledge explosion and the "shrinking" globe produced by technological advancement teacher education programs, teachers must find ways to engage in global-local connections (see Price-Rom & Atiyat, this volume).

Chances are that these same topics will continue to impact your practice during the next 25 years. Be aware of them and be able to discern how the "new" proposed ideas are for sure based on very "old" historical underpinnings that have been part of the fabric of our profession during the last century.

WHAT DO WE KNOW ABOUT SCHOOLS?

So, what do we know about schools and their historical impact on our practice? As we have explained before, schools are impacted by societal forces but they also impact the way that teachers practice their craft. Some school districts create their own interpretations of the societal mandates reacting to their own "clients." We know that enculturation of students was, is, and will be one of the major goals of public schooling in the United States. Schools are primary social agents that create an atmosphere where enculturation of the young into the larger mainstream national identity is encouraged (see Grinberg & Weisz, this volume). Another important and sometimes overlooked topic is school funding. It is clear from the chapter on funding how race, gender, and socio-economics, among other factors, impact public school funding. (see Murray & Frank, this volume). Furthermore, STEM instruction, a "new" initiative in most public schooling during the last decades, is an area where the chapter authors explain how decisions about the content, tools, and goals of school curriculum benefit some and not others (see Maloney & Powell this volume). Finally, we also know that progressive education has been viewed as a pendulum between "traditional" education and "progressive" forces since the inception of public schooling in the United States. The authors also analyze the tensions, contradictions, and commonalities of progressive practices manifested in certain practices such as learning communities and child-centered practices among others. Those powerful contradictions will be part of our ongoing conversations in the schools of the 21st century (see Grinberg & Wells, this volume).

Schools will be reacting and changing based on the overall public debate about their role in the 21st century. This section of the book establishes some communalities and future trends that will be important to remember while engaging in school-wide professional development or practices.

WHAT DO WE KNOW ABOUT TEACHERS?

So, what do we know about teachers and their historical impact on our practice? As we have established, teachers play a central role in the development of curriculum, activities, lesson plans, and assessments (among others) to enact the understandings and conceptualizations represented in the society and the school sections. We know that good teachers integrate different aspects of their life into holistic ways of being and they ethically advance the facilitation of their authentic voice as part of their practice (see Levanon & Adelman, this volume). Moreover, teachers are at the frontline in the enforcing and applying, changing understanding of ability and disability into their daily practices (see Baglieri et al., this volume). Another issue that is a permanent aspect of teaching revolves around evaluation and measurement of students' learning. What is assessed and how it has been deliberated and discussed since the inception of public education. Therefore, understanding the historical and societal forces that influence teachers' evaluation of students' achievement is crucial (see Dacey & Mills, this volume). A new development during the last decades of the 20th century is the importance of parent involvement in schooling. The development of National PTA standards is one of the issues that this section is highlighting as an impactful aspect of teaching and teachers in the 21st century (see Barrios & Barrios, this volume). Finally, creativity in learning and teaching has been sometimes overlooked and sometimes emphasized in teaching during the last decades. Supporting creative behaviors in teaching and learning is a priority for the 21st century that teachers should approach as a clear goal for their practice (See Tinio & Tinio, this volume).

Teachers have a major role to play in enacting and sometimes opposing pedagogical practices that are being "tested" in their classrooms and schools. Reflective teachers know that most of these "new" ideas have been tried before with sometimes terrible results. It is important to promote teachers' autonomy and reflectiveness to be able to adopt and reject curriculum and practices presented to them based on their own interpretations of what good teaching is. In the next section, we encourage YOU to become an active member in our professional field.

Your Turn—your proposed personal action plan!

Following is the plan of action we have created and followed in the book—use it to your advantage—we believe it has the potential to be useful as a road map for you!

1. Start by identifying the new issue that you and your colleagues want to reflect or act upon. Find a "simple" definition—try to avoid complex "jargon" as much as possible. Make a conscious effort to relate its relevance for laypeople in your community. Try to gather conceptual information about the glocal understanding of the phenomenon. We found a table that summarizes the information as a graphic organizer very useful.

	Global	National (United States)	Policies	Understanding of the Phenomenon
Topic/issue 50 years ago				
Topic/issue today				

2. Engage and document a dialogical analysis between you and a colleague. Find a critical friend in your current professional community to "bounce" ideas with each other. You can find any texts by conducting a "Google" search of the terms or some other ways to center your conversation on some concrete ways, which is highly desired but not required. The discussion between colleagues should be then showcased or shared in a professional development (PD) opportunity in the school setting, or at a school district meeting, and so on. Action is central to this dialogical conversation that we are advocating here. Finally, develop clear and practical implications for lay leaders and colleagues to better understand the topic at hand.

CONCLUSION

We are hoping that reading this book has helped you cement your decision about whether becoming a teacher is something that you would like to be during the next 25 years of your professional journey. As you can see, we do not think that teaching is easy because we have summers off or because of the great benefits that are offered to teachers. We believe that teaching in the 21st century is of crucial importance to continue to ensure democracy in the United States and to foster a more just and inclusive society worldwide. The power of teachers and schools has the potential to influence society. It is our intention to encourage you to join in the journey with open eyes. Some of the challenges have been with teachers since the inception of public schooling in the United States and will remain part of your professional arena. Yet, some challenges may become opportunities depending on the way that we react to them.

Each journey starts with a very important first step—thank you for choosing this book to be one of YOUR first steps in your academic journey!

POSTSCRIPT

REFLECTIONS ON WHAT NOVICE TEACHERS NEED TO KNOW ABOUT TEACHING, POLICY, AND CONTEXTS: A CONVERSATION WITH JENNIFER ROBINSON

JENNIFER ROBINSON WITH JACLYN WEISZ AND
JAIME GRINBERG

The following is a conversation conducted with Dr. Jennifer Robinson. She shares her reflections about what novice teachers need to know about the relationships between teaching, educational policy, and social, historical, cultural, and political contexts. Dr. Robinson is the Director of the Center of Pedagogy at Montclair State University and Professor in the Department of Secondary and Special Education. She has served as an adviser and member of numerous task-forces and committees for the State of New Jersey, for the National Network for Educational Renewal, and for the American Association of Colleges of Teacher Education. Coinciding with this, she has consulted for the U.S. Secretary of Education and Congress, among many other activities. She has been the recipient of numerous awards and recognitions for her work and advocacy.

Weisz: The historical perspective of New Jersey—What three things would you whisper to a teacher at the beginning of their career? What are the most important things to know about based on your experience?

Robinson: *First, I believe it is important that teachers understand their role in providing their students with access to opportunities and resources in their community, city, country, and beyond. At the classroom level, new teachers need to understand that some of the curriculum they will be given may not benefit all of their students. An educator understands her role as a "steward of best practice," who gives students access to all the possible knowledge, resources, experiences, and opportunities. A new teacher may have to make wise decisions and have the courage to choose the best options for her students. If the curriculum does not provide students with "mirrors" that reflect their assets, and open "doors" of opportunity beyond the classroom, students will not be able to see a positive future for themselves. When I see closed, run-down, and barred schools in low-income neighborhoods, I always ask myself, "What is the role of the school in this community?" The community and educators have to decide <u>together</u> how to solve the challenges in the community and how education can be used to offer* *access to new possibilities. It might mean that a teacher must discard or modify the traditional curriculum so there is room for students to address the problems of the local community.*

One person from whom I learned this lesson in the mid-1980s was Claude Winfield, principal of Horace Mann Middle School (real name not used) in Brooklyn, NY. When he first became principal, graffiti covered the school and neighbors paid little attention when windows were broken or garbage accumulated around the school. Mr. Winfield made it his goal to change residents' perceptions of the school in the community. He believed the school in any community essentially belonged to the people. After much negotiation, he convinced district leadership to allow his staff to open the school earlier than required by law and keep it open beyond normal school hours so that he could run community activities to benefit the students and their families. First, he made the school a polling site for local elections, effectively drawing neighbors inside as this was where they had to vote. He also offered evening courses to adults in the community who wanted to learn more about technology and improve their English language skills. He then challenged teachers to come to school early or stay later to assist their students with their schoolwork. Teachers began taking field trips to city, state, and out-of-state sites because students began appreciating the education they were receiving at the school. Over the span of a year, Mr. Winfield changed the perception of the school as a place where everyone could gain access to a world beyond their neighborhood. This sentiment prevailed so much that neighbors, even those without children, began taking responsibility for the well-being and safekeeping of the school. Families no longer hesitated to enter the school for a variety of reasons, graffiti did not return after it was removed, and school grounds were cleaned up as a result of one educator's efforts.

Second, I would tell new teachers about the importance of being aware of how resources are distributed, particularly how state funding for schools depends greatly on zip code. New teachers in New Jersey need to understand that, unlike other parts of the country, the state formula for funding schools uniquely impacts the quality of education its children and youth receive. This means where new teachers eventually teach is seriously impacted by how government in the state distributes funds, which typically is across socio-economic status (SES) lines. The big challenge in NJ means that <u>where</u> you teach is highly impacted by the way in which funds are distributed. In Newark for example, the adult education program was closed due to lack of funding. Despite residents' desire to improve their educational status and opportunities, the district did not receive enough funding to benefit the adults who have the greatest potential to elevate the city's SES standing. City residents and teachers banded together, spoke up, and the City miraculously found a funding source that enabled the District to once again open the adult school. As a result, the teachers involved in this fight learned that education is a very political matter and they must be aware of how education in their community gets funded. Not coincidentally, funding for NJ schools at present falls along SES and racial lines. Local community taxes pay for schooling and therefore, upper-income families desiring high-quality education for their children, demand to have local control of education. This is why school funding is a factor in the type and quality of education students may receive. Sadly, local control may conflate some residents' desire to create segregated schools in the state. This leads to the third secret I would whisper to new teachers, especially those being prepared at institutions like ours that value social justice education.

I believe it is important for new teachers to understand that, much like the rest of the country, New Jersey education is deeply affected by our continuing battle against segregated schools, equity, and racism. Despite the fact that NJ is a gateway state for new immigrants, we have some of the most segregated schools in the country. This in part is why MSU students receive preparation that promotes social justice education and equity for students. But new teachers need to understand the larger system that mitigates against equity in schools and how they must develop a social justice stance in their classrooms, their schools, and in the profession as a whole.

While teachers as a group have the capacity to address educational inequity, I do not see the professional association in New Jersey moving in that direction. However, nationally, professional associations across the country are beginning to fight for competitive salaries as well as equitable education for P-12 students and youth. For example, after teachers in Oklahoma won their battle for better pay, the sole Hispanic teacher from a school that is one-third Latino, organized a 110-mile March for Education. She also intends to run for elected office to help change what happens in the Oklahoma state house on behalf of educators. In her own words, "For my students. For my community. Because all students deserve an equitable educational experience, regardless of race, socio-economic status and gender." In Kentucky, one teacher is leading an effort in conjunction with *Emerge Kentucky* to elect over 40 female teachers to the Kentucky state house.

Another Oklahoma teacher decided to fight to keep open the most innovative school in the state after funding to that school was cut. She determined that she could not stand by and watch public education become decimated by special interest groups. "I went to public school all my life, I'm a public-school product and I can't imagine not having my daughter in a public school," she said. "It's so much more diverse. I just didn't get my book smarts from there, but I got my worldly view from public school and I just can't imagine robbing my child of that."

In Phoenix, Arizona, teachers organized not only to bring their salaries in line with neighboring states, but to secure more funding for students. Arizona was cited as among the worst states in the country for public school spending per student and by pupil-to-teacher ratio.

New Jersey has not fully faced its challenges with racism in the schools. While the NAACP has raised this as a serious matter, the professional associations have been silent. Until NJ teacher association leadership moves away from provincial notions of education in very individualized and segregated ways, we won't see large-scale improvement and equitable education for our neediest student populations. Some schools work to address the achievement/opportunity gap, especially in communities that have taken on that challenge as a whole and formed organizations to address racism and segregation, but there aren't enough of these across the state, and it is not being led by teachers. Clearly, new teachers have to look through multiple lenses and recognize that teachers individually and collectively have a role to play in radically changing the institution of education in NJ.

Weisz: There are a number of young people who would like to be teachers, but are not convinced about the profession due to certain factors. Why should someone go into this profession?

Robinson: *Healthy young people are full of desire to make a difference in their world on both a small and large scale. They are eager, energetic, intelligent, aware that their parents' generation does not have the answers to society's challenges, and often interested in and creative about seeking solutions. This generation is particularly caring and willing to help and serve. These are all reasons why young people should enter the teaching field, if only for a brief (1–3 years) period of time. Teaching provides the opportunity to do what most other professions do not allow. It couples youthful talent and inspirational energy with the needs and promise of a generation that is looking for answers to help a very desperate world.*

One very concrete example of what I mean is a program hosted by the Center of Pedagogy at Montclair State University called Jumpstart Children First. Jumpstart is a national organization that leverages partnerships between higher education institutions, community-based pre-schools, and school districts to address kindergarten readiness. The program was originally started over twenty years ago by four college students who believed they could improve the trajectory of young children from under-resourced communities by giving them essential academic and social skills—the "jumpstart"—they need to succeed. We were introduced to Jumpstart about seven years ago by a colleague who hosted the program on her college campus. Jumpstart recruits and engages community members and college students who learn early language and literacy strategies, which they will use when they go into early childhood centers and public school classrooms to read and interact with young children.

Many university-based teacher education programs do not reflect the diversity found within the campus community itself. That is certainly true at Montclair State University. We have found that Jumpstart has been an authentic way to attract a very racially and ethnically diverse corps of young adults who have a willingness and desire to give to under-resourced communities. They receive high-quality training and learn about how to build key literacy and language skills that help prepare preschoolers for kindergarten. What's more, Jumpstart is a leadership development organization that focuses on team building so that the young people who volunteer naturally become stronger, more self-confident, and advocates for their young charges. In a way, Jumpstart provides college students with a taste or "jumpstart" to the field of education as a profession, which is why I like the program so much. In fact, as I talk about this program, I am reminded of the Black Panthers' Free Breakfast for School Children programs that began in the 1960s, which was meant to accomplish a similar goal—to harness and inspire young people to volunteer and give community service.

I believe teaching brings together a community of young people who can "touch the future" by going into the classroom. THAT is the possibility of becoming a teacher—bringing hope to children and youth. Young teachers can bring their students hope beyond what they see in the immediate future. Teaching really does enable a person to touch the future—a saying that Christa McAuliffe coined in her brief, but impactful life that is actually true.

Grinberg: *I decided to become a teacher when I was a teenager. I realized it was not just "babysitting" and saw that I could change the world and the hope of the students. A teacher has so much power in their class, despite the inequities and can create a little paradise in the classroom.*

Weisz: What is the reality of teaching and being a teacher in NJ?

Robinson: *We are a state that does a very good job of educating its youth. Many teachers in New Jersey are great, which is evidenced by New Jersey education standings nationally. The reality in New Jersey, however, is that the general public doesn't believe that there are long-term teachers who still want to make an impact through education. Very experienced teachers with high expectations are still very active and not burned out and they want to make a difference for the children and youth they teach. I see this regularly through our school/university partnership, the Montclair State University Network for Educational Renewal (MSUNER). The teachers who are heavily involved in the MSUNER attend workshops, engage in teacher study groups, and action research. After they spend a year studying about teaching, they make presentations to each other at a summer conference, which hosts over 300 teachers. Teaching is extremely hard work and not for the "faint of heart" because you have to fill many roles that are lacking or absent in students' lives. Teachers are often charged with challenging mediocrity that we sometimes see in schools.*

Weisz: Why do you think so many teachers get "burned out" early in their career?

Robinson: *"Burned out" is a term that means something pretty horrible. The field of psychology uses the term "burned out" to describe someone who is in a state of chronic stress that leads to physical and emotional exhaustion, cynicism, and detachment. I would hope that anyone who is in that severe a state has taken steps to remove themselves from being in the presence of children and youth. Teachers who feel "ineffective and lacking accomplishment," another aspect of being "burned out," are severely fatigued and need a break from the job—for some temporarily and for others permanently.*

There are a lot of reasons for teacher fatigue. For one, I think we need to examine how we prepare and nurture teachers throughout their career to overcome teacher isolation, which leads to fatigue. We tend to blame the individual and not the system for failure. Teaching has become a profession where support for beginning novice teachers isn't the norm and it is sorely needed. One way that we are addressing this issue in a very simple way is to prepare teacher candidates in cohorts. This helps them form bonds and become socialized into the profession as a group. When they complete preparation and begin as teachers of record, they need to be placed in teams as well because you need a team of people to help you address the challenges of starting out as a teacher. I team taught my first few years and found that it was extremely helpful to have a colleague on hand to whom I could share ideas and address challenges. We are just now (and only on a small scale) recognizing the importance of providing support for new teachers in their work.

In Newark, where we have been working intensively over the past 10 years, we have developed a cadre of energetic, seasoned educators who can help novice teachers. They are helping us prepare our pre-service teachers and they are helping their principals induct new teachers into their buildings. Principals have to retain their teachers and make school a place where teachers want to come to work. That, coupled with other administrators who also see the importance of nurturing their students, staff, and faculty, can make school a powerful place for everyone to learn.

Another reason why we see teacher burnout is that some people went into teaching for the wrong reason or have unrealistic expectations. Perhaps they were not prepared well and the work is much harder than they thought it would be. They may leave because they realize they can make much more money with less stress. Or the work environment and conditions are not optimal. It really is sometimes difficult to determine the "leavers" and "movers" in education. Teacher mobility as a whole is something that I think we will see more of, not only because of the factors I expressed earlier, but also because this is a workforce that tends to be mobile. People are not staying permanently in a single job or profession for as long as our parents' or even our generation. This may have an adverse effect on our schools, especially those in high-need communities where staffing stability is critical.

Grinberg: We see different situations in other countries. Finland retains teachers by paying high salaries. And we see better creativity in other places. Belgium's policy of having team teaching situations where females can teach part time when also raising a family is more realistic. Freire said that younger teachers abandon the profession because they see that they are not good at it or because they say they cannot teach "these" students. The social context seems to also disable the way we can do the job. Some societies have been more creative in retaining their teachers.

Robinson: *Speaking of the social contextual reality of teaching in New Jersey, I will say that since we as a state have been focused on testing students, we have created less nurturing schools and really need to change our practice to make schools more learning and learner centered. We need to give students opportunities to engage in deep learning to nurture their curiosity and not be afraid to be challenged academically. How can we make the time in school more valuable for students? Let students explore their interests in the younger grades and give them the tools they need to develop and hone their interests and skills as they progress through the grades.*

Getting back to teacher retention, I am intrigued by your reference to Friere's assessment of why teachers leave. If you look at the way teachers develop, we understand that pre-service teachers are egocentric, meaning the complexity of the work itself causes one to be quite self-conscious. Indeed new teachers may become discouraged because teaching is not as easy as it looks. Very quickly, novice teachers come to realize they can't solve every problem. They have the challenge of needing to be in control of the classroom and even their students' learning, which we know is impossible. So, for example, when I teach our pre-service teachers the elements of cooperative learning, I have to explain that they have to trust their students if they want them to be in control of their own learning. Pre-service teachers also come to understand that it is developmentally appropriate for them to want to step in when their students are struggling with a concept or skill. Teachers need to be facilitators of learning rather than controlling, which is a delicate balance to strike. It takes time and experience, but it is possible.

Grinberg: What would it be like if we had larger school districts that have schools from all over and different SES backgrounds? How would it be different than what we have today? People moving from one place to another to get the best possible education.

Robinson: *I think your idea is an interesting one, but I still think we have to be committed to the true education of our students. I have seen where school districts, influenced by economic factors, have made poor choices for its students at the expense of its most vulnerable population. This is where we can take our cues from countries that are doing this right. We all need to place greater value on our children, just like the people of Singapore. Several years ago, that country made a conscious decision to invest in its only natural resource—its children. The leaders of that country decided that no expense was too great if it meant generations to come would see better lives. Today, Singapore is a thriving society of well-educated people. We can change schools to make them student-centered and restructure schools so that children (and teachers) can thrive.*

Weisz: How did the edTPA evolve? What came before it and what do you think will replace it in the future?

Robinson: *The Stanford Center for Assessment, Learning, and Equity (SCALE), which is where the edTPA originated, has been at the forefront of the development of Teaching Performance Assessments for many years. Historically, however, we have to go back to 1998 when the California legislature signed a regulation requiring all candidates for licensure to pass a state-approved performance assessment with demonstrated validity and reliability. Several institutions of higher education (including Stanford) formed a consortium to create a portfolio-based assessment that evolved into the Performance Assessment for California Teachers (PACT), which was approved in 2007 by the California Commission for Teacher Credentialing. The PACT, used by over 30 California higher education institutions, requires candidates to demonstrate pedagogical content knowledge and critical thinking through a Teaching Event that includes a demonstration of the candidate's skill in Planning, Instruction, Assessment, Reflection, and Academic Language.*

In 2010, SCALE in partnership with the Association of Colleges for Teacher Education (AACTE) created what they call "a **support** and **assessment** program for teacher candidates that could be used around the country" (Stanford University, 2014). The edTPA developed from that partnership, and one can see that it is modeled heavily after the PACT. States across the country with Race to the Top funding began adopting the edTPA as one way to hold teacher preparation programs accountable and the several non-RTTT states followed suit. Now, over 40 states across the country, including New Jersey, have adopted the edTPA as the state-approved performance assessment as part of program completion. Although SCALE is the sole developer of the edTPA and Stanford owns the edTPA, many in the teacher education community have negatively focused attention on Pearson because of its operational and administrative support of the edTPA and the enormous financial profit made as a result—especially at the expense of those trying to enter the profession of teaching.

Prior to the edTPA, individual universities used their own performance assessments including portfolios, exhibitions, and teacher and student work samples. There has not been a nationally validated teaching performance assessment system that states could use to license their beginning teachers. Though there have been a range of responses opposing and supporting the use of the edTPA as a high-stakes assessment, it is the first "nationally accessible teacher performance assessment that gives states, districts and teacher preparation programs a common framework for defining and measuring a set of core teaching skills that form a valid and robust vision of teacher competence" (NCATE, 2010).

I think it is also important to add that the NCATE Blue Ribbon Panel Report, which was generally embraced by the teacher education community as ground-breaking, cited both the PACT and the development of the edTPA as "promising practices," in hopes that a teacher performance assessment, developed by the profession and for the profession, would be adopted nationally. In addition, the NCATE Blue Ribbon Panel made strong recommendations that we are seeing enacted in many states (including ours) and in teacher education programs across the country, which I believe will continue far into the future. For example, the Blue Ribbon Panel called for "linking performance assessments to state licensure requirements." It also urged accrediting bodies to "define areas of expertise to be evaluated, including content knowledge and the skills of teaching specific content areas, and clinical skills of practice such as pedagogical expertise, the ability to analyze and make changes to one's own practice, problem solving, interpersonal and communication skills, professional decision making, and collaboration" (NCATE, 2010).

Weisz: *What are some crucial education policies that you think teachers in NJ should know about? What about national and federal policies? Are the educational policies in NJ better or worse than the policies in the nation as a whole?*

Robinson: Teacher education candidates, especially those at the graduate level, should be made aware of education as well as social policies (e.g., immigration) that may affect their students positively or adversely, and prepared to engage in advocacy as well as decision-making at the district level regarding the education of their students.

Historically, I would say that the Obama administration policies and Race to the Top (RTTT) ushered in an era of education regulation that has not been seen in the nation, let alone New Jersey in a very long time. Under Education Secretary Arnie Duncan, we saw for the first time a successful effort to align state oversight of student achievement, teacher assessment and accountability, and teacher education program accountability as they directly link to federal funding. That is what Race to the Top did on a large scale and why so many states were able to quickly revamp their statewide infrastructures, including student and teacher databases, and systems for monitoring student achievement. The RTTT funding to states also largely supported the major overhaul of teacher evaluation systems. In New Jersey, where we did not receive large amounts of RTTT funding, we were still under the pressure—politically, socially, and financially to make the same sweeping changes to our education systems statewide.

At the same time several states, with significant corporate and private funding, successfully disrupted teacher association power by promulgating a negative narrative about teacher effectiveness. We saw the systematic de-professionalization of teaching with this emphasis on teacher evaluation based upon student performance, as measured by standardized tests alone. No one disputes the fact that teachers should be accountable for student achievement, however, using measures such as "value-added" as a way to assess and hold teachers accountable is not appropriate.

And, despite the absence of data to substantiate the claim that teachers, schools, and districts are/were failing, an atmosphere of competition was created and there has been heavy introduction of charter schools, especially in urban communities. Depending upon who you speak to, the introduction of charter schools is good as it affords parents, especially those who live in low-income communities, with few options and for their children to obtain a high-quality education. Others who have studied the national proliferation of charter schools, assert that charters are no better (or worse) than non-charter public schools. The differences identified are often related to the fact that precious resources (everything from bricks and mortar to human resources such as school social workers) have been systematically syphoned from district public schools to charter schools, causing an imbalance favoring charters over non-charter public schools.

Weisz and Grinberg: Thank you Dr. Robinson!

REFERENCES

National Council for Accreditation of Teacher Education (NCATE) Blue Ribbon Panel on Clinical Preparation and Partnerships for Improved Student Learning. (2010). Transforming teacher education through clinical practice: A national strategy to prepare effective teachers. Washington, D.C.: NCATE. Retrieved from caepnet.org/~/media/Files/caep/accreditation-resources/blue-ribbon-panel.pdf

Stanford University, 2014. About edTPA. https://scale.stanford.edu/teaching/edtpa

CPSIA information can be obtained
at www.ICGtesting.com
Printed in the USA
BVHW091727160120
569662BV00009B/29

9 781524 990183